MW00397179

FROM A BOY ON A HORSE TO A MAN WITH A GAVEL

FROM A BOY ON A HORSE TO A MAN WITH A GAVEL

THE AUTOBIOGRAPHY OF FORMER CHIEF JUSTICE FRANK X. GORDON

Text Former Chief Justice Frank X. Gordon

Copyright © Former Chief Justice Frank X. Gordon

Design Adeline Media, London

Text is private and confidential

Second print January 2017

 StoryTerrace·

www.StoryTerrace.com

CONTENTS

ACKNOWLEDGEMENTS

A very special thanks needs to be given to Robyn Snyder, my former secretary, who has spent countless hours typing, re-typing, revising, and gently prodding me to finish this book. I don't know anyone who could have helped more.

Another very special thanks goes to the law firm of Roush, McCracken & Guerrero, who so generously hired me after my retirement from the bench. It had been so long since I had practiced law that they did not require much actual work from me, and for that, I am grateful. It was a very happy time for me working for these special people.

1

MY PARENTS AND
THEIR FAMILIES

I was an only child, born to Frank and Lucille Gordon
on January 9, 1929, in Chicago, Illinois. My mother,
Lucille Gburek, was born in Chicago in 1897, I believe.
Her parents, Thomas Gburek and Mary Sterma Gburek,
were both immigrants from Poland. Her father was a whiskey maker in Bialy Orzel (White Eagle) Orwa, Poland. He
smuggled himself and his wife out of Poland before 1878,
because he, like other Polish males, would be forced to join
the German Army.

Lucille was the eighth of 12 children born to my grandparents. The first Gburek born in the United States was
most likely mother's oldest brother, John, who was born
around 1878. Her brothers and sisters in order of their birth
were: John; Frank; Veronica; Mary; Francie; Martha (died
at 11 years); Mike; Lucille; Stanley; Anthony; Tom and
Sophie. After coming to America, the Gburek family first
settled in New York City, but soon moved to Chicago and

lived on Frye Street. Mother's father died at age 73 years and
her mother at 83 years. There is a statue erected to them in St.
Albert's Cemetery in Chicago.

As with most Polish immigrant families, music played a
great part in Mother's life. All six of Mother's brothers were
musical. Stanley played the trumpet; Tony, the sax and clarinet;
Tom the piano, drums and accordion; Frank, the piano; John,
the violin; Mike started violin but had to quit to work, so he
became a dancer. My grandfather, Thomas, played the flute.
Mother had a beautiful soprano voice when she was young
and received some formal operatic training from a Mrs. Nerr-
ing, a concert artist in Chicago. She was a soloist in several
Catholic churches in Chicago. Her favorite religious piece was
Gounod's "Ave Maria". Mother also must have performed in
several operas, as I found pictures of her in operatic costumes
with medals she had won.

Even later in life, Mother made occasions for singing, either
alone or in groups with her friends. In the summer months of
either 1936 or 1937, when I was seven or eight years old, she
received additional voice lessons in Beverly Hills, California,
from Harold Hurlburt. We stayed in an apartment somewhere
near Hurlburt's studio. Mother taught herself to play the accordion at the same time and became quite accomplished on
that instrument. I remember that a then famous movie actor,
Dick Powell, received voice lessons from Mr. Hurlburt in the
lesson hour right after my mother. He would pull me around
in a little wagon on the sidewalk in front of the Hurlburt man-

sion while we waited for my mother's lesson to be completed.

Mother was a very beautiful young woman, about 5' 3" tall, and with very dark brown hair, brown eyes and a ready smile. She had rather little formal education as a child, completing only fifth or sixth grade. Even with her limited schooling, she was very intelligent and quite artistic. Her sewing, crocheting and tatting were of extremely high quality. Joan and I still have many of her tablecloths, napkins, towels, pillowcases, quilts and other things she made.

Not having had much formal education before she was married, Mother took advantage of every educational opportunity she could during her later life. She was a serious student of everything that she took up, and quietly insisted that I should do my best in my schoolwork also.

Mother learned to draw on a copying device while in Chicago. She also loved working with ceramics, and painted on china. That encouraged her to take up painting on canvas, which she did while in her fifties. She spent the better part of two years in Phoenix, living in an apartment, studying under Jay Datus, a highly respected artist who did murals in several important buildings in Phoenix, including a mural depicting the Seven Cities of Cibola in the First National Bank Building. According to some artists, Mother had considerable innate talent. I think her greatest skill was in watercolors, although she was most fond of oil painting and thought that her best medium. For several years after her training, she painted prolifically, mostly landscape scenes. She did thirty or forty major

My mother Lucille Gordon née Gburek

paintings, and had several shown in juried Phoenix art shows. For some reason her interest in painting waned, and she quit as abruptly as she had started. Father was very supportive of her art training, and was proud of her accomplishments. Mother continued her needlework, however.

Mother also went to Lamson Business College for a year in Los Angeles to learn typing and shorthand to be my father's legal secretary. Her penmanship was beautiful, even to the last. I am not sure whether this training was before or after she took voice lessons.

Although I believe Mother was a very affectionate woman, she did not display affection in public. I can only remember a few occasions on which my mother and father kissed each other in my presence. She was very sociable, however, and appreciated clubs and social activities and the warmth of close friends. She loved to dance, and always had a big smile and kind word for everyone. Mother had a dramatic way about her. She dressed well and stylishly. People noticed her when she came into a room. She noticed and acknowledged them also.

I think Mother's favorite group in Kingman was about a dozen couples that celebrated their birthdays together. The "Birthday Club" boasted some of the most well-known people in Kingman at the time, such as Shorty and Liz Hafley, Johnny and Edith Mullen, Elsie Gallup and Ted Wallace, Kirk and Rose Tatum, Ray and Lutie Atherton, Bernice Richardson, Hank and Ollie Belle Searcy, Lloyd and Pearl Clinkenbeard.

13

Their birthday celebrations usually consisted of dinner parties at different homes with the group singing late into the night, accompanied by Lutie Atherton on the piano. These late-night songfests made a strong impression on me. Some of the old tunes I heard lying in bed, sung in fair harmony, were: There's A Long, Long Trail Awinding; Red Sails in the Sunset; When the Moon Comes Over the Mountain; K-K-K-Katie; Over There; Lily Marlene; Moon Over Miami; Don't Sit Under The Apple Tree.

Mother was a wonderful cook and loved to entertain with large dinner parties. Many political figures of the times were guests in our home at 537 East Spring Street. It was in that beautiful old stone and stucco gingerbread-type house that I had my fondest memories of growing up, from grade school through high school. We lived there from about 1937 when I was just eight years old until I left to attend college. The house had two levels above ground and a full basement.

It was built in 1917 by a wealthy early Kingman merchant, S. T. Elliot, who spared little expense in building it. It probably was one of the most elegant homes in Kingman at the time. It had a steam boiler that heated the home with radiators, and was stoked with coal by hand. Later, during World War II, when coal was difficult to obtain in Kingman, my parents converted the boiler to burn oil. Until then, I remember shoveling coal in the boiler and worrying whether the steam pressure gauge was accurate. The clanking of the radiators and hissing of the steam was welcome music on cold mornings.

The house was also originally installed with a central vacuum cleaner powered by a five-horsepower electric motor in the basement. In each room were at least four baseboard wall-plugs in which you could attach a flexible wand and turn on the vacuum motor in the basement, where the dust and dirt was directed to a bag in a collecting canister. The system was so strong that it would almost suck the rug off the floor. Central vacuum cleaning was touted as a recent innovation in home-building in Phoenix in the 1970s, although I had known of it decades before.

The house had oak floors throughout, and fine custom-built oak cabinets with leaded glass doors in the living room, dining room and hall. In the winter we slept on the first floor; in the summer, we moved to the basement where it was cooler. I don't believe we had a swamp cooler while I was growing up. The house was quite cool most of the summer due to its thick stone walls. Opening windows almost always ensured a comfortable evening cross-draft. During my high school years and the summers that I returned from college, I slept in the upstairs bedroom, which had its own bath. My parents continued living in the house until they sold it to Elmer and Helen Graves in the late 1960s.

Mother was a faithful member of the Ladies Auxiliary of the American Legion Post in Kingman, and at one time held a high state office in that organization. I believe she was state Chaplain. I found many of her typewritten prayers used to begin the meetings. They were beautifully written, showing

15

great concern for the goals of the Auxiliary. I believe King-man hosted the Arizona state convention of the Legion Auxiliary one year when I was four or five. The meetings were held in the old Elks Hall. Shirley Lewis and I, both the same age, were dressed up in formal attire to deliver flowers to the State President of the Auxiliary. My tuxedo was homemade by mother, and the pins holding it did not make it through the evening.

My father died in 1968, and mother really never got over the shock of being alone. They had been exceedingly close and mother was very dependent on him. Until my father died, she had not maintained a checking account of her own. She never learned to drive a car, although she tried once and almost killed us by running off the road. Mother developed a small tumor in her breast soon after father died. It was removed and she underwent radioactive treatment, which was very hard on her. She never really regained her strength after that. She died of congestive heart failure in 1971.

In the three years that she lived after my father's death, Helen Graves who lived across the street, was a great help to mother, visiting her almost daily, and helping her by doing shopping for her and taking her places. Mother looked forward to seeing her each day. I am extremely grateful for Helen's care of my mother, as I was busy being a Superior Court Judge during this time, and tried to visit my mother as often as possible, but not nearly as often as Helen. She was truly an angel sent by God to help my mother at that time.

My father, Frank X. Gordon, was born in Chicago, Illinois in 1898, I believe. He too was born to a recently immigrated Polish couple, and was one of eleven siblings, although I only know of two. He had a brother Steve, who owned and operated a shipbuilding yard in Chicago, and a sister Lottie. Lottie lived in Boulder City, Nevada, for quite a few years. I believe both she and her husband are now deceased. My paternal grandfather's given name was Xavier Leszczynska and his mother's was Joanna Magierski. I believe my grandfather worked for the railroad, but later sold coal from a cart to heat houses in Chicago.

I am sorry I know very little about my grandparents or my father's siblings. I never met either of my paternal grandparents or my mother's father. I don't even remember my parents telling me when they died. The most information I obtained about my mother and father's respective families was from my Uncle Mike Burke (Gburek), my mother's brother, after my parents died. I am sure part of my ignorance was due to lack of interest on my part in my youth. But my parents rarely spoke of their families. To my recollection, only Aunt Lottie and her family, and Uncle Mike, visited us in Kingman. My father never returned to Chicago after he left, and mother returned twice – once in 1938 when I was nine years old, and again later when her mother died.

I went with her the first time when I was nine years old, and met my maternal grandmother, Mary Gburek, for the first time. She was stocky and seemed to be less than

My mother and father, Frank and Lucille Gordon, with the Atmos clock on mantle, Kingman

five feet tall, with long, silver hair braided and wound tight around the back of her head in a bun. At nine, I was several inches taller than she was. I remember walking with her to a fish market, where she bought a large sack of smoked white-fish from Lake Michigan. I can still smell that wonderful fish. I roller-skated all around the neighborhood, which was made up almost entirely of Polish immigrants. They loved food and song. One man had a sort of xylophone made of glass bottles filled to different levels with water and strung by strings on a wooden frame. He could play almost anything on that contraption by striking the bottles with different-sized wooden mallets.

During our visit in 1938, my mother and I stayed for several weeks at my grandmother's house on Leavitt Street. I believe the address was 2200 North Leavitt. There was a vendor that came through the neighborhood that sold chocolate-covered frozen bananas on a stick for a nickel. He also sold a large waf-fle-type cookie that was marvelous. At that time, stores sold huge dill pickles for a penny; movies cost a nickel, and you could stay to see the movie over and over. During this visit, I met most of my aunts, uncles and cousins, who numbered it seemed close to 100. We never kept up with them, except for a few by Christmas card exchanges. Looking back on it, I felt it was strange not to keep in touch with family, but for some unspoken reason, we didn't. My parents only spoke Polish when they did not want me to understand things. As I grew older I was sorry that they had not taught me the language. I also wished they had filled me in on the reason or reasons that we had isolated ourselves from their families.

As an aside, Uncle Mike was a very interesting person. He was the last survivor of Mother's family, who visited Joan and me in Phoenix on several occasions. He was a tall, spry, simple man, who was retired for over 30 years from the printing trade. He loved his beer and cigarettes, but had to give up the latter at about 80 years of age on doctor's orders. He also had to give up polka dancing at about the same time, which he had done regularly once or twice a week. Mike died in 1992 at over 90 years of age. To the end, Mike had a full head of coal black hair. He attended both Trey and Candy's weddings, late in his life. His wife had died before then, and he had at least one fiancée that he lived with thereafter.

Mike had enlisted in the regular U. S. Army in 1912 at 19 years of age. He served 2 ½ years in Texas City, and six months in the Panama Canal. He was in France for over a year in WWI, in the 86th Blackhawk Division. During his Army duty in Texas, he was in the Engineer Corps, and was involved in map making. He told us that they sometimes measured distances on horseback – so many paces of the horse to the mile. He said during that time in Texas, quite a few movies were made about the war with Mexico, and he had a bit part in the movie *War With Mexico* leading a mule.

His wages as a soldier were $33 per month. French soldiers got seven cents per day. Mike paid nine cents for a quart of wine when he served in France. He was discharged in Camp Grant, Illinois, in 1918. Thereafter he worked in a machine shop, married and had four children. Two of the children died within five days of each other with "black diphtheria." The other two were Norbert and Dorothy. Norbert helped Mike maintain an apartment house they owned, and Dorothy lived at 1412 South Orange, Fullerton, California. He came from Chicago frequently to visit Dorothy, and spent his last years with her.

My father attended law school at Northwestern University in Chicago, Illinois and served in the U. S. Navy during World War I at the Great Lakes Naval Base on Lake Michigan. He told me about the great influenza epidemic of 1917 on that base, when hundreds of sailors died. He said it was quite common to wake up in the morning and find that the sailor on the next cot had died during the night. According to father, the only medication available to counteract the flu was a licorice-flavored medicine that was given to them on every possible occasion, even on street corners in Chicago. He served only a short time in the Navy, and the war ended in 1918.

After an honorable discharge from the Navy and graduating from Northwestern School of Law, father practiced law for a short time in a small firm in Chicago, handling civil matters. I do not remember the name of the firm. He was evidently quite successful in his practice, as Mother and he owned a beautiful three-story home on Hansen Court in Chicago. Uncle Mike said the home cost $50,000 at the time, which would have been a great deal of money in the mid to late 1920s. In the basement of this home was a complete ballroom, fully equipped with all the instruments necessary for a dance band. Father told me he had a 1918 LaSalle four-door Cabriolet, equipped with metal covered spare tires on each side of the engine hood just forward of the front doors, and a special compartment for his golf clubs just behind the back door on the driver's side. Father said gasoline was a dollar a gallon then, and the car got very few miles per gallon. Several times when I have been in Chicago I have imagined how grand Mother and Father must have looked then, driving down the main streets of Chicago in their LaSalle, attending concerts, operas and light operas, all of which mother adored.

I met Steve, one of Frank's brothers, while visiting my grandmother Sterma. He was retired, but had been quite successful in the boat-building business, and had a yard on the Chicago River. Dad told me he built a large boat for one of the Wrigley family, and on the day of its launching into the river, something went wrong with the way the boat was going into the water. Mike reached for the winch and somehow got his hand caught in it and lost three fingers. According to Dad, that did not stop the launching festivities, and after it was completed, Dad took Steve to the hospital, where he remembered he had left a large amount of cash in his coat pocket at the yard, which was the final payment for the boat. Dad was sent back to get it, and it was still there.

For some reason still not clear, Dad left Chicago suddenly and went by train to Los Angeles, California, leaving mother and me behind, when I was just a few months old. We were to join him later. It wasn't until after my parents' deaths that Uncle Mike told me that Frank may have become involved with something improper, perhaps being accused of using some union money that he had no right to, and he had to leave town right away. It may have been at this time that he changed his name to Frank X. Gordon, as before that time it was Lecien (perhaps a contraction of Leshinsky), which is the name that appears in his Law School Annual from Northwestern, which has his picture and name in it.

I thought about leaving this part of Frank's life out of this monograph, as it seemed unnecessary, in light of there being nothing further that came of the incident. But if any of our children or grandchildren thought about doing a family genealogy, I didn't want them to bark up the wrong family tree and mistakenly think that we had a Scottish background, as the name Gordon might imply. Actually, I do not really know why or when Dad changed his name, or how he settled on the name Gordon. It is entirely irrelevant to me now, as everyone who knew my father in Kingman knew him by the name Gordon and thought highly of him in every aspect of his character. I do not have a birth certificate showing my parents' names, but obtained a delayed birth certificate after my parents' deaths with Uncle Mike's help and affidavit.

After leaving Chicago, Frank became associated with an attorney named Charles Rosin in Los Angeles who owned property in Kingman, Arizona. Rosin was interested in establishing a business in Kingman, which was very novel at the time – the business of writing title insurance on real property transactions. Until that time, people who purchased real estate were assured that the seller of the property had a title that he could convey by hiring a lawyer who searched the county records and found that the seller indeed had a title through proper conveyances from predecessors, and that the title was not encumbered by any mortgages, judgments, liens or leases of record. The buyer relied on this "Lawyers Opinion on Title," and if it ended up being wrong, the buyer's only recourse was against the lawyer.

Under the new system, the title company would search the records and if the title were proper, would issue a policy of insurance guaranteeing that the title conveyed was merchantable and could in fact be passed to the buyer. Frank was to come to Kingman, rent office space, equip it, hire people to do the title searches, train them, set up the business, and then come back to Los Angeles and practice law. Within a short time, Dad came to love Kingman and figured this was a good place, perhaps a very safe place, to bring his family. In the summer of 1929, he notified my mother, who with me in her arms only six months old, boarded a Santa Fe train in Chicago bound for Los Angeles, with Uncle Mike and her brothers and sisters seeing her off. Uncle Mike said they didn't want

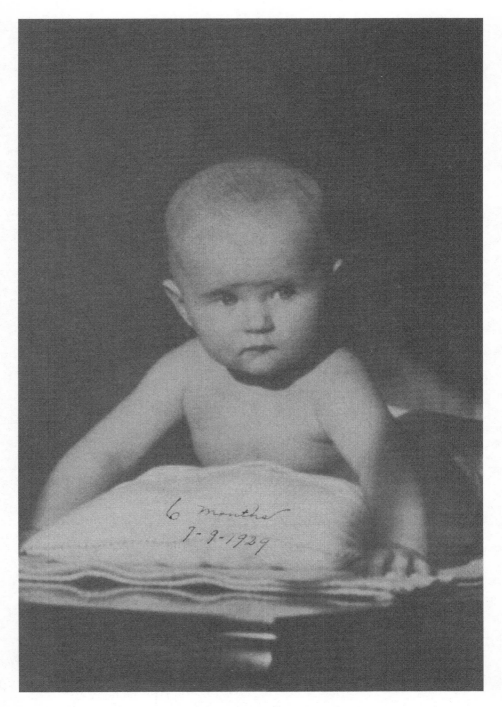

Yours truly, six months old

to let Mother and I go out there to the West, where they knew we would not return.

Mother and I arrived in Los Angeles, and father drove the family by car across old Highway 66 to Kingman. It was as hot as August could get crossing the desert. The car had no air conditioning. Mother was worried about me, so we stayed overnight in Needles, California, where they bathed me with cool water in a motel sink before making the rest of the trip to Kingman. The next day they drove through the thriving mining towns of Oatman and Goldroad, arriving in the little town of Kingman.

Mother was a big city lady accustomed to the luxuries and high cultural events of Chicago. Kingman was then a windy, dusty, sleepy little railroad town of about 1,500 or 2,000 souls, few of which had ever attended an opera or even knew what it was. The Central Commercial, the only general store in Kingman, I am sure was a disappointment to her, compared with the fashion stores in which she was used to shopping. I understand Mother was very depressed when she first arrived in Kingman. Ultimately she came to accept Kingman, but I don't think she ever felt totally at home there. She took every opportunity to spend time in Los Angeles, Phoenix or Las Vegas to go to school or shopping.

Father came to truly love Kingman, and became an important part of the community. He bought the title company business, then called, I believe, Security Title, from Mr. Rosin. He also became an insurance agent for some major companies including New York Life. Dad served as a commissioner on the Arizona Highway Commission, and an appraiser for the loan programs of the National Recovery Act (NRA) made to farmers and ranchers under the early Franklin D. Roosevelt redevelopment plans. In 1932, he took and passed the Arizona Bar Exam. He ran unsuccessfully for County Attorney of Mohave County in 1936. He served on the Selective Service Board during World War II, and was an ardent supporter of incorporation of the City of Kingman. The Gates family, who owned and operated the Central Commercial Company, was staunchly opposed to incorporation, and Jay M. Gates, Sr. and Dad were frequently involved in public debates over the issue. In either 1951 or 1952, after a successful incorporation vote of the citizens of the town, Kingman became an incorporated city. My father became Kingman's first City Attorney, and Herb Biddulph was its first elected mayor.

Whatever the dark reasons were for Dad to move to Kingman, he became and was one of the most respected lawyers not only in Mohave County, but in the State of Arizona. He served many years on the Board of Governors of the State Bar. He was a lawyer because he loved to help people solve their problems. When they needed his help, he was ready to give it to them, whatever the time of day or day of the week. To the end, he resisted requiring appointments to see him in his office.

Dad worked in his office until late in the night, most often coming home just in time for the ten o'clock news. He loved his work. I can still see him sitting at his desk, pecking with three fingers at his manual Remington typewriter, smoking a cigar, composing a draft of a will, contract or lease. He was very meticulous in his draftsmanship, and felt no title company should be allowed to draft deeds, contracts or other property conveyances. He passionately but unsuccessfully resisted the passage of a constitutional amendment in Arizona that allowed title companies to do this. I remember he was proud of the fact that only in Mohave County did the measure fail for lack of votes, whereas the measure won by a landslide in all other Arizona counties.

Father's skill and patience were stretched a little too far one time. His job one Thanksgiving day was to carve the turkey at the table in front of the many guests, which he did not like to do. After a few slips and slides of the large turkey, it was coming off the platter and onto the tablecloth. Guests began to watch quietly. Then, without a spoken word, father picked the turkey off the table where it last fell and drop-kicked it off the floor and through the kitchen door out into the backyard. Father then took the whole party out to a restaurant to finish the dinner. Mother never asked him to carve again.

Rotary International was a very important part of my father's life. Mother enjoyed it as well. Frank became District Governor of Rotary International from the District of Arizona, which also included a club in Needles, California. He served as District governor in 1954 and 1955, the first year I returned to Kingman to practice law with him. He and Mother made the required personal and official visits to each Rotary Club in the District during that time, which I believe then numbered about 27. Each visit took about three or four days, including a social get-together in the evening, a formal meeting with the officers of the club on the following day to go over current policies and practices of the club, and then his formal visit to the club at its regular weekly meeting. At that meeting he addressed the members of the club, giving his appraisal of the club's compliance with the goals of Rotary International, and suggestions for improvement in areas needed.

Dad and Mother loved those club visits so. They made many long-lasting friendships all over the state and country. Each club would present them with a gift on Dad's official visit. For his services as Governor, the district gave them an Atmos clock, which wound itself by barometric and temperature changes. Joan and I still have the clock, which has worked continuously since 1955.

Dad discovered he had diabetes while I was in high school. At that time local doctors in Kingman knew little about the disease or how to treat it. He treated it with pills rather than hypodermic injections. He obtained information and medication at the Sansum Clinic in Santa Barbara, California. Dad also had glaucoma during later years. Neither of these conditions seemed to affect his work or personal life, although his feet were very sensitive. He couldn't even stand to have a bed sheet touch them. Dad had suffered from diabetes from

My first best friend, two years old

*Me in tuxedo made by my mother for the Arizona state convention
of the Legion Auxiliary*

middle age, but otherwise seemed healthy and vigorous until his first, and last, heart attack.

Dad died in October, 1968, of an apparent heart attack. Joan and I were on a deer-hunting trip, camped out in the southern end of the Peacock mountain range when he died. The Sheriff was not able to locate us, although I had left a detailed handwritten map in case of emergency. When we returned from hunting on Sunday, we were advised that Dad had died the Friday night before.

Mother continued living in the large house she and Dad had built at the end of Spring Street until she died in 1971. The house was much too large for her to keep up, but she would allow no discussion about her moving to an apartment closer to us, so that we could help her and she could have frequent visits with her three young grandchildren. She was very lonely and depressed after Dad's death. Most of her old friends had passed away before she did, and she had very little social life. She frequently said she did not want to live without Dad, and when she developed congestive heart failure in the months before she died, she indicated she just wished she could be left alone to join her husband.

Both Mother and Dad were important contributors to the early history of Kingman and Mohave County. It was primarily through Dad's efforts that Kingman incorporated as a city, and he was very instrumental in helping Mohave County locate the Ford Proving Ground in Yucca, south of Kingman. He served as the first City Attorney for the City of Kingman for almost two years before I succeeded him in 1954. His strong leadership served the City well and started it down the path to success. Both Dad and Mother acted as unofficial ambassadors of good will on behalf of Mohave County and the City of Kingman wherever they traveled. They are still remembered fondly and with honor by many old-timers in Kingman.

2

EARLY KINGMAN
(PEOPLE, PLACES
AND THINGS)

Kingman already had a long and illustrious history prior to our family settling there in 1929. Then, it was a bustling community, the county seat of Mohave County, and had a population of about 1,500 to 2,000. Oatman, Goldroad and Chloride were then larger, thriving mining communities, each boasting about 5,000 or more residents. Kingman existed primarily to serve those mining communities. Most people living in Kingman worked in the trades related to the operation or serving of the mines, as well as the ranching, farming and railroad industries then flourishing in the area. Huge chuffing steam locomotives brought raw materials and goods several times a day to Kingman for the mines and ranches, and left loaded with gold, silver, copper ore and cattle. It was only in the 20s or early 30s, that gasoline-engine driven trucks began delivering the timber and equipment that had arrived by train to the distant mines, supplanting the horse and mule teams that had done this work before.

The streets of Kingman were either graded dirt or gravel. The main commercial streets were wide enough to allow the 20-mule or horse freight teams to turn around on them. The main street, then called "Front Street" (now Andy Devine Avenue) eventually became U.S. Highway 66, connecting Chicago to Los Angeles. I am not sure when it became paved or black-topped, but in 1929 it most likely was the only sur-faced road or street in the community when I arrived. Before becoming Highway 66, the main east-west road came into Kingman on the north through White Cliffs, where the ruts of wagons in the soft sandstone still exist showing the path used by the wagons of the pioneers. Back then, the road was known as the "Old Trails Highway." It crossed the railroad tracks at Fourth Street and went south through town. On the southwest corner below the railroad tracks was the Old Trails Garage, then a large service station and repair garage for cars and trucks.

Ethnically and culturally the community was very diverse. Chinese rail workers who had come to help construct the railroad, remained in Kingman after the completion of the construction of the railroad. They had a tight-knit community on both sides of Front Street from First Street to Third Street. A large Chinese steam laundry existed next to and just north-west of the old abandoned steam generating electric plant, which was south of the old intersection of Highways 93 and

66. The White House Cafe, a fine Chinese restaurant, operated next to the old Kingman Drug Store on the east side
of Fourth Street and Andy Devine Avenue. It had been one
of the town's best eating places since before the turn of the
century. It is said that many underground tunnels connected
the White House and other Chinese establishments within
the downtown area, so that the movements of the Chinese
would not be readily known. There are tales of opium dens
being operated underground in these tunnels. Many opium
pipes have been found in the basements and outhouses of the
downtown buildings.

The Hualapai tribe had an encampment on the hill west
of the downtown area, about a quarter of a mile from the
old county hospital building (now some county offices). I
am not sure how many lived there, but there were quite a
few who did, living in tents and wickiups. They had many
horses and burros that strayed throughout the town. Some
would meet the trains near the Harvey House restaurant
just west and across Fourth Street from the railroad depot.
There they sold blankets, baskets, pottery and some jewelry to
the tourists arriving on the trains. At that time trains stopped
at towns for water for their steam locomotives and even
for passengers' meals at the Harvey House, which was
one of a chain of restaurants along the line that imported
comely young ladies to wait on the customers. Several of these
"Harvey Girls" stayed on in Kingman, marrying ranchers
and miners.

37

Jewish merchants established clothing stores and tailor stores in this growing mining community, as well. They too maintained a close ethnic group, although to my knowledge they did not have a temple for religious worship. I think they worshipped together in their homes. The Spector family (Albert and his brother Ned) lived in the large rock house behind our Spring Street home. The Van Marter family later bought their home.

To my knowledge, no African-Americans lived in Kingman. As late as the 1940s I can remember signs on the highways that said Blacks were not welcome in Kingman. They could not find a place that would serve them food or lodging in the town. I was told of cross-burning ceremonies at night to warn the African-Americans to move on. It wasn't until World War II and the establishment of the Kingman Army Airbase with its thousands of gunnery cadets living on the airfield that they were grudgingly allowed into town and commercial establishments. Even then, off-base habitation of African-Americans was discouraged.

Mexicans made up a significant portion of the population of Kingman, as were the Hualapai. I attended school with members of both of these races and was not aware of any overt discrimination toward them. Some Mexican children were especially good marble players. Marble playing was what most boys did after school or during recess time. There were no organized athletic programs in grammar school. The only grammar or grade school in Kingman was at the north end of

Fifth Street, and it went up to the eighth grade. I believe it is now called Palo Christi School.

Kingman had only one movie theater when I arrived. It was Lang's Theater, located on the northwest corner of Fourth Street and Andy Devine Street. It is now a vacant lot. It was a two-story building like the rest of the buildings on that block. At one time, there was a bowling alley on the second floor. The same motion picture usually played each evening for a week, and the strong light to project the images on the screen was made by electric arcs between two fountain pen-shaped carbon rods about a half-inch in diameter and six inches in length. The projectionist usually threw these into the street when they became too short to use. These stubs made great carbon pencils for the graffiti of the day, written usually on what few sidewalks we had in town. As we had no television in those days, going to the movies was a big event for kids. On Saturday afternoons there were kid's matinees, with serial stories that continued from one Saturday to the next. Some of the favorite serials of the time were Flash Gordon, the Shadow, the Lone Ranger and the Green Hornet.

On the nights that you didn't go to the show, you played games in the streets under one of the few streetlights, such as Kick the Can or Hide-and-Go-Seek. Later, Spin the Bottle was a favorite in mixed groups at parties. In that game, the boys and girls sat around on the floor in a circle, and the boy whose turn it was to spin the milk bottle got to kiss the girl it ended up pointing to. Then the girl got to spin the bottle.

After you had seen the weekly movie, you had to find things to do. No one did it for you. Kids then were able to do that, without television. Girls sewed, painted, and cooked. Boys made model airplanes, hunted with B. B. guns, played football or baseball in the streets, made sidewalk carts, roller skated, or went fishing. It was a fun time in children's lives. Parents were not worried about drugs, or child molesters or cars running over the kids in the streets.

During my childhood, streets north and south of Andy Devine or Front Street were dusty and dark at night. What few streetlights there were, were at intersections and rarely in residential neighborhoods. On the nights when there was no moon or starlight to light the way home after the movie, I remember walking in almost total darkness up the street toward home, with my arms extended in front of me to make sure I didn't inadvertently bump into a sleeping burro or horse standing in the middle of the street. Although normally docile and friendly, rudely awakened burros were likely to kick.

Mrs. Cohenour, who was quite old at the time and who lived in a large home on the hill north of the courthouse, drove an electric car around town. She frequently startled us as we played baseball or football in the street. The vehicle was so silent we would not hear it coming. I think she took great pleasure in sneaking up on us. She would wait until she was very near us and then honk her loud klaxon horn (Oo-ooogah!). Now that I think of it, she had a little smile on her face as we jumped out of her way.

My parents lived in several homes during the first few years after they moved to Kingman. I believe the first one was a rock and stucco home on the north side of Spring Street just east of First Street. Then they moved to a small frame house on the south side of Beale Street between Fifth and Sixth Streets. I remember we were snowbound in that home for several days in either 1936 or 1937. The snow was over six feet deep. You could not even see your car in the yard. All our pipes were frozen, and we had to melt snow to drink and to cook and bathe. Our stoves and home heat ran on wood cut from trees in either the Cerbat or Hualapai mountains. Most families cut their own wood with saws and axes.

Next, we lived in a very interesting green and white wooden two-story house that was located where the Masonic Temple is now, on Fourth Street just south of the old post office. It had a large combination living room-dining room, a bedroom, and a kitchen and bath on the ground floor. There were two bedrooms and a bath on the second floor. To go upstairs, one ascended a very grand wooden staircase with lathe-turned balustrades. Heating in that home was by kerosene or oil burning portable stoves that we moved from room to room. That home had a wonderful screened-in porch on the front part of the second floor, overlooking the street below. We slept there in the summer to catch the cool breezes of the evening. The screened porch also was a wonderful place to shoot water pistols at people walking on the sidewalk below. The screen was dark enough in color that it was difficult to see through to tell what was happening. The targets would look up in surprise, wondering if it were beginning to rain.

Because there was then no home delivery, everyone had to go to the post office each weekday to pick up the mail. The post office was a very popular meeting place in the morning, where many gathered to visit and show off prize vegetables and melons. Ranchers gathered there to discuss how long it had been since the last good rain and how the feed was growing. As an aside, it might be interesting for you to know that the climate in the Kingman area changed greatly from the middle of the 19th century. An early pioneer, Greeley Clack, Betty Grounds and Ollie Bonds' father, successfully grew winter wheat in Golden Valley in the 1880s without irrigation. Also, when the first cattlemen came into the Hualapai Valley south of Anteres Point, the grass was tall enough to brush the stirrups of the cowboys' saddles.

The lawn in front of the post office was also the place where hunters proudly displayed their biggest deer or elk killed during hunting season. Once in a while a large mountain lion or rattlesnake would be shown there. I remember seeing a huge wild boar (feral pig) being shown off there by Howard Hill, then a very famous archer, who had killed the pig with his bow, near what later became Bullhead City. The boar must have weighed over 500 pounds. (There were two broadhead arrows placed close to each other right between the pig's eyes.) The Rucker family, parents of Ray and Ellis Rucker, raised pigs south of what is now Bullhead City. It is thought that the wild pigs that were hunted near the river may have been descendants of the domestic pigs that got loose from the Rucker farm. Feral pigs revert to primitive form when some time passes after they escape, growing long hair and huge tusks in their mouth. They can be quite aggressive and dangerous when startled or cornered in thick underbrush near the river, especially a sow with a litter of piglets.

The wooden home we lived in on Fourth Street was where I first became aware of what my father did for a living. One of the bedrooms of the house on the first floor, just inside and to the right of the front door, had been converted into his law office. It was there he kept his few law books, old typewriter and mahogany desk and chairs. Although I was only about seven or eight years old, one of my chores with which I earned my allowance was to empty the wastebasket in Dad's office, and to dust and put red Old English oil furniture polish on the desk, chairs and cabinets. I still recall the smell of that furniture polish, and the pungent odor of Dad's cigar lingering on the furniture and papers in the office.

I remember people coming to talk with my father to ask his help in disputes, and to have him draw legal instruments for them – wills, deeds, mortgages, bills of sale, mining agreements, etc. The clients would come in, almost always without appointment, any time of day, sometimes even while we were eating dinner. Father would never send them away to come back another time. He would usher them into the office, smile, and ask how he could help, take notes and then prepare the necessary documents or pleadings for court action. I would sometimes sit on the well-polished wastebasket and listen to the discussions between lawyer and client.

Even at that age, I sensed the tension some people had when they came to Father for help. I watched as he assured them, kindly, thoughtfully, and respectfully, and reduced their tensions. I recall being proud that my father could do such wondrous things that made people feel better, much like those which a doctor did. I think it was then that I had my first thoughts of becoming a lawyer.

This was during the Great Depression, the mid-1930s, when most people in the cities were out of work, had lost their savings through bank closures, and were greatly concerned about their future. Many had to sell their homes, their farms, and other property just to raise enough money to feed their families. People in Kingman did not fare much better. Father's legal bills were frequently paid with chickens, eggs, sides of bacon or a quarter of beef. It was my recollection that Father never refused anyone his services merely because he or she could not pay and he never brought legal action against clients who he thought could pay but didn't.

My mother told the story of how one day during the Depression, they were broke. They were literally down to their last dime. I was just a small child then and needed milk. Father said he would go to the store and use the dime to buy milk for my dinner. Mother was very proud and did not want anyone to know that we were in financial trouble. Instead of my milk,

Mother insisted that Frank walk down to the drugstore and buy the best cigar that this ten-cent piece would purchase. (In those days that was a pretty good cigar.) He did in fact go to the drug store, carefully chose an elegant cigar, put the dime down on the counter and walked out of the store looking every bit the successful and prosperous lawyer. As he stood by the curb, lighting the cigar, a man walked up to him and asked if he were a lawyer. Dad said he was, and the man asked if he would draft a deed for him to convey some property. In those days, the legal fee for drawing a Warranty Deed in Joint Tenancy was $5.00, which the man had the money to pay. Mother said they were so grateful for that fee that father typed the deed himself, and decorated it with the then-customary ribbons and hot-wax-seal. Father always felt that this was the turning point in their lives, when things got better for them financially. Those five dollars could then feed our family for a week.

During this time, my father held a position with the U.S. Government similar to that of a U.S. Magistrate. He dealt with initial appearances for people charged with federal crimes, mostly misdemeanors, set bail, arranged prisoner transport by federal marshals and held or arranged other preliminary legal proceedings. At that time it was illegal for a Native American to buy, sell or consume any alcoholic beverage except tulapai, tiswin or corn beer, which weren't commonly made by the Native Americans any longer. Because of the frequency with which they got caught with illegal liquor and had to appear before him, my father became a very respected and feared person in the community, at least from their perspective. They did not want to be on the wrong side of "Judge" Frank Gordon.

For this reason, when as a young boy I would wander into the Hualapai camp on the west side of town, I was treated very special. I was given melons and jerky, and if I asked to ride a burro or horse, I almost always was given permission for extended periods of time. At the time, I had no awareness of why I was being so generously treated. I naively took their actions as signs of pure friendship. Whatever the motivation, and unaware as I was, I appreciated the friendship given me by the people and got to know a lot of them quite well. I also was allowed to be present at several of their events I now feel other Anglos would not have been permitted. Hopefully, the initial reason for their courtesies to me finally gave way, I believe, to a genuine liking of me as a person. My great empathy toward Native American people came about as a result of these early contacts.

When I was about eight or nine years old, a Hualapai elder, whose name I cannot recall, asked permission for me to accompany him on a horseback ride in the hills near town. He evidently had the respect of my father, who agreed. I arrived at the camp before sunrise on the appointed day. Still in the gray dawn, we rode horses somewhere out of camp into the mountains. It was just the two of us. I can't even recall the direction we took, but we traveled for a while until we came to a rather high mesa, on which was a large circle of boulders. We arrived there just as the sun was rising. Later as I thought about it, the place was obviously one where the Hualapai met or worshipped.

The old elder got off his horse and sat on one of the rocks, silently staring at the rising sun for what seemed to be a long time, ignoring me totally. He made no sounds or gestures. He just sat there in silent meditation. Then he got back on his horse and we returned to camp. I did not know what he was thinking, but within days I was told that he had died. Looking back now, I am convinced that this act of friendship to include me in these personal moments was not a random act. I sincerely believe that he sensed that one day I would be a person that might be in a position to wield some influence regarding Indian people, and that he wished to share an intimate, personal experience with me in order that I might later feel a close bond to his race and culture. I shall treasure that silent period of communication as one of the more important and significant experiences of my life.

One of the most important structures in Mohave County was and perhaps still is the Mohave County Courthouse. It was a beautifully designed and impressive building when constructed in 1915, right after Arizona became a state, in 1912. The courtroom within the building was of dramatic design. It had high wood-paneled walls, a large Tiffany-style stained glass skylight giving light to the room, Tiffany-style lamps on the bench, oak hardwood bar and decorated bench, over

100 connected wooden spectators' seats with tilt-up bottoms under which were wire hat racks for men's large hats. There were also brightly polished brass spittoons at the end of each row of spectators' and jurors' seats. The Court reporter's seat, counsel table and judge's bench also were also equipped with spittoons. To my knowledge this courtroom still has the largest spectator capacity in the state of Arizona. It was wisely designed that way in order to accommodate the large crowds of people that would come to witness the important events that occurred there. In those days, trials were scheduled as much as possible to occur after fall roundup and harvest and before spring roundup for branding and planting, so that ranchers and farmers could attend trials and serve as jurors, as well as spectators. Also, the building had no cooling, so that period of time was the most comfortable one for trials to occur.

Some very interesting trials were held in that courtroom. For example, one was the method of counting and challenging handwritten political election ballots in the county elections. Another case was how far the owner of a hard rock mining claim could pursue the veins of ore that began within his claim but pursued the veins below his neighbor's surface.

Another old case that I was told about was about three Chinese defendants from California who were charged with murder. They supposedly killed a local Chinese cook from Kingman, and were caught before they made it to the California line. The defense attorney for all three defendants requests were denied for a week. All three were convicted and hanged within a short time. If that is true, trials are certainly not delayed in Mohave County.

Public jury trials were tremendously important occasions in the community, and that courtroom was generally looked to as being the final answer to all community disputes. It was well attended by all local citizenry who were then not distracted by home-entertainment centers with televisions, videos, video games and compact disc players, or the Internet.

The Mohave County Courthouse has a balcony on the south side of the second story courtroom, from which I can recall having witnessed from below debates between the then Judge of the Superior Court and the County Attorney or some other public official over issues of law, politics or morals. The metal statues depicting World War I servicemen in the south courtyard of the courthouse was then surrounded by a fishpond with many beautiful goldfish in it. The cool grass lawn shaded by bearing mulberry trees served as an amphitheater for many people who sat on the lawn in the evening to hear these debates. They were important learning experiences of the day.

Campaigns for state and local public office were held in Kingman, Wikiup, Chloride and Oatman, using head-to-head personal debate between the candidates at public barbecues, steak-fries or cornbakes. In 1936, when I was seven, my father ran for County Attorney. I accompanied him on these campaigns, heard him debate, and slept out on the ground on a trip to Short Creek (now Colorado City) on the "strip" north of the Grand Canyon, where most of the people at that time were self-exiled polygamists or outlaws running from law enforcement. At more than one gate, we were met by several men on horseback with rifles on their saddles, asking why we were there and whom we had come to see. Obviously these people were cautious about being spied on by law enforcement officials.

Public officials, and those who wanted to become public officials, in those days could not rely on ads on television, radio or in newspapers to campaign for office. They had to knock on doors and discuss issues with people in person. Politicians were much more personally known and were held more accountable than they are today.

The lobby of the Beale Hotel was a place of great interest and importance on election nights. It was there on election nights that the latest polling-place results were recorded on great sheets of paper on the walls of the lobby. Many people stayed up all night in order to find out who won the elections. Precinct officials around the County would bring their vote tallies to the County Recorder's office and this information was telephoned to the Beale Hotel where the results were placed on the paper sheets on the walls. Precincts on the strip had to deliver their vote tallies in person in order to be official. The results sometimes did not get to the Courthouse until late the next day, and in close elections these precincts were very important. Many elections were not decided until midnight the day after election because of the length of time it took to get the official results from Mount Trumbull, Wolf Hole, Tuweep or Short Creek precincts north of the Grand Canyon.

I grew up knowing some very interesting local politicians. We had several early judges of the Superior Court who were impressive to a youngster like me. First, there was Judge Carl J. Crook, who served as a territorial judge before Arizona became a state, and then as Mohave County's first Superior Court Judge after statehood.

Crook – what a name for a lawyer or judge! His name was an anachronism, however. He was a very highly educated and greatly respected lawyer in his early days. He got his under-graduate degree in Minnesota, but attended Oxford University in England for his law studies. That was very unusual in those days. Crook originally came to Arizona as a mining prospec-tor, but then decided to hang out his shingle as a lawyer in the territory of Arizona. He was very active in mining cases and represented the Tennessee-Schuykill Mine in Chloride, a very big silver producer in the 1920s.

By the time I became aware of Judge Crook, he was quite old, but still handsome, with long, carefully combed straight white hair and a very fair, ruddy complexion. He usually wore a three-piece brown suit and fancy tie with a gold stick-pin. He lived in a stone house where the J. C. Penny's building is now downtown, and walked with great strides two miles each morning. He married Mary, who became his secretary, and had an office in the second story of the old Central Com-

51

mercial Building. He had the largest collection of law books of all local lawyers, except for the official County Law Library. Late in life, Judge Crook's mind and memory left him, but slowly and by degrees. He continued to practice, however, and represented many clients in court. Sometimes Judge Crook forgot which side he represented right in the middle of trial and the judge or other lawyers would have to remind him. All lawyers in the County revered and respected Judge Crook and protected him against his own forgetfulness, even to the last. After he died, Mary Crook, his widow, continued his practice of the law in the Judge's old office for many years, although she was not licensed. She continued to draw wills, partnerships, corporations, powers of attorney and other legal documents.

By the way, in the Courthouse are pictures of every Superior Court judge that has served since statehood in Mohave County, but not including a Judge Ellis, who refused to allow his picture to be taken. Ellis ended up in prison later. In collecting the pictures of all the old judges, I even tried to get a prison picture of Ellis, but couldn't.

After Judge Crook, there was a Judge Dolman, who had a short left leg, and wore about a four-inch wooden extension on his shoe so he did not have such a pronounced limp. I remember playing marbles or floating a wooden boat in the street after a rain and hearing his wooden foot come clumping down the street. He was otherwise unremarkable. I think he was a justice of the peace at the time.

There was a Judge E. Elmo Bollinger, a roly-poly curly

haired good-natured man who had defeated my father in his race for County Attorney. He served as a Superior Court judge later, and some question later came up as to the appropriate disposition of funds he collected in the sale of Townsite Trustee lots during his administration.

The next interesting judge was Judge J. W. Faulkner, who served a record twenty years as Mohave County's Superior Court Judge. Faulkner was so morally offended by the practices of the polygamists living on the strip that in 1952 or 1953, he convinced Arizona's Governor Pyle to get then-Attorney General Ross F. Jones to raid Short Creek, arrest the men who had more than one wife and take away all their children. If it weren't such a tragedy to the families involved, that raid could be considered an absolute comedy of errors.

For months the residents of Short Creek knew the raid was coming. Months in advance, dozens of people in Kingman were deputized as Special Deputies Sheriff (members of a Posse Commitatus) to assist in the raid. These people could not keep their special status secret, so their roles were well known in the whole county. The raid was most dramatically scheduled to occur on the night of a total eclipse of the moon, in complete darkness, ostensibly to maintain an element of surprise. The approach to the small backwoods community was to be made by all these vehicles on a dirt, single-track back road into the community, and being led by our then-Sheriff Frank L. Porter. The Arizona Attorney General officially made the raid, but Porter insisted on being the first car in.

On the evening of the raid, the Deputy Attorney General who actually organized and led the raid, Paul LaPrade, a law classmate of mine, held a press conference in the Flagstaff High School Gym, where previously invited television, magazine and newspaper reporters were gathered and briefed on the upcoming raid, and were allowed to accompany the law enforcement officers in their official cars and in buses provided. At that time, I was told the Arizona Highway Patrol, our official state police department, had only 55 cars on the road in all of Arizona, and 51 of them were committed to be used in this raid, leaving only 4 to patrol the whole highway system of our state during the two or three days of the raid. As a third year law student, I personally asked Governor Howard Pyle how he justified this use of that many state cars when he spoke to the law school in Tucson in 1954. His response was that Mohave County law enforcement could not do it all and that this was a matter of statewide safety. This didn't convince me.

The raid was made on what I was told were charges of "open and notorious insurrection against the State of Arizona," claiming that these peoples' communal religious practices were essentially communistic acts dangerous to the state. The real reason for the use of that type of criminal charge was at that time (and I believe at the present) there was no law against polygamy in Arizona. There were laws against this practice in Utah and a U.S. statute proscribed it. Mormon families have successfully defeated efforts to

54

criminalize polygamy in Arizona because it would be embarrassing to their families and ancestors who had practiced that
form of plural marriage.

After the press conference and around midnight (the
appointed time of the eclipse of the moon), the long column
of law enforcement cars, buses and trucks, spaced several
minutes apart, started down the road with no headlights, pur-
portedly to avoid detection. Sheriff Porter in the first car heard
what turned out to be a dynamite signal charge on a hillside
off to the side of the road. The blast so frightened Porter that
he attempted to turn his patrol car around in the middle of
the one-lane mountain road and got it stuck, thus blocking
the entire column for almost an hour. When they finally got
Porter's car straightened up and going again, the whole army
of law enforcement officers, state, county and special deputies, finally arrived in the town of Short Creek in the pre-dawn
darkness. There, the entire community was waiting for them
in the schoolyard: men, women and children, singing religious
hymns. Their children were checked for contagious diseases
(of which none were found) by Dr. Arnold, our county physician, and then transported by school bus to waiting foster
homes in Mesa. The men were arrested, tried and convicted
and put on probation.

Later, the procedures used by Judge Faulkner and Maricopa Juvenile Court Judge Lorna Lockwood in the juvenile
proceedings were set aside by the Arizona Supreme Court,
Justice Struckmeyer writing, declaring that the judges had

deprived the children of due process by not allowing their attorney to properly defend them. These children were then returned to their parents after almost two years of absence, without even an official apology. Judge Lockwood went on to become a justice on the Arizona Supreme Court, and later she became the first woman to be Chief Justice of any state Supreme Court in the United States.

The whole Short Creek raid was such a fiasco that Governor Pyle and Attorney General Ross Jones both were defeated in their bids for re-election the following year, and Judge Faulkner quietly resigned from office, as he had planned to do anyway. Both Pyle and Jones expected to gain political advantage by carrying on the raid, but it backfired dramatically on them and ended their political careers.

The judge who followed Faulkner was Charles P. Elmer, a highly respected and intelligent jurist. He had maintained a very successful private law practice in Kingman, specializing in mining law. Judge Elmer had emphysema and other bronchial problems from being gassed while in the Army in World War I in France. In the last few years of his term as judge he had great trouble climbing the stairs to the courtroom on the third floor of the courthouse. There was no elevator at that time. I was told that Elmer's political rival, the County Attorney, would not allow the Board of Supervisors to pay for a health chair or lift that the judge could sit in and which would follow the stair bannister up from the basement. Judge Elmer's health got so bad that he retired in May 1962, and I was appointed by Governor Fannin to succeed him.

Other interesting early Mohave County politicians were state Senator Earle Cook and state Representative Jim Glancy. Both of them were known to run out of words in civil debate on the floor and challenge their opponents to fist fights in the hall. Glancy was a contractor and almost always wore a painter's hat to caucuses or voting sessions.

State Senator Robert Morrow always seemed a wise and morally upright man, until it became known that he and Senator Giss from Yuma County had each been on a $500 per month retainer (or consultant's fee) from Robert McCulloch, the entrepreneur/developer who ended up buying from the state (with Morrow's and Giss's help) all of the land upon which Lake Havasu City sits. This took a lot of wrangling, as the state and federal land all had to be blocked out solid as state land, requiring an exchange of lands between the State of Arizona and the U.S. Government. Then, the state had to arrange through appropriate legislation (again with Giss's and Morrow's help) to bypass certain existing laws that would have given military veterans preference to bid on any lands sold by the state.

From the standpoint of culture in early Kingman, I am not aware of much in the way of community-supported cultural events. No opera house was constructed, as had been done in other mining towns such as Silver City, Nevada. Performances of traveling orchestras or solo performers sometimes occurred at the high school auditorium. Reading groups were organized at the little red schoolhouse public library. Dances were held at the school gym, and in the American Legion and Elks halls.

The booming towns of Oatman and Goldroad had professional, uniformed baseball teams and large uniformed bands, which came to Kingman and put on performances in the baseball park, which was where the steam locomotive now stands. The Hualapais from Peach Springs had a band that also came to play at baseball games and parades.

On the 4th of July, and on Armistice Day (later known as Veterans Day) there were wonderful parades, with bands and marching veterans. Later there were picnics, footraces in the street on the north side of Central Commercial, and hard-rock hand drilling contests by brawny workers from the mines. Patriotism was very high in the community. No one would dare remain seated for the passing of the flag during a parade or the singing of the Star Spangled Banner. A derogatory remark about our president or our country during those holidays could well cause a fistfight.

People really enjoyed dancing in those days. My parents would take me to Oatman for dances at the old Honolulu Club, or the ranchers' dances at the Wickiup or Hackberry schoolhouses. The Wickiup dance was always an exciting experience. It was said that people attending divided into three shifts: one shift danced, one drank, and the third fought. Dances in Chloride were held at the local brothel run by Rosie, who ran a bar and house run in a big barn on the main street of town. Rosie later married the game ranger C. B. "Kirk" Tatum, who much later was elected Clerk of the Superior Court. Kirk was Clerk for several years after I became Judge. He could not take shorthand and wouldn't let anyone else cover open court proceedings. The courtroom minutes sometimes were strange indeed.

The dances at Rosie's Barn were well attended and enjoyed by all. No one seemed to be concerned about what the principal business of the place was. I remember learning about dances such as the Varsovienne, and the Drunken Schottische, which is much like a modern line dance, but to different music. I was too little to take part in the dances, so I would ride my tricycle or wagon around the edges of the dance floor or in the yard. There were many other children there doing the same and it was lots of fun – much laughter and happy music.

The Mohave County Bar Association was a very active organization during the 1930s and 1940s. Early members, in addition to my father, were judges Crook, Bollinger, Faulkner, Elmer, lawyers Carl Hammond, Louis L. Wallace, and O. Ellis Everett. The Bar frequently had dinner meetings with their spouses. These were held at what was called "Frenchy's Café," which was a rather elegant restaurant run by a French couple and their daughter at the top of El Trovatore Hill on the west side of the road, just about where the Terrible Herbst gas station was. I remember how very intellectual and

formal these evenings seemed compared to the dancing at
Rosie's dance hall.

3

MY YOUTH

Some of my earliest recollections were while we lived in the house on Fourth Street, next to the old post office. I remember the good smells of food being cooked by Mother in the kitchen, as I played in a sand pile in the back yard, or floated miniature wooden boats down the street in front of the house after a rain. I remember my father's office and the seriousness of that place.

Grammar School

I can recall that when I became school age, I didn't want to go. My parents' coaxing was to no avail. Then my father came upon a plan to frighten me into going. He took me up to the courthouse and introduced me to Sheriff Ernest "Ernie" Graham, who showed me the jail where people who break the law go. Ernie Graham was, as most sheriffs of small counties then were, a former rancher or farmer. He was short, portly and reputedly a very good shot with a pistol. The jail was the small two-story concrete historic building that still stands just east of the courthouse. It had about six cells upstairs and two larger "drunk tanks" downstairs. Dad and Sheriff Graham then introduced me to Charles Adams, who was the Mohave County Truant Officer and I think also the only adult and juvenile probation officer for the county. As Truant Officer, his duty was to see to it that all school-age children were in school when they were supposed to be. Adams was a small, thin man with grey hair and a hatchet-like face with a moustache. He looked mean to me, like a rat. He always wore a gray suit with a vest, a bow tie, hat and a gold watch chain. Both Sheriff Graham and Truant Officer Adams told me that children who would not go to school would have to live in the jail. I was convinced that school had to be better than that. I went to school the next day and never considered dropping out again.

Our Kingman "grammar school" was where Palo Cristi School is now. All eight primary grades were taught there. Duncan McRuer was the principal of the school. He was a stern, gray-haired man with a ruddy complexion who ruled the school with an iron hand. He had a soft voice with a Scottish burr. Paddling children was not done. However, if you were really bad, Mr. McRuer would smack the palms of your hands with a ruler. One time he took a small metal water pistol away from me and stomped it flat on the concrete floor. I was in the second or third grade and felt I had been unfairly treated, as I had not squirted anyone with it at the time. (At least not that day.) I was careful not to be disciplined in school,

Bobby and me, approximately 11 years old

because my father told me that whatever sanction I would get in school would be nothing compared with what I would get when I got home.

Although I was a thoroughly spoiled only child, I did occasionally get a deserved paddling. The ultimate threat by my father was that I would get a spanking with his razor strop. The strop was a pair of leather straps about three feet long and about four inches wide used to sharpen straight razors, which men used for shaving in those days. This was before safety razors and blades were popular. Electric razors were to be invented much later. The strop was always used as a threat, but never applied.

One time I had done something my mother thought was particularly bad and she told me she would tell Dad to spank me. When Dad got home, mother told him what I had done and he agreed that a spanking was in order, but decided that he would do it after dinner. In my opinion, that was cruel and excessive. I had to wait for a few hours before the punishment would be administered, and I was sure he was going to use the razor strop. The more time that went by, the more apprehensive I was. I decided I would hide the razor strop. My method of hiding it was to flush it down the toilet, which of course stopped up the plumbing and the toilet backed up all over the bathroom floor. Dad called the plumber who found the problem. He pulled the razor strop out, all soggy and curled up. Dad was pretty angry with me, but sensed my apprehension and the humor of the situation. He and Mother sat down and had a good laugh. I don't think I even got a hand-spanking for that, which was probably deserved. Dad said that I so skillfully talked him out of punishment on that occasion that he knew then that I had the potential to be a convincing trial lawyer.

I do not remember too much about early grades in school, or many teachers. I do remember a large, raw-boned, red-headed woman Ms. James, who was my teacher in third grade and then followed me into fourth and fifth grades. Penmanship was a big thing in school in those days. Ms. James was particularly strict about our handwriting. My penmanship was not good then, and has become progressively worse ever since. Ms. James would rant and rave about those of us who did not write well. She used some of my work as bad examples. Still, I liked her. She made each of us believe we had great potential, and she strove to make us reach it. In a small town, parents and teachers were often social acquaintances or even close friends. Teachers considered it their personal obligation to see that each child did his or her best.

The playground at the grammar school had no grass on it. We played marbles or baseball on the gravel, getting skinned up and dirty each day. Mr. Bill Ball was our shop teacher in a separate building behind the school. As I recall, he was the only male teacher in grammar school. Tall, muscular and handsome, Mr. Ball supervised playground activities and was our early male role model. He had a great sense of humor. Occasionally when the bell would ring ending class, he would stand in the door of the building and say that we had to push him out of the way before we could leave. We would pile on him and he would resist enough to make it fun but not enough to discourage the kids. He was a private plane pilot who gave flying instructions on the side. In 1990 Mr. Ball came to see me in Phoenix. He was still teaching driver's education and was concerned about the lack of state standards in driving schools. He looked great. He even remembered some of the things that I had made in shop, such as a pair of bookends and a table I had made over fifty years before. My work must have really been bad for him to remember it so.

Two of my best friends in grade school were Clarence (Casey) Cummings and Jerry Rawlings. We were in the same class all the way from first grade through high school. We got along just great and shared all the wonders of growing up together. Casey lived in a modest wood frame home on the north side of Oak Street, the second house east of Fifth Street. I remember it as having a cool yard shaded by chinaberry trees. The house had a large front porch with a steel-framed cot on it. Casey's parents were Eva Cummings (previously Harris) and George. George was a retired mule-skinner who had spent most of his time freighting supplies from Kingman to Oatman and to the mines. Casey had an older brother, Donald.

The Cummings were kind and gentle with all children, welcoming all at their house. Eva thought nothing of feeding several extra children lunch or dinner. There were wonderful meals of beans and ham hocks, with homemade bread or biscuits. Water came from an "olla" hanging on the back porch. It was a clay pot hanging in a burlap bag that was kept wet, cooling the water. George was a great woodcarver. I would watch raptly as he took a pine board and transformed it into a lifelike replica of a long-barreled revolver and gave it to one of us. One time, he made me a life-sized wooden replica of a 30-30 Winchester saddle gun that I prized for many years. George also inspired me to whittle, which I would do by the hour with Casey and his father on their front porch. We would whittle and watch people and cars go by while listening to George's stories of the old days.

One time in 1939, while Casey and I were in his front yard, a large black touring car pulled up in the street in front of the yard and a tall, dark, good-looking stranger got out. We both recognized him as Clark Gable, the famous movie star. Carole Lombard, who was soon to become his wife, was with him. Gable came up to the wood picket fence and said to us, "Boys, do you know where the Methodist Church is? We want to get married." After we stopped gaping at him and the beautiful lady in the car, we finally were able to answer that we did, and directed him to go one block north to the corner of Fifth and Spring Streets where the old Methodist Church was at the time. Of course, we ran along after them, watched them go into the parsonage to get the minister, and went into the old church to witness the celebrated marriage of Clark Gable and Carole Lombard. After the ceremony, the couple spent their wedding night in Oatman at the Oatman

Hotel. It is said that the couple were extremely happy together. Carole was killed in an airline crash in the mountains near Las Vegas, Nevada in the early 1940s. By coincidence, my parents had taken me to Las Vegas on that weekend, and I was in that city when Clark Gable came to Vegas to claim his wife's body.

Casey and I were adventurous little brats. I think we tried everything together. Our first smoking adventure was sucking on a smoldering grapevine. Yuk! We had BB guns and were remarkably good shots with them. Like most kids of those days, we killed birds, bugs, lizards or anything else we could get close enough to. I am not proud of that now, but it seemed exciting at the time.

When we weren't hunting, whittling or playing marbles, Casey and I were interested in airplanes. At about age eight or nine, we carved solid small wooden replicas of planes. Then later, aged 10 or 11, Casey, Jerry and I got to be pretty good at assembling balsa wood model airplane kits that were glued to-gether on a pattern and covered with special paper. We would fly the completed products off the highest place we could find, which was usually the top of the stairs to the second floor of the Elks Building. Flying those models made us dream about being able to fly ourselves. We decided it was possible. To that end, we designed and built a contraption of our own, which we felt was sure to make us human gliders. It consisted of three major components: a fairly large pair of wings (about 5 feet long by about 1 ½ feet in width, made of balsa wood and doped paper, with holes in one end of each of them where you could insert arms and grasp handles); and a pair of pants that had a piece of cloth between the legs to act as a stabilizer, with a rudder attached to the middle and back part. Visualize the gliding position: arms outstretched, perhaps flapping; legs spread, facing down with tail stretched above. To us, it was the perfect design. We painted it all black. (One might ask how all this was accomplished without our parents learning about our project and putting an end to it; I honestly don't know.)

There was an old rusty tin garage behind our house on north Fourth Street, where the Masonic Temple is now. To Casey and me it seemed the logical place for the maiden flight of our plane. Both of us were eager to be the test pilot, but we could not decide who would have the honor. We flipped a coin and Casey won. I stood below, watching as Casey stood at the peak of the garage (about nine or ten feet above the ground) in all his glory. Smiling from ear to ear, Casey said, "Here I go!" flapping his arms grandly. All went very well for the first one or two flaps, but then as I recall he did a sharp bank to the left and started losing altitude very quickly. He made a 180-degree turn before he crashed on his left shoulder. Perhaps it would have been better for Casey if we had thought about building landing gear. Thankfully, Casey was not badly hurt. Just bruised. Laughing, he said, "Now Francis, it's your turn." I recommended we make some design changes first, and my turn never came.

Our home at 537 East Spring Street was just across the street from the mountain rim rising across the northeast portion of town. The mountain or hill was fairly steep and had lots of big boulders to climb. Chuckwallas and other lizards, as well as chipmunks could almost always be seen sunning themselves on top of the big rocks in the spring. It was fun chasing them.

We used to make sidewalk coasters out of roller skates nailed to the bottom of two-by-fours. These had a wooden box standing in front with wooden handles to hold onto. You would put one foot on the two-by-four and push with the other. Casey and I would terrorize pedestrians along the sidewalks in front of the courthouse, as we ambled clackety-clacking down Fifth Street in front of the Methodist Church, in front of the old firehouse, and clear to Central Commercial.

From sidewalk coasters we graduated to making four-wheeled hill coasters. We cleared trails down the mountain across the street from our East Spring Street house. We extended them almost up to the steep solid face of the mountain. Occasionally we would be successful in navigating the twisting gravel course all the way to the pavement on Sixth Street. If we made it that far without crashing, and made the turn onto Sixth, then it was a clear, fast ride from there all the way down Sixth Street, across Oak and Beale Streets, clear to Highway 66. We didn't stop at stop signs. We just hoped no one was coming. (Still no punitive action taken by parents.)

Roland and Courtney Paup, Dr. Paup's two boys, were really good at making hill coasters. They made elaborate ones, with steering wheels instead of ropes, with roller-bearing pneumatic wheels, not hard rubber ones. Casey and I were envious. We saved up and finally built one like the Paups, except it was even better. It was enclosed with three-ply plywood sides and top. Once in, the driver looked through a steering wheel and out and forward through a four-inch opening in the streamlined wooden body. The driver could see only forward. We painted it all white. It was frighteningly faster than any of our previous models. It also was more difficult to steer. Once built, we had to try our coaster out on the steepest paved hill in town, which was the road running north from the back of the courthouse. I think the street is an extension of Fourth Street. I know it ran steeply up the hill for about two blocks. There was a cross street between the top of the hill and the courthouse.

The courthouse then, as today, was surrounded by a strong two-rung black steel pipe fence about four feet high. The street we wanted to come down dead-ends into the courthouse, turning right and left between what is now the new jail and the juvenile detention center. There was always some gravel in the intersection for some reason. The plan was to coast down the two-block street and turn right to continue coasting toward Third Street, which was also paved.

With great effort Casey and I pulled and pushed our new super-coaster to the top of the hill. From that vantage point, the people around the courthouse looked very small. It was mid-morning, the streets were quiet, and the perfect

71

time for the coaster's maiden voyage. Again, who was to be the test-driver? We flipped a coin and again Casey won. He was to be privileged to test our pride and joy. I helped Casey into our wooden wonder, closed the canopy, and wished him well. Down the hill he went, gathering speed quickly.

Almost as soon as he started, I saw a Central Commercial lumber truck coming from the west, approaching our test run intersection. There was nothing either Casey or I could do. The coaster didn't have brakes, and I couldn't run fast enough to catch him. The lumber truck reached the intersection just before Casey and was fully stretched across the street when Casey got there. His only alternative at the time was to go under the truck in front of or behind the rear dual wheels of the flatbed truck. Fortunately, Casey was able to steer to the right of the wheels and go under the bed of the truck just behind the rear wheels.

That crisis over, Casey was at maximum speed when he came to the "t" intersection ending the street behind the courthouse. He turned the steering wheel to the right as he crossed the gravel. The coaster turned sideways, but instead of turning the corner, it slid sideways at about 15 miles per hour all the way across the intersection and crashed into and through the pipe fence. The coaster seemed to explode and plywood and other pieces went into the courthouse yard, leaving Casey draped over the lower rung of the pipe fence. Luckily, Casey again escaped serious injury. I think he lived a charmed life. There was not enough left of the coaster for Casey to insist that I take my turn.

Oftentimes, I was included in Cummings family hunting and fishing trips. At that time, all one had to do was drive out to Slaughterhouse Canyon south of Kingman to hunt quail. Quail and cottontail rabbits were so plentiful then that it was no problem to come back with a gunnysack full of birds. There was no bag limit at that time. Fishing at Temple Bar on Lake Mead was the "in" thing then. Hoover Dam (then Boulder Dam) had been recently completed and Lake Mead was only partially filled. Large lunker bass were common then. The Cummings did not have a boat, so we fished from the bank and camped on the shore. I remember eating Spam sandwiches and pork and beans right out of the can next to evening campfires.

I started working during the summers at about nine or ten years of age. I was not forced to work, but I think my father felt it would be good for me to learn the value of money and how hard it was to buy things. What I earned I could spend for whatever I wanted. First, I washed windows at the Babbitt Brothers Trading Company Store on the southwest corner of Fourth and Beale Streets. That building burned much later. The next year, I began as a stock boy at Central Commercial. My job initially was to unpack glassware, furniture, food and vegetables and stock the shelves. One or two summers later, I was promoted to assistant sales clerk in

73

the furniture department under Burton Porter, my department supervisor.

One of the reasons I started working was so that I could buy a horse. The Gates family, Jay Gates Sr. and Jay M. Gates, Jr., owned and operated a large and very good general mercantile store. You could buy anything there, from horseshoes and wagon parts to food, clothing and building materials. It was fun. Central was staffed by neat people. There was no minimum age or wage requirement then, so I worked for about fifty cents per hour to begin with. Burton Porter was kind to me, and helped me learn to cut and lay linoleum, fix window shades and screens, put furniture together, and a world of other useful tasks.

Jay Jr. was just out of college then, and had horses. I wanted one in the worst way, and my father said I could have one if I saved money for the horse and necessary tack, such as saddle, bridle, and other things. Jay Jr. sold me one of his horses for $30. She was a young unbroken filly about nine months old when I first got her. She had never been ridden or even saddled.

Now I had a horse and old saddle. Where could I keep her? It was either 1939 or 1940, just before World War II, and there were no zoning restrictions about keeping horses in town at that time. Burros and horses frequently were seen roaming the streets. But to build a corral in your yard might cause problems with the neighbors. There was room for a small corral just behind our garage, next to the dirt road that curved around the garage and became Sixth Street. I got the consent of our neighbor to the north, Mr. Seeley, who also worked at Central Commercial, to build a corral there, directly across the street from his white wooden house, on the condition that I keep the corral clean and odor free. I think my father and I built the corral ourselves. It was about 20 feet long and 12 feet wide, with a manger and water tub at the east end. The north side of the garage formed one wall of the corral, the three sides made of two by fours, and corner posts four by fours set in concrete. The gate was on the west end. The little bay filly fit the corral very well.

I knew nothing about "breaking" or training a horse, so I inquired from friends. I think I got most of my information from Leonard Neal and one of his nephews, a schoolmate of mine, Clifford Neal. At the time, there were only two ways of breaking a horse. One way was to "gentle break" her, by gradually making a pet out of the horse and slowly getting her used to having things put on her like a blanket, a bridle, and a saddle, then ever-so-gradually getting her used to having you lean on and over her so that you could eventually climb up on her back without frightening her and making her buck. The other way was to tie the horse to some strong post, blindfold her, put a saddle and blanket on, and climb aboard, without all the other formalities. Usually in the latter method the horse attempts to throw you off, and you keep up the process until the horse decides you are never going to quit trying and she gives up. Gentle breaking is the best way, as the horse ends up expecting only love and good things from you, not rough treatment which breeds fear.

I was having some success with the filly, having spent several weeks getting her confidence by petting and brushing her. I had progressed to the point where I could lean on her, lie across her back and put a hackamore bridle on and lead her. One day, Jay Gates, Jr. rode by on his stallion and told me I was wasting a lot of time. He said he would saddle and ride the filly at his home. Not knowing any better, I took the filly to his house, where he snubbed her to a post and put a blanket on her. She was used to that. Then he put a brand new saddle made by Porters in Phoenix on her and cinched it up tight. The filly didn't do anything more than express surprise at this new feature. Jay untied her and climbed on. The filly came unglued. She started bucking violently and spun around. Jay and the new saddle slid down on the filly's side, and Jay fell off. The filly went west down Oak Street at a gallop with the saddle under her belly and bridle reins flying. We had no other horse saddled to chase her, so we couldn't find her that day. Jay's brand new saddle was found in several pieces all through town, and the filly was found the next day near the Country Club none the worse for wear, at least physically.

I had trouble training her from that point, however. She was terrified when anyone came near her. She would kick me anytime I came up on her left side. I later found that sometime earlier something had injured her left eye and that she was developing something like a cataract in that eye. She probably only saw cloudy images on that side and not knowing what they were, would lash out with her back legs at anything coming up behind her on that side. Finally, it got so bad I couldn't handle her and sold her to Clifford Neal, who had much more skill and patience than I did. He was able to make something of her.

My next horse was a five- or six-year-old solid black gelding that I got from Choc Hamilton, who was quite a famous local roping champion. In fact, I was told he won ribbons for his roping in Madison Square Garden in New York City. I will call this horse "Jim", as his actual name was two words, the first of which was a colloquial reference to the black race, no longer politically or socially correct. Jim was a fully trained roping horse that Choc could not use any more because he had become "locoed" – he had eaten a great deal of loco weed and it apparently permanently affected his brain. I understand this is common. Jim was not predictable in stressful situations any more, and Choc couldn't count on him when needed. He would suddenly shy away from things he normally would not pay attention to. He would stubbornly refuse to turn or speed up.

Still, Jim was a gentle kid's horse and wouldn't intentionally hurt anyone. So I had a wonderful riding animal that became a real pet. Jim loved to be petted, brushed and played with. He became so friendly that he would follow me around like a dog and would let any amount of children ride him that could climb on his back. Although I rode with a saddle most often,

My pal Jim and me, approximately 13 years old

I sometimes rode Jim bareback. I liked riding bareback better. You feel closer to the horse, and can anticipate his movements better. I think the horse likes it better, too.

I think I was 12 or 13 years of age at this time, still in grade school and before my interests turned to girls. I had a small mixed-breed brown and white dog named "Bobby" who was my most constant companion, next to Jim and Casey. Bobby was some kind of a Cocker Spaniel-Airedale mix.

My parents sensed the closeness that existed between me and Jim. Although they knew nothing about horses, they were aware that there was a very special bond between us, and they did not worry about me when I was out in the desert with Jim. Sometimes I would take Bobby and my .22 caliber single-shot rifle, and ride Jim out in the hills and stay overnight. I remember once we went to Beale Springs, then about a mile or so west of Kingman. That was before they fenced the springs in and people out.

I can recall that I shot a rabbit that day and cooked him over an open fire at the springs. I ate watercress from the springs as a salad with my rabbit, sharing some with Bobby. As darkness came, I remember lying down on Jim's saddle blanket, watching the stars overhead, and listening to the trickling sounds of the little creek. Jim lay down on the ground next to me, and I laid my head on his rear leg. Bobby, Jim and I all fell asleep together, as close as we could get to each other. I awoke at daybreak and Jim was gone. He was grazing about a hundred yards away, with no ropes or hobbles on him. If he wouldn't come to me when I called, I had a long walk home ahead of me carrying a saddle, bridle and rifle. As soon as I whistled, Jim raised his head, whinnied and came trotting over for his morning greeting. What a great day and wonderful memory.

Jim was also gentle with other kids. Sometimes when a group of us would be playing outside at night, one of the boys would say, "Let's go for a ride on Jim." We would go to his corral, wake Jim up, put a rope around his head and lead him out of the corral. He would let each one of us lope him around the block bareback, until each boy had his turn. If someone tried to take more than one turn, he would gently buck him off, and return to his corral, lie down, and refuse to get up again no matter how much you coaxed.

When I cleaned Jim's corral, I would open the gate and let him out. He would graze around our yard or down the street while I shoveled manure into a box to be used in the rose garden. When I wanted Jim to get back in his corral, most of the time I would only have to whistle, but sometimes he would play hard to get and trot away. I could always get him to come back by tempting him with an apple. When he would see the apple he would come jogging back, and sometimes I would play hard to get also. I would run away, with Jim chasing me around the yard, our car, our fruit trees, or even run into the garage with him hard on my heels. Eventually, before he became tired of the chase, I would give him the apple when he returned to the corral. One time, while I was cleaning the corral and Jim was loose, a boy came around the corner tossing a baseball into the air and catching it. Jim apparently thought this was an apple and that the boy would give it to him. Jim took off after the boy, who did not know what the game was. He was terrified to see this huge black horse bearing down on him at a gallop, coming right at him. The boy screamed, which stopped Jim in his tracks. I yelled at the boy to get behind the telephone pole and to throw the ball down. He did. Jim came to the ball, smelled it, and turned away, obviously disappointed.

Helen Kristich, a female friend my same age, had a quarter horse mare. We used to ride together a lot. We sometimes raced our horses at the old rodeo grounds south of the railroad tracks where the little league field is now. As a prize, the loser of the race had to buy the milkshakes. Helen's mare was a fast horse, usually jumping out to an early two or three lengths lead at the beginning of our race. Jim would easily catch up, but then loaf along beside the mare, not obeying my urging to pass and win the race. I had paid off several milkshake bets before I figured out a way I thought would make Jim put forth more effort at the appropriate time.

I bought a ten-foot length of one-inch thick cotton rope, and tied a huge knot in each end. I doubled the rope and put it on my saddle. The next time Helen and I had a race, Jim as usual caught up with the mare and refused to pass her. I took the rope and gave Jim a hearty whack across the backsides with it. The rope was too long. It went around Jim's back legs and under his tail. Surprised by the rope, Jim clenched his tail down tight on the rope while I tried to pull it out. It didn't work. Jim bucked me off at a dead run, ran about a hundred yards, turned around, came back and nuzzled me as I dusted myself off. I gave up racing. I knew that some cowmen wore spurs to make a horse more responsive, but I thought that might hurt Jim, and I couldn't do that.

I owned Jim for about two or three years, and sold him to Matt Hanhila, a teacher at the high school, who had several small children.

During the time that I had horses, I rode with and came to know many interesting people who were ranchers or horsemen. Some of them were: Choc Hamilton, Leonard Neal, Johnny Mullen, Judd Bishop, Bud Cornwall, the Odle brothers, and Chet Cofer. There is something very special about these people. People who love and care for horses and who train them have special qualities. They appear to be calm and patient with animals and people. I still like that kind of person.

My parents had some friends named J. Terrell and Edna Johnson. Terrell was a pumper on the Santa Fe Railroad. That was when the trains were powered by steam locomotives, and the railroad had wells frequently along the line where a pumper saw to it that the water tanks were kept full to fill the tanks of the locomotives. The big metal tanks on the south side of Andy Devine Avenue between Fourth and Fifth Streets were put there for that purpose. The Johnsons were originally stationed at a pumping station at Hackberry. They were moved to Goffs, California, which is about thirty miles west of Needles on the Santa Fe line. They had a very warm and friendly home in Goffs that was provided by the railroad. It was wood-frame with a large fenced yard right next to the railroad tracks. They had chickens in a pen in the backyard, and several huge fig trees that shaded most of the yard, and yielded the most luscious black figs. The fig trees always had a sweet smell about them that attracted huge numbers of birds that ate the figs, and tarantula-hawk wasps that ate the overripe fruit.

The Johnsons heated and cooked with kerosene, used Coleman gaslights, and kept their food cool in a large out-door wooden box with burlap sides that were kept wet. The breeze cooled the contents by evaporation. The support legs of the cooler stood in coffee cans filled with water to keep ants from invading the food. This device was amazingly effective, even in summer. The railroad provided an ice-house across the tracks. It was a pit dug about eight feet deep into the ground, with a wooden roof and dirt over it. Inside, large 300-pound blocks of ice were stored with wood sawdust over, under and around them. Sawdust is such a good insulator that the ice would keep in that house indefinitely without melting. I remember going into the ice-house during the heat of the day in summer to keep cool, while my parents played cards or visited with the Johnsons. I can still smell the cool, damp sawdust.

When I was maybe seven or eight, Terrell taught me how to shoot a .22 rifle. Theirs was the only house in

Goffs, so their backyard was desert for miles on the south side of the tracks. Terrell would line up tin cans and bottles about 50 yards outside the fence and we would plink at those during the evenings. When I was 10, he bought me a double-barreled Winchester .410 shotgun and taught me how to shoot it. We would hunt quail together. He fooled me one time by saying that if you wanted to make the shot from the shell spread in a larger pattern than normal, so that you could get more birds with one shot, you should shake the barrel of the gun just at the instant of firing. I remember trying that a few times. Of course that did not work, and I am sure Terrell had a lot of fun watching me try.

Edna was a wonderful cook. Her cook-stove was fueled by kerosene, which was funneled into the stove drop by drop from an inverted one-gallon glass bottle. There was always a slight but not unpleasant smell of kerosene in the house when she was cooking. She could fry chicken and bake apple pies so well on that stove I looked forward to going there just for the food. Terrell was very short. He probably wasn't much over five feet. Being heavy also, he was almost round. He had a ruddy complexion, short red hair and big calloused hands. He almost always wore bib overalls. Terrell smiled most all of the time and jiggled when he did. I remember one time he played Santa Claus at Christmas, in full costume and beard, at a nearby school. He made a picture-perfect Santa.

When diesel locomotives started replacing the steam driven ones on the line, the railroad cut down on the number of pumping stations. Goffs was closed and moved to Newberry Springs, near Barstow, California. The Johnsons moved there, where Terrell was the pumper for a few more years until there were no more steam engines and even Newberry's pumping station was closed. Terrell took retirement and lived out the rest of his life there. After he died, which was while I was in law school, Edna moved somewhere near Los Angeles, where she lived several more years.

I still have the .410 shotgun, and prize it very highly. Even after law school, I was able to go quail hunting with that small shotgun alongside many other hunters with large-bore automatic shotguns.

My folks and I were visiting with the Johnsons in Goffs on December 7, 1941, when the Japanese bombed Pearl Harbor. We got the news on the Johnsons' battery-operated radio, while my folks played cards under the Coleman light. I remember how shocked and silent the grownups were for a long time after the announcement on the crackling, static-laden radio broadcast from Los Angeles. The next day, we listened on that same radio to President Franklin Delano Roosevelt as he addressed the joint session of Congress with his famous "Day of Infamy" speech, prior to Congress' formal declaration of War against Japan.

Things seemed to change quickly in my life from that time

forward. I was twelve years old when WWII began. Kingman itself changed drastically soon after the war began. The Kingman Army Air Base, located where the Kingman Airport and Industrial Park is now, was built by the government soon after the war began. It was a huge operation. From time to time there were over 3,000 air force gunnery trainees stationed there at one time. They were trained in the use of machine guns for use air-to-air, air-to-ground, and from ground-to-air.

Wooden barracks were dotted around all over. Cadets from big cities, some of whom had never even held a gun of any kind, were sent there to be trained as gunners in fighter planes and bombers. I think their training session was six to eight weeks. In that period of time, the cadets started by learning to shoot a BB gun at targets. As I recall, these were the same Daisy air rifles most children at that time had as youngsters. Then they were introduced to .22 rifles, then .410 shotguns and on to .12 gauge shotguns. Somewhere in there they used a machine-gun BB gun that shot plastic pellets. Then they got to shoot 30 caliber machine guns and eventually 50 caliber machine guns. Even the officers had to go through this type of training.

The government forced neighboring ranchers to "lease" their ranches to it, although they were paid very little. All of Hualapai Valley within about a 5-mile radius of the airfield was under government control. The west side of Highway 66 was the weapons training site. The part of the base on the east side of Highway 66 was devoted mostly to living facilities.

The officers had a swimming pool and officers' club and a mess hall. The enlisted men (no women trainees) lived in the barracks and had their own separate swimming pool, club and mess hall. There were a few women military nurses on base serving in the base hospital. They even had a very large movie theater on the northern part of the base. Part of that theater is now the American Legion Post meeting hall on Oak Street in Kingman.

The cadets usually trained five or six days a week and stayed on base. They were allowed, finally, to come into Kingman on weekends. Kingman then had only about 3,000 inhabitants. There was some resistance at first to having the military personnel in town because there were quite a number of Black cadets. Kingman at that time was very bigoted. There were signs posted along the highway as you entered town that advised Blacks (or Negroes, as they were called at the time) that they would not be allowed in town after dark. No motel or hotel would give them lodging, and few, if any, restaurants would serve them. Finally, greed overcame prejudice, and the soldiers, all of them, were greeted with open arms in the few stores, bars and the movie house we had at the time. There were not enough bars or restaurants to handle them.

Business began to boom as new stores, bars and restaurants were built. I remember feeling sorry for some of the young cadets. They were far from home, wherever that was, and they had next to nothing to do in Kingman. I'm sure rural Kingman left a lot to be desired for the cadets from

large cities. They wandered the streets by the hundreds on
Saturday night, dressed smartly in their best, freshly pressed
and starched uniforms. Some came to high school dances and
were told they were not welcome. They could come, and did,
to the public dances held at the high school auditorium. The
high school girls really liked the soldiers, but most were kept
from dating them by their parents. The high school boys were
jealous because the girls were attracted to the older, more so-
phisticated soldiers, who knew different dance steps and were
more mature.

I learned later that at that time there was a thriving business being operated south of Kingman a few miles north and
east of Yucca. It was a brothel operated on a pig ranch owned
by Harry Caesar Nipple. (Can you believe that name? It's
true, I swear it!) Harry had several "girls" at his farm and
the soldiers would take a taxi to his place. We used to call it
"Yucca University", "Yucca School of Mines" or just "Yucca
U." Harry was looked down on by all the righteous in Kingman society, and was finally put out of business by the sheriff
on a civil charge of running a public nuisance, a bawdy house.
Harry tried to get my father to represent him as a lawyer in the
lawsuit, but Dad would not take the case.

Harry was truly a character out of a comic book.
Thin, emaciated, with false, ill-fitting teeth and long black
unkempt hair and beard. He wore a derby-type hat,
three-piece suit and a string tie. He smelled just like he
had rolled in the pig-pen. Some say they were sure he

had chicken manure in his beard. Harry finally died still running pigs on the ranch, the four-legged kind.

I think I was in eighth grade when the Air Field began operating. There was a riding stable operating then near where the fairgrounds is now located. Some cadets liked to ride horses when they were on leave. It was something to do with their spare time in a town that had little of interest for them. The horseback riding business grew so much that the stable had about 100 horses, and cadets were riding them all over the desert. I was offered free board for my horse if I would ride with the cadets to see they did not get in trouble, run the horses too far, or on pavement or otherwise abuse them. I met some of the most interesting people there. I went fishing with two of them at Topock. They were from Idaho and were really homesick. One had a funny name: Twitchell.

One group that I met was most memorable. They were fliers from China who were being trained in gunnery in the U. S. Some could hardly speak English. I remember the first time they came to ride at the stable. The head wrangler didn't like "Chinks," as he called them, and was going to make them look bad. He saddled up one of the roughest horses he had, hoping that the first Chinese would be thrown off and they would leave. What he did not know was that these were Manchurian Chinese, and very skilled riders. Some had ridden since they were very small children.

When the first rider boarded the bronc he was given,

the horse started to buck. The Chinese rider handled him well and could not be thrown. When the horse stopped bucking, the rider started doing tricks on him, running the horse around the corral as he did cartwheels on both sides of the saddle and under the horse's neck. That wrangler was not only surprised, but embarrassed! The Chinese were better riders than he was.

I rode with these young men several times and they took an interest in me. I was asked to their o ff-base apartment near the cemetery on my fourteenth birthday for a birthday dinner they personally prepared for me. It was a meal I will remember always. They had a separate, different dish for each year of my age. How they found the ingredients in little Kingman, I don't know. But they did, and I am sure at great expense and effort. There was a small Chinese population living in Kingman at the time, and possibly they helped. The evening was even more enjoyable because of the Chinese cadets doing sleight-of-hand magic tricks and singing songs of their homeland. What a night! I often wonder what they told their friends and relatives about me when they returned to China.

There were also quite a few officers of the Jewish faith stationed at the base. We had very few Jews living in Kingman at the time. The ones who lived there were primarily in the clothing business. The Spectors, who lived behind us, were Jewish, and invited many officers and cadets of that faith to huge dinners on religious holidays. They

90

had a son my age, whose name I cannot recall. It was fun to go to the Spectors' home on those holidays and listen to their songs and chants. Some were accomplished cantors or religious singers.

Another job I had during the war was in the Gibbs Jewelry Store on Fourth Street between the barbershop and drug store. I think I was in the eighth grade then. Alarm clocks were impossible to buy during the war, as clock manufacturers were building military equipment, bomb timers, precision chronometers, watches, etc. for the armed services. Electric clocks were either non-existent then, or a novelty. Wind-up alarm clocks were the norm, and were durable pieces of machinery. When they wore out it was usually wear on the main gear that was first in line pressing on the strong main spring. Mr. Gibbs found that in most brands of alarm clocks, the main gear could be made like new by merely turning it upside down, facing the reverse side of the gear to the gear holding the mainspring. To do this one had to compress the main spring and take apart the two brass frames that held the gears in place to get at the main gear. Once the worn gear was reversed and the gears replaced in the brass frames, the clock usually operated like new for the same amount of years that it took to wear out.

I liked working on clocks and other small mechanical things, so Gibbs gave me this job at $1.00 per hour. The whole repair on the clock would take maybe thirty minutes, and Gibbs would charge the customer $5 for the cleaning and repair.

That was a lot of money then. Gibbs was the only jeweler in town though, so he had a corner on the clock repair market. While there, I worked on some wall clocks and small watches. It was nice, clean indoor work, and he was a good person to work for. Besides, a dollar an hour was almost grownup wages then.

High School

Mohave County Union High School was the only high school in the county when I entered as a freshman in the fall of 1943. It was located at the west end of Oak Street in Kingman. It consisted of two concrete buildings: one a three story classroom building facing First Street; the other, just north of it, was the combination basketball pavilion and school auditorium. Behind the auditorium stage was the band classroom. The grass football field was west of and behind the classrooms.

In those days, it was a true rite of passage to go from grammar school to high school. Freshman boys and girls were subjected to all sorts of indignities by the sophomores upon initiation, held the first week of school. We were dressed in costumes, face-makeup on both boys and girls alike, and paraded through the main part of town with the high school band leading. We were paddled at almost any provocation and forced to eat chili peppers. We had to call the sophomores "sir" and "ma'am." Now I understand why those who made us do these silly things are called "sophomoric."

As a freshman, I walked or rode my bike to school. Even

when we were old enough to drive, very few students could afford to own or operate a car. Gas rationing was in effect during the war, and the weekly allotment per family was five gallons per week, except for certain medical emergencies. Families usually had only one car. There was plenty of gasoline, but you could not buy it without ration stamps. I think the price of regular gas was $.17 then. Ethyl was $.21. Food was also rationed. You had only a certain amount of stamps for different items of food. Sugar and coffee were very scarce. Every household saved all their bacon grease and rendered fat in cans for the "war effort." Somehow it was used in explosives. Aluminum pots and pans were turned in to be melted down to make airplanes. I don't think any Japanese families lived in Kingman. It would have been very hard for them if they had, as prejudiced as we were then.

My freshman class, the class of 1947, numbered in the forties. I think there were only about 100 children in the whole school. Most of the male juniors and seniors finished school and then enlisted in the Army or Navy. Some enlisted right away and came back later to get their diploma. The war ended in 1945, so some of these suave and worldly-wise guys came back during my junior and senior years. They were so smooth and mature they were the most popular guys in school. One of these was Ervin McBrayer. He came back from the Navy and was one of our star football players. Betty Brady and he soon became serious and were married right after graduation. Ervin had a 1934

Ford coupe and for some reason took an interest in me. He wore a white sailor cap, so I did too. He drove a gas station to Wickiup, to the only gas station around, to fill the tanks of ranchers. He was very mature and I both admired and emulated him. We sometimes went fishing for catfish in the Topock slough.

I was a tall, skinny, bookish kid as a freshman. I had no athletic ability, but because almost every boy went out for football, I did too. The high school band played at half-time during football games. The school was so small that some of the football players were also band members. They had to change into and out of their band uniforms to play during halftime activities.

Matt Hanhila, a great educator and one of my idols, was the coach of all sports at school and later the principal. He was very patient with me as I tried out for football. I weighed about 135-140 pounds then. "Hanny," as we called him, probably hoped a strong wind wouldn't come up during a game, as I might be blown away. I went through shin-splints and bruises as I tried to build myself up to play. I could barely run the laps. Matt tried me at halfback and that didn't work. I wasn't big enough to stop the defensive backs. He tried me at end, and I played only a part of one competition game at that position. After receiving a pass, I was tackled by a Las Vegas back by the name of Jim Monachino, who later became an All-American at University of California. My ankle was so sprained that I was out for the rest of the season. I could not even run on a basketball floor during that season. So much for my athletic pursuits in high school.

I signed up for band, starting with the clarinet. I took private lessons in the afternoon from Joe Coppa, the band teacher, and became second clarinet behind Jim Haynes until he graduated and then I became first clarinet. Casey Cummings also was in band, playing saxophone. Our penchant for getting into trouble together continued.

One time after school we rubbed smoked herring in the mouthpieces and bells of all the brass instruments stored in the band room. (We really worked on the sousaphones, trombones, trumpets, and French horns. I think we even got the saxophones.) We came to band the next day, all innocent-looking. As soon as the brass players took out their instruments, they almost wretched. I'll never know how, but Coppa knew instantly who did it. He chased us both out of the band room. I outran him down the back stairs. Casey jumped off the staircase and almost broke his leg. I think we were required to clean out the instruments.

Because my mother had insisted that I take piano lessons as a younger child, playing a single-note instrument was easy. I became a fairly proficient clarinetist. I got superior ratings twice in state competitions at the Northern Arizona Music Festivals in Flagstaff. They were held at the old Armory which is now a furniture store across the street and west of Northern Arizona University. I later taught myself to play saxophone and trumpet fairly well. Casey, who played tenor sax, and another band member who played drums, and I formed a small band and even played for a couple of study-hall dances. Some of our better numbers were "Don't Fence Me In," "Rum and Coca Cola" and "The Beer-Barrel Polka." I think we only could play four or five numbers. The dancers had to listen to them over and over again, but it did not seem to matter. We were all they had and we were free.

My summer job between freshman and sophomore years was at Earl Duke's Packard Garage on Second Street between Andy Devine and Beale Street. Earl was a master mechanic who gave me a chance to learn about cars. He was also a good friend of my parents. Earl was a small but strong man with a mustache and a pronounced leg limp. He always chewed gum. He was very active in the Elks, and was a sponsor for the Antlers youth organization, which I joined. That group of boys was allowed to use the Elks lodge one afternoon and evening a week, with adult supervision. I learned to play pool then.

We had our meetings on Wednesday evenings in the Elks' meeting room. We also learned adult Elks' initiation ritual and were taken to other lodges for ritual competition. We traveled in a bus to Las Vegas, Prescott and Phoenix for these competitions. It was great fun and Elks activities largely took the place of a teen-center. The girls had Rainbow Girls, an organization sponsored by the Masonic Lodge. Some of the men who were active sponsors for Antlers were Curley Leonard, Burton Porter and Earl Duke. I wore Burton Porter's tuxedo in the ritual competitions.

Working for Earl Duke was a happy experience. He was the only one in the garage, besides me. Like most boys, I was interested in cars and eager to learn about them. Cars were so much simpler then. You didn't need a computer to work on one. My first responsibility was to clean and polish the heads on cars being overhauled. Cars outlasted their engines then. Rather than buy a new car, people usually rebuilt their cars' engines. Earl would pull the heads off in preparation for removing the pistons, rods and valves. I would use a wire mesh polisher on an electric drill to remove the carbon deposits from the heads and tops of pistons and valves. When I got good at that, Earl allowed me to dismantle braking mechanisms and replace the brake shoes, then made of asbestos composite. No one worried about lung cancer caused by asbestos then. I was not paid much, but enjoyed Earl's company immensely. He was a very ethical man who would never overcharge his customers. He did his work well and charged only for work he actually performed. In those days, a car would run for only about 50,000 miles before the engine would need to be overhauled or replaced. That was before car lubrication systems were operated under pressure from a pump.

A better lubrication system evidently was the development that made cars run better and longer. Earl Duke was so good as a mechanic that there was always a waiting list of customers. No car ever left his garage without a quart of Rislone being added to its crankcase. He swore that it increased lubrication efficiency and longevity. Rislone is still sold in larger stores. I used it in our cars and our boats for many years, with apparent good result.

Earl's "tow truck" was, in reality, a handsome 1936 or 1937 twelve-cylinder black Packard four-door sedan, which was so powerful it could pull any car out of a ditch in second gear. It was a beautiful piece of machinery. No car manufacturer produced as high quality a product as Packard did in those days. His tow truck was kept in mint condition, shiny and purring like a cat. One time he scratched a fender and I was given the job of sanding down the bruised area in preparation for repainting. I was to use the finest Carborundum sandpaper and "feather-edge" the paint out to its first coat of primer. There were six coats of lacquer on the car, plus its primer coat. It had mahogany and velvet trim in the interior, and the seats were high enough that you needed a running board to enter the car. Many times I have wished I had the means to have purchased that car and to have stored it for the future. It would probably be worth well over a hundred thousand dollars now.

I also worked in a gas station during the war, and in that job became more popular as a person than any other job I think I ever had, including Chief Justice. As I mentioned, gasoline was being rationed, and at the end of each shift of work at the station, the gallonage of gas sold had to match the ration stamps in the register. But gas tanks rarely filled at precise 5-gallon increments, which was the denomination of the gas rationing stamps. If you filled up a tank and it took 13 gallons, the attendant had to receive three five-gallon stamps. That meant that at the end of the day there were two gallons that were left over from that transaction. The smart buyer would ask for five or ten gallons at a time. At the end of the day, there were usually fifteen to twenty gallons that could be purchased by my friends within the stamps that were left over. Boy, was I important! Upper-classmen that had not spoken to me before suddenly became my best friends.

Drugs were unknown in those days in Kingman. No one took pills to get high, mainlined heroin or methamphetamine. No one even had heard of marijuana. We did imbibe the occasional beer, however. During the war all the good beer went to the servicemen. Victory Ale was usually the only beer that we could get. Being underage, we would have a returned serviceman buy it for us, and then we would go out in the boonies and two or three of us would consume a quart of beer together. Then we would eat Sen-Sen, a breath cover candy, so no one would know. (We thought.) But no one got rowdy with drink, as that would be a giveaway. Also, we didn't carry weapons. Disputes rarely ended up in fights. In the few that did occur in school, Mr. Hanhila would take the disputants into the empty auditorium, put boxing gloves on them, and tell them to go at it. No one except Hanny would be there to watch them, and it was usually all over within a few harmless blows later. Then the combatants came out, arm in arm, all injustices being forgiven. Moral — no audience, no fun in a fight. I shudder to think of the lawsuits that would be filed if that method of dispute resolution were used today.

High school dances were usually to a juke box on Friday night in the auditorium. Some boys played basketball at one end of the floor while the other boys and girls danced. Once you came in, you could not leave. It was suspected that if you did, you would smoke or drink beer. Most of us as junior or seniors did sneak cigarettes. I hope kids now are smart enough to know how unhealthy and dangerous that is, and that it really isn't cool to smoke. I even tried chewing tobacco once, and got caught in the dance with it, when I tried to leave to spit. Hanny knew what we were doing and made us stay inside and we had to swallow it. Ugh. Never again.

In my senior year in high school, I had a lead part in our senior play, the name of which I cannot recall. I played a doctor, who had to administer ether to some patient before surgery. To make the act realistic, I went to the local drug store and after explaining the need for realism, the pharmacist for some reason sold me a can of genuine ether. After the successful running of the play and refusals of a further future as a thespian, I didn't know what to do with the ether. This was still during the time of gasoline rationing.

My friend Don McNulty had a Model A Ford which seemed to be losing its vitality, so he suggested that we add the ether to his gas tank to revive it. Not knowing just how powerful such an additive would be, we poured the can of ether into the tank of the car, which was located in front of the windshield. Model A's did not have a fuel pump, as gas was gravity fed from the tank to the carburetor. Ether is much

100

heavier than gasoline, so after being added to the fuel tank, it sank to the bottom and did not mix with the gasoline, and was fed pure into the carburetor. It took just about three seconds from the time the car was started until the pure ether hit the pistons of the A and was fired like jet fuel. The A was in first gear at the time, luckily, and took off just like a jet, squealing smoking tires for about fifty feet until the piston rods went through the engine block and froze everything up. So much for realism. Ah, but what a wonderful ride while it lasted.

Girls in school then were outwardly sweet and pure. They did not smoke or drink (in public). A girl who got a reputation for going to bed with boys, might attract a certain type of boy, but she was not considered a serious marriage candidate after that. Chastity was an important societal value then, which apparently now is of very little value.

The normal progression was for boys and girls to go to college, marry right after, and have a family. The boy was to support the family and the girl was to stay at home, keep the house and nurture the children. I can remember only two girls that were pregnant while they were in school. As soon as it became known, they either got married to the father or left school.

During the years I was in high school, over 85% of our high school graduates went on to college. That is really a high percentage. Most of those that did go on to college did not return to Kingman, as there were very few high-paying jobs available then. You could be a store clerk, gas station attendant, farmer, rancher or motel maid. That was about all there was beside the medical and legal professions.

At that time, we were very fortunate to have some wonderful teachers in high school that took a personal, after-school interest in their students. These teachers were truly positive influences on their students, shaping their lives in the future. Some of those teachers, and some other adults in Kingman that affected me in such a manner were:

Matt Hanhila

Every boy learned to love and respect this big, athletic man of Finnish descent. He was tall, muscular, and wore his pure-white hair in an immaculate crew-cut. He had only one good eye, although few people knew. Hanny taught algebra, geometry, trigonometry, calculus and physics while I was there. I had a terrible time with algebra. My mother developed a perforated stomach ulcer when I was a freshman, and was sent to Santa Fe Hospital in Los Angeles, where she had most of her stomach removed. She was in the hospital for a month or six weeks and barely survived. During that time, my father spent most of the time in Los Angeles to be with mother, and I lived by myself in our big house on Spring Street. Hanny noticed the difficulty I was having with algebra, and took pity on me by offering free tutoring at his home on north Grandview Avenue, just north of Joe Coppa's home. I spent an hour or two several days a week at Hanny's home after school and football practice, which he coached while he tried to show me the logic of algebra. He was only minimally successful, and I think he displayed considerable charity by awarding me a "C" in that class. I took geometry from another teacher, and for some reason that subject was easier for me. Nowadays it would probably be rare for a teacher to offer free after-school tutoring to any student.

We didn't have air conditioning in the old high school building, and it was quite warm in the fall. Hanny would leave the class windows open and it was balmy. Flies would come in the classroom and provide Casey and me with some distraction. We found that if you came up with your hand slowly behind a fly on your book, you could make a quick pass with your hand and catch them in your hand once in a while. For some reason they didn't seem to see well backwards. Then it was fun to throw them into the algebra book and slam it shut quickly. An almost dime-sized blot of blood and fly-guts would result. If you left the book closed for a day or so, the adjoining pages would be glued together. One time, Hanny asked to see my book and promptly showed the class my special talents. I was awarded the honor of being the best flycatcher in algebra, but also given the privilege of paying for that honor by buying a new book for the school at the end of the year.

Other classmates, mostly football and basketball players, liked to try to trick Hanny by putting thumbtacks on his chair in class. Even though he had only one good eye, he usually spotted the tacks and laughed as he avoided them. One time the culprits drove a thin needle through the bottom of the wooden chair so that he could not see it. Although I was not in the class at the time, (pure luck, or I would have been blamed), the story was that Hanny sat on the needle and jumped up. He good-naturedly said, "Well, you got me that time." Thereafter his habit was always to run his hand over the seat before he sat down.

Hanny was the chief male role model for boys in school. He inspired honesty, integrity, industry, fairness, pride, physical fitness, and respect for both man and animals. Hanny later became a principal, moved to Phoenix and served as principal for then trouble-ridden South Mountain High, then on to Superintendent of the Paradise Valley School District. He was instrumental in developing Glendale Community College in Phoenix, where he served as Executive Dean. (Our son, Trey, went to Glendale one year while he was there.) Then, still fit in his sixties at least, Hanny boasted that he could beat any teacher there at the college at handball except one, and he was working on him.

For a summer job between my sophomore and junior year in high school, I was assistant lifeguard at the one and only swimming pool in Kingman, the public pool on Grandview. Hanny was the manager at the pool and George Grantham, then a senior, was the senior lifeguard.

For some background, before that swimming pool was

built, there were no pools in town, and if people wanted to
swim, they would have to drive south of Kingman about
five miles on Highway 66 to Goodwin's Pool, where Hanny
taught me to swim when I was about seven or eight years old.
The only other pool was at a motel in a community called
Crozier, on Highway 66 between Hackberry and Peach
Springs. This pool pre-dated Goodwin's, but was not kept fil-
tered or chlorinated. Although the water there was really cold
spring water that flowed through the concrete pool constantly,
the pool was usually slimy on the bottom with moss. Goodwin's was much better and larger. It also had change rooms
and showers. Like Crozier, the water was always cold.

Kingman needed a pool, and during the war a man by the
name of Howard Dungan, who owned slot machines, made
an offer to the county. If he could place slot machines in all
places of accommodation in the county, he would divide the
revenue with the county, and the county could build a new
spiffy public swimming pool. Gaming, even slot machines,
was illegal in Arizona at the time. But the Mohave County
Attorney, Carl D. Hammond, gave his approval to the pro-
posal, evidently feeling that beneficent purpose overshadowed
illegality. No one complained, and everyone enjoyed the machines which were in every bar, restaurant and club in town.
The servicemen contributed substantially.

Within one or two years, I believe, the county had
raised enough revenue through its share of the slot machine
profits to build the pool and buildings. I think Hanny told me

the total cost was around $125,000. Then Dungan and the county parted ways and slot machines became illegal again, although some reappeared occasionally at the Elks or Legion halls. When they did reappear, if someone complained the Sheriff would make them disappear again into the basements. To my knowledge, no one suffered greatly as a result of this temporary immorality except a few inveterate gamblers who lost more than they could afford. One of those was a lady who was at the time the elected County Treasurer. She loved to play the quarter machines so much that she started dipping into the county's tax revenues to feed them. She was such a constant fixture in the various clubs that suspicions quickly arose and after an audit of the county's funds, she "fessed up." Her bonding company negotiated a settlement with the county. I think the sum paid to reimburse the county's losses was about $10,000. But after all, this was just a shift of funds from one county pocket to another, as part of the profit was going to the county anyway. I wonder if the insurance company took that into consideration.

My first year as guard at the pool, Hanny and George Grantham played a trick on me that Hanny loved to tell at every opportune occasion. After the pool closed in the evening, we would clean the restrooms and sidewalks and close up. One night after closing, Hanny suggested we turn off the lights and we would take a skinny-dip. I remember his saying "the last one in is a rotten egg" as he turned off all the lights and we raced to see who would be first in the pool. What I didn't know was that Hanny and George had conspired to let me win that race and when I was the first to hit the water they turned on all the lights, thus illuminating me for all passing by on Grandview to observe. I quickly flattened myself against the near pool wall and pleaded for mercy. It was granted as soon as Hanny and George could stop laughing. The lights turned off again so I could make my naked escape from the pool.

When I was the senior guard between my third and fourth year in high school, it was my job to prepare the pool for opening at 1:00 p.m. each day. I would arrive early, clean the pool edge with Dutch cleanser, check the chlorine and add Clorox if needed, bring out the cash register drawer with change, and open up. The pool had a sand filter which needed changing several times each summer. When we did that we would drain the pool dry and scrub the bottom with soapy water and Clorox. Then it would take a full 24 hours to refill the pool after draining. Filling the pool was expensive and would deprive the county of a whole day's revenue, so we would delay the operation as long as possible and try to keep the water clear with the filter and chlorine. Still every two or three weeks we had to change the water. At the end of the period before cleaning, sometimes the water in the deep end would become cloudy enough that objects on the bottom would be hard to distinguish.

One weekend someone cut the football-tackling dummy down from its moorings at the high school field and threw it over the fence into the swimming pool. It was a life-sized canvass dummy from the shoulders down, and sunk readily when saturated. In the murky water with its canvas straps dangling from the top, the dummy looked much like a body lying on the bottom in the deep end of the pool. I was not aware of this prank as I came to open up the pool, and when I saw what looked like a drowned or drowning person in the deep end I dived in ready for the rescue. As I approached the object in the cloudy water, the floating canvas straps looked much like intestines coming out of a dismembered body. I grabbed the object with much trepidation, and only then realized what had happened.

Hanny had been out flying a private plane that morning and had flown over the pool. From above he could see the sunken dummy and after looking at the football field knew exactly what had happened. You would have thought that being the good person he was, and knowing how it would startle me, he would have called to warn me about what to expect when I went to open up. He didn't however, and looked forward to my reaction when he came to work at the pool later that day.

As you can see, Hanny had a marvelous sense of humor and loved to put one over on you if he could. That's why others tried the same on him. One time, as we sat watching the pool on an August afternoon, just before Labor Day and the September primary election, a small plane flew over town a couple of thousand feet up and dropped some leaflets. We saw them floating down, small specks like snowflakes. I pointed them out to Hanny and he said "Oh yeah. I think I can read them from here with my one good eye. "They say 'Vote for Earle Cook for State Senator.'" I was amazed when I found one that had floated down later. They were exactly as Hanny had said. I temporarily thought that Hanny's one good eye was indeed a telescope. What I discovered later was that earlier in the day Hanny had helped load the plane with the campaign leaflets.

Another one he pulled was on Jay Gates, Jr., who was building a new home and corral on hilltop. His contractor came to Hanny to figure out how many gallons of water a tank that he had available would hold for Jay's home and horses. Hanny took down the measurements and figured out the answer on paper for the contractor, who went away satisfied. Later in the day, Hanny met Jay Gates, Jr. in Central Commercial and Jay, not knowing that Hanny had already figured it out, asked Hanny how many gallons of water a tank of these measurements would hold. Hanny paused, stroked his chin, gazed skyward for a moment and said "exactly 12,543 gallons," remembering his previous calculations. Stunned, Jay challenged Hanny on his figure. Hanny asked for paper and pencil and proceeded to work out the exact answer for Jay, who was then convinced that Hanny was a human mechanical calculator. It wasn't until the next day that he found out what had happened from the contractor, and then both he and Hanny had a laugh together.

Matt Hanhila's warmth, love of children and good humor touched the lives of many young men and women in Kingman. He died after being struck by a car in Phoenix, crossing the street to help a neighbor. His hearing had gone and he did not hear or see the car coming. He had just recently given a humorous talk about my youth at my retirement party in 1992, where he again told the story of how he and George Grantham played the "skinny dipping" trick on me.

Howard Cate

Howard Cate taught chemistry and photography at Mohave County High School. His wife, Eleanor and their children lived only a block or so away from the school on Oak Street, in a wood house with a large garage. Both Howard and Eleanor were artistic people. Howard was an expert photographer and Eleanor painted and sculpted. Howard had a wondrous sense of humor. Both of them laughed a lot and it was fun to be around them. Howard encouraged all of his students to live up to their maximum potential, but he showed special attention to those that were serious about their studies. A lot of the "jocks" in the school were not that serious about studies, and didn't especially care for Howard's insistence on 110% performance.

Don McNulty and I somehow achieved favor in Howard's eyes. We were invited to Cate's home in the evenings, where there was always a pot of coffee on and lots of fresh cookies. We would drop by several evenings a week to visit, pondering what we considered the great current issues of the day. Eleanor would put a piece of clay or charcoal in our hand to see what we could fashion or sketch. Although we resisted at first, believing we had no talent, Eleanor persisted until we forgot our self-consciousness and tried to create. Nothing of show quality resulted, but Eleanor was always very complimentary. Eleanor treated us to our first taste of poetry at their house, and we also learned a little about the lives of some of our greatest classical authors.

The Cate's home, as cluttered as it was with materials for photography, sculpting and painting, with children running through, playing noisily and almost without inhibition, was a warm and inviting place to be. The Cates treated McNulty and me as grownups. They invited and encouraged discussion and debate. They made us feel like adults and welcome in their home. Howard later was a teacher in Guam and retired to Hawaii. One of his children spent time in a Japanese prison because he freed some porpoises that were to be slaughtered. He was an excellent scuba diver and active Green Peace supporter of creatures and the environment. That grown son later drowned in a diving accident and Howard continued support for Green Peace by being an administrator of the organization until he died in the early 1990s. I believe Eleanor still lives on the island of Hawaii.

Bill Freiday

Bill had worked at the Kingman Army Air Base as an airplane mechanic. He married Mildred after the war and returned to Kingman, working as a mechanic and flight instructor at the Kingman Municipal Airport. He was one of the greatest vehicle mechanics in the country. He was extremely intelligent, although he did not have much formal schooling. His innate abilities allowed him to become a very successful heavy equipment operator and civic leader. At the time I was in high school, he was a nut about cars and hotrods. I met him when I took a few hours of flight instruction at the airport in a Piper Cub airplane. I received enough instruction to be allowed to solo (six hours), but was too young to do so. You had to be sixteen.

At the field I met Bill because of our mutual friendship with several of the local Arizona State Highway Patrolmen. I was entranced by Bill's hotrod, which he raced frequently in local events. Because it was available at the airport, Bill used aviation gasoline which was extremely hot. I would ride with him on unused airport runways while he tested his latest car adjustment. Big blue flames used to shoot out of the exhaust ports down below the engine as we raced down the dark runway at night. Both he and I were sure that Bill's car could outrun any car in Mohave County. He proved that one time by outrunning his highway patrolman friend Sam Marbell, who was on duty at the time. Freiday left the patrolman behind in second gear, attaining over 90 miles per hour up Coyote Hill west of Kingman, without bothering to go into third gear. Of course, Sam knew who he was chasing, and he simply went to Freiday's house and waited for him to come home so he could deliver his speeding citation.

Bill and Mildred also seemed to run a feeding station for teenage boys while I was in high school. Their children came

112

later, so they kind of adopted a bunch of us. Mildred always had huge pots of fresh popcorn and coffee on and available when we would drop by. If the lights were on in their house, we always assumed we were welcome. They never said differently. Their home was behind the old fire station on Fifth Street between Oak and Beale Street, next to the Odd Fellows Hall.

Floyd Cisney

Floyd Cisney was an Arizona State Highway Patrolman when I first became acquainted with him. He later was Sheriff of Mohave County. Floyd was quite effective at steering teenage boys away from trouble. He knew boys with cars liked to try to see how fast they would go, and sometimes under dangerous conditions. Cisney was an amateur hot rod driver in his spare time, and was a fair mechanic.

He endeared himself to almost all boys who had cars in Kingman by acting as a friend to you, not an enemy. He would pull up to you when you were stopped in your car and ask you about the car. He would get out, look at your engine, praise you on your equipment and its cleanliness. He would ask you what it would do, and if you weren't sure he would suggest that he clock you on some lonely paved road, where there was no traffic. There were no citations. He would let you know that he expected you to obey the speed and safety laws except when you were under supervised racing conditions, which he tried to arrange for us whenever we felt the need for it. At one time he arranged with Mohave County to use an old abandoned airstrip at the airport to time cars with a stopwatch. Occasionally, he would supervise a two-car drag on that strip for a quarter of a mile. We got to know and respect Floyd and most of us would not want to embarrass ourselves by getting a ticket in town, because that would disappoint him.

George Stinson

Through Floyd Cisney, I met George Stinson, another Highway Patrolman stationed in Kingman. George continued Floyd Cisney's friendly approach toward teenage boys. He was a handsome, tall, dark-haired policeman who even the high school girls liked. Very few schoolgirls had their own cars. George befriended girls and boys alike. He let some of us boys ride with him on routine patrols, and we frequently met him for coffee at the El Trovatore Restaurant or at the City Cafe on Hilltop. El Trovatore had the best pecan pie I have ever eaten. The cherry pie was popular, too. It was a favorite stop after dances or with the patrolmen.

Richard L. Whitlow

Dick Whitlow was the next Highway Patrolman I met and became friends with. I spent more time with Dick than any other patrolman, and Kenny Hudson and I became close to he and his wife Ruby. Kenny was a Navy veteran who returned to finish high school. He bought a 1932 yellow Model A convertible roadster that became our favorite mode of conveyance. It was no racer, but was a wonderful fixer-upper. We were constantly working on or painting that car. Ken was my closest friend during my senior year. We separated during college, he becoming a newspaper reporter for the Mohave Miner, and a newspaper in Colorado Springs, Colorado. He finally worked for the San Diego Union in California until his retirement. He developed Parkinson's disease and died in the summer of 1998.

Dick was a tall, blond ex-marine who fought in hand-to-hand combat against the Japanese in the south Pacific and in the caves on Okinawa. He was a soft-spoken tough character that no one in his right mind would cross. He was universally respected by all public officials.

In those days, Arizona had a 60 mile-per-hour speed limit. Dick drove the usual Ford Interceptor with a hopped up engine. He was tough on drinking or sleepy drivers, but gave warnings to most speeders if they were tourists. In his slow, soft voice he would convey to them that he was concerned not only about their welfare, but that of others on the road. He would give them either a written or a verbal warning and tell them that he would be calling the next patrolman down the road and letting him know that this person was coming his way and to watch for him. That usually did the trick, even without the radio message.

The police car radios in those days were very primitive AM radios, with limited range. I can remember that you could not reach Kingman from Yucca or even Union Pass sometimes, but you might be able to catch a policeman on "skip" in Maine, and ask them to call Kingman on the telephone and send an ambulance to a wreck just a few miles away or over a mountain from Kingman. One time Dick and I were in Golden Valley and overheard on skip two Royal Canadian Mounted Policemen from Canada talking to each other car-to-car near Vancouver. They were talking on their radios about mutual girlfriends, but were far enough from their home base that they could not be heard there. Dick keyed the mike and said "RCM #__ and __. This is Arizona Highway Patrol Unit #__ near Kingman, Arizona advising that we read you loud and clear." There was silence thereafter.

One time when I was riding with Dick, we were called to an accident on Union Pass on the way to Bullhead. A car had run off the highway and there were some serious injuries, although we did not know it until we got there. Dick told me to take the car back to the ranch house belonging to Lon Ferrar at the east base of the pass to use the telephone to call for an ambulance while he stayed to administer first aid. I drove the car back to the house and rushed through the gate, so excited that I didn't see the "beware of dog" sign. About two steps inside the gate a large Doberman dog came running full speed and jumped up at me. Somehow I grabbed the dog by the neck and swung him around and off the ground just in time to use him as a shield against the second Doberman that was running at me. Talk about scared. About that time a man I later found was Mr. Ferrar called off the dogs, and calmly said , "Young man, don't you know to 'haloo' the house before you come through a gate?" I didn't then, but I certainly do now.

Once while with Dick, he answered a general call at night to help the Sheriff in Kingman find some burglars who had stolen some money, stamps, tickets and an addressograph machine from the Santa Fe Depot in downtown Kingman. The burglary must have just happened as one of the thieves was found under a railroad car just a block or so from the depot. Dick cuffed him behind his back, put him in the front seat and asked me to sit in the back seat of the patrol car and hold his riot shotgun on the guy while he kept looking for the second suspect. In those days there was no wire cage or protective glass between the front and back seats of highway patrol cars, as they weren't usually used to transport prisoners.

At age 17, sitting in a patrol car at night, alone with a handcuffed prisoner, looking forward into the car headlights, I was one nervous boy. I thought about what was in the front seat that the suspect might use to escape. It suddenly occurred to me that there was a fire extinguisher on the front floorboard between the driver's and passenger side of the patrol car. The prisoner began leaning forward slowly. I didn't really know what to do, but I knew I better do something. I put the barrel of that riot gun right behind the prisoner's ear and said as authoritatively as I could, "You better lean back slowly and be still if you want your head to stay in this car." With that he leaned back and told me where his buddy

was. I was able to call Dick and relay the information and the other man was captured by the deputy
sheriff. That's as close as I have ever been to having to
kill someone. I think I was frightened enough to do it,
if I had to.

Dick was the ideal highway patrolman. He would rather be
patrolling and hunting down bad guys than anything else that
I knew about at the time. Ruby said he would sleep better if he
had a steering wheel in his hands in bed. He was transferred
to Holbrook and while I was in college, I visited the Whitlows
there. One of the local officials was the brother of the Arizona
Attorney General at the time. He tried to bribe Dick into not
reporting gambling operations just outside of town. Dick refused the bribe and turned him in. I thought Dick would lose
his job over that, as the Attorney General had considerable
influence over the Highway Patrol at the time. On the contrary,
rather than being discharged or demoted, Dick was promoted
to Inspector and lived in Phoenix until his retirement, when
he went back to driving — gasoline tanker trucks — all over
the State.

Dick was still with the Patrol in Tucson when I started law
school at the University of Arizona. He was with me at Tucson
Medical Center when Trey was born in 1951. Dick and Ruby
were there for Joan and me when we needed them. They
showed us around town to find a place to live while we were
going to school. They also introduced us to our first authentic
Mexican food in Tucson. Dick and Ruby later divorced. He

died and I lost track of Ruby, although she lived in Phoenix for many years.

Bob Broan

Bobby Broan was a state agricultural inspection station agent when I first met him through Dick Whitlow. Bobby was a young, handsome veteran working in the "bug station" or agricultural inspection station that used to be located just east of the Smokehouse Bar and Restaurant, now the Dambar, on Highway 66. Bob wanted to be a Highway Patrolman but had to put in his time at the inspection station until another opening came. At that time there were fewer than 50 Arizona Highway Patrol cars on the road. Bobby idolized Stinson, Cisney and Whitlow, and they considered him a gullible young kid at the time. They pulled all sorts of tricks on him.

One time, Stinson had some blank pistol cartridges he had obtained when he did a bit part in a movie shot in Sedona using uniformed officers. I think it was Cisney and Stinson that decided to scare Broan silly. While Broan was inspecting the trunk of a New York tourist's car stopped under the awning of the inspection station, Stinson came up behind Broan and said, "Okay, Broan. I've taken as much off you as I can and I won't stand for any more. Go for your gun!" With that, Stinson drew his pistol and fired of two or three blank rounds within 10 feet of Broan before Broan could get his hand on his weapon. At that time, the owner of the car from New York was standing by the driver's side of the car, outside the car. He slammed the door before he realized he was still outside. He then dove through the open window and took off burning rubber down the road, sure that the Arizona police had gone berserk. Broan could not speak for some seconds before he realized he was not dead. When Cisney and Stinson started to laugh, Broan finally caught on. It took a long time until Broan could forgive those guys though. I wasn't there when this happened, but was told about it by Whitlow.

Besides riding with Highway Patrolmen, my friends Mc-Nulty, Hudson and I found that being with girls was fun too. Marion Acuna, who worked for the Spectors and was several years older than I, tried to teach me to dance when I was a freshman. She was very patient. Between her and Claudia Ricca and Jeffie Duke, Earl's daughter, they were somewhat success-ful. What is it about older girls that make them want to teach younger boys to dance? Other girls I liked and dated were Sue Spaw, Shirley Lewis, Antoinette Melles, Virginia Leonard and then there was Montie Coe Smith, who was my serious steady through my junior and senior years. "Going steady" at that time meant any time you spent with a girl when you couldn't find something more interesting to do, like fixing and riding in cars, going hunting or fishing, or riding with highway patrol-men. Montie Coe and I were an item in school, a topic which was referred to in our Bulldog High School annual of 1947.

High school days then were happy times. The war was over. The world was at peace. Most people were employed. Mothers had time to nurture their children. Teachers had the time and the desire to encourage their students to stay in school and plan their futures. The community wanted to be proud of its youth, and every child knew that and cared. Other than being reckless sometimes in cars, kids did not try to find ways to self-destruct through drugs. And all of us looked forward to going to college. What a wonderful time of life.

There was another real character I got to know in high school through my friendship with Ken Hudson. That was his aunt, Lila Chamberlain. This crusty old lady was a child of an early Navajo trader on the reservation, who married the manager of Babbitt Brothers store in Kingman. She was a very proper Anglo lady, well educated, and very stiff and formal. She spoke Navajo fluently, and operated a curio store on northwest corner of Fourth Street and Andy Devine. The Indians of the area loved to deal with her, as she spoke their language and recognized good jewelry.

My friend Ken lived with Lila after he returned from the Navy. Lila thought because she had lived in Kingman for so long that she need not comply with newly passed City of Kingman ordinances, especially traffic laws. She constantly refused to stop at stop signs or traffic lights, and continued to park in her usual parking place on the corner next to her store on Fourth Street, even when the City painted the curb red for some distance from the corner. Her car had scratches down both sides from coming too close to the rock gate posts at her home, which she explained as someone else's fault. Whenever we saw Lila Chamberlain's car coming down the street, most of the people pulled over to let her by.

4

COLLEGE YEARS,
1947-1951

My father had so programmed me to go to college that there was never a doubt in my mind that I would. Between my junior and senior years in high school, my parents took me on a trip to visit the campuses of University of Southern California, U.C.L.A., Stanford, University of California at Berkeley and University of Washington in Seattle, Washington. The choice was to be mine, but my parents were partial to Stanford, as at the time that school was rated tops on the west coast with high academic standards, and was the western equivalent of Harvard, Yale and Princeton.

I was greatly impressed by Stanford's reputation and its spacious, farm-like campus. The choice was made in favor of Stanford, although it remained to be seen whether I could get in as the school was very exclusive. We later heard that Stanford was only allowing two students that year from Arizona to enter as undergraduates. Although I did not know it at the time, the cost of attending Stanford was quite high compared with other schools and it would have been quite a financial sacrifice for my parents to send me there. Funny, but neither my parents nor I seriously considered my attending any Arizona college. Both Northern Arizona University and Arizona State University were then "Normal" schools, which were accredited universities but were geared toward training teachers. Although the University of Arizona was a good undergraduate school at the time, my parents felt I should go to one more prestigious.

The entrance exam for Stanford was given in several cities in Arizona that year: Phoenix, Tucson and Prescott. My parents took me to Prescott to take the test. Only two took the exam there at that time. Some young lady from Prescott whose name I do not remember was the second applicant. She was not accepted, but a young lady from a ranch in southeast Arizona, Sandra Day (later to become Sandra Day O'Connor) did.

I was advised of my acceptance to Stanford during my senior year, and was elated but a bit concerned. Palo Alto, California was over 500 miles from Kingman, and I had never been that far away from home alone. Although I thought I was qualified academically to go to such a prestigious school, I also knew I was just a skinny kid from a small town in the backwoods of Arizona, without much in the way of a cultural or social background. I think that is exactly why my parents wanted me to go there. They wanted me to be exposed to a

124

social and cultural scene that they felt would not be available at any school in Arizona.

When the time came in the fall of 1947, my parents accompanied me to Stanford for pre-registration and orientation. My residence for the first year was to be in Encina Hall, the freshman men's dormitory located on the south part of the campus. Encina Hall was a four or five-story stone dormitory built in the shape of an "E". It housed about 500 young fresman men and their dorm supervisors. At that time, the school had about 3,500 undergraduate students and almost that many additional graduate students in well-respected medical, engineering and law colleges. Freshman girls were usually housed in Roble Hall, on the north side of campus. At the time, there were about eight male students for every female student. Because of the shortage of girls, most boys looked for dates at other colleges, either Mills College near Oakland, which was strictly a girls' school at the time, San Francisco State in San Francisco, or San Jose State College about 30 miles south of campus.

But dating was the last thing in my mind at that time as I learned that Stanford graded "on the curve." That meant that at least 10% of the students in each class would be given failing grades each year in each class. That was the school's method of retaining only the students with the highest academic achievement. You had to keep climbing the ladder academically as the rungs of the ladder were being cut off below you each year. Stanford prided itself on admitting the cream of the academic crop, but you still had to prove yourself worthy of staying there.

First year Stanford students quickly learned that you were very lucky to be allowed to study there, and that you could be expelled from the school for any "conduct unbecoming a Stanford student." That could mean a lot of things, all the way from failing your studies, to having committed a crime, or merely doing anything that would embarrass the school. You were also expected to be very ethical about how you handled your exams. The motto of the school was "Let the Winds of Freedom Blow." At the orientation, you were told that you were free to study for your classes in any way that you felt best prepared you for your final exams. You could pick up your exam paper in class and go anywhere you wanted to in order to answer the questions. You could take the exam back to your dormitory to type the answers, sit on the library steps, anywhere. You were on the "Honor Code." Cheating on an exam would be considered the ultimate dishonor to the school. Expulsion would be expected. In fact, the school considered anyone who even observed someone cheating on the exam and not reporting it to be as guilty as the one that cheated. I would assume Stanford still requires that level of ethical behavior, although very few other schools today could expect that level of honesty.

At Kingman High School, it was the practice at that time that if your grade average in a course was an A or B + through-

My father, mother and me, enrollment at Stanford University

out the term, you did not have to take the final exam at the end of the year. Your class attendance, participation, and mid-term exams demonstrated that you were a superior student, so it was felt that you did not have to prove yourself by taking a final exam. As I maintained an A or B+ average in almost all my classes in high school, I did not have to take many final exams. So even though it took some pressure off me in high school, it was not a good practice in college as Stanford based almost all your grades on your performance on the final exam. You were not required to attend classes if you thought you could pass the course with book study alone. In fact some of the classes, biology for example, were so large (200 students or more) that professors did not even take attendance.

My parents helped me register for my classes as most parents did in those days. They also helped me move into Encina Hall. They met my new roommates, Bill Street and Carl Abercrombie. Bill was the son of a wealthy merchant from Seattle, and Carl was the son of a dairy farmer from Madera, California. Our room was #345 and was on the third floor. In it, we had three cots, three desks, and three wardrobe closets – comfortable, but not overly spacious. You were allowed to decorate the room as long as you did not damage it.

Showers and bathrooms were at the end of the hall. The freshman men all ate together in a communal dining hall, where abundant and very nourishing food was served, which was included in your room and board. I think tuition was

$125 per quarter then, and $150 room and board per month. Now, I think tuition and room and board for a freshman at Stanford is over $40,000 per year.

When my parents left that weekend, they surprised me by leaving me our family 1947 new blue Chevrolet 4-door sedan. I had not had a car of my own before and was really surprised. My parents told me that they were giving me this car because they were proud of my being able to get into Stanford, and that I should have a car in order to be able to come home to Kingman occasionally and to take advantage of some of the sights nearby. I also understood that I might not be able to keep the car if my grades didn't stay up.

Before they left to go home to Kingman, my father took me aside and told me that although grades were important for me to stay at Stanford he believed that I would learn a great many important things by getting to know as many of the students in my class as Stanford was such a cosmopolitan school. We had students from all over the world in my class. He told me to set a specific time each day to take a break from the books to go down the halls of Encina and meet new people and find out all I could about them, which I did. My father really knew what he was talking about. Excellent advice from a wise man.

Some results of that practice were that I came to really enjoy meeting people, finding out about their families, their cultures, their values and beliefs. Most importantly, I learned to be a good listener. These traits stood me in good stead for the career that followed later.

Stanford life was a wholly new world for me. For the first time in my life I had to learn how to manage my allowance, balance a bank account, budget my expenses, as well as my time and interests. I had to learn to do my laundry and plan for clean clothes. Corduroy pants and jeans were standard wear for men then, with t-shirts or sweat shirts. Dress up was in jackets and slacks for dances and trips to the city (San Francisco). Long hours of studying were assumed. You had to plan time for relaxation.

Physical Education was required for all four years. Because I was a fairly good swimmer, my first P.E. was swimming. Stanford was (and is still) world renowned for its swimming and water polo teams. My coach evidently felt that I had the potential to be on the swim team, and so I trained for the sport. I would swim twice a day. Free-style Australian crawl was my best stroke, although I was pretty good in back stroke and side stroke. In the morning, you swam a mile crawl, and also a quarter-mile on a kick board using legs alone. Then, in the afternoons you would do wind sprints — several 50 and 100 yard dashes; then the coach would have you swim a few races. I was really in good shape then, and began to put on weight. When I graduated from high school, I was about 5 feet 10 inches tall, and weighed 140 to 145 pounds. My first year on the swim team (and eating in dining halls) resulted in my growing four inches and putting on 30 pounds. When I came home after my first year, my body change surprised almost everyone.

My first year in college taught me several things. First, in college teachers do not force you to learn anything. It's all up to you. No one is going to constantly nag or encourage you to do your best like your parents did. You are the only one responsible for your grades. If you want to waste your opportunities at Stanford, that's your decision. Second, being thrown in with the cream of the academic crop meant that I was going to have to really work hard to stay cream, staying at the top of the container, rather than becoming skim milk and sinking to the bottom. Third, there were really some neat new things to experience in college, mostly girls. That may have been one of my problems.

My first quarter's grades were not good. I got a D in Biology, and a C in Western Civilizations (history). I got B's in the rest of my classes, but that D made me ineligible to compete in intramural swimming. That was a shock as I had never considered that I would be ineligible for any activity. I had to re-assess my priorities. After that, although I was not a top student, I made it through my courses with better-than-average grades and stayed ahead of the curve.

One of the classes I took was Expository Writing. This was an English course taught by the now-famous author Wallace Stegner, who wrote the famous novel "Angle of Repose." In that course, we were to write a paper that would demonstrate our skills in writing, and our ability to clearly explain a serious topic that required research. As I was pretty certain

I was going to law school, I chose to write on a legal topic — "The Diversity in Divorce Law in the United States." My father sent me some information about how different divorce law was in some states, and I wrote a serious (but probably very nerdy and boring) paper on that topic. My roommate, Bill Street, taking the same course, wrote a very humorous paper on the "Sex life of an Earth Worm." Bill got an A from Stegner on his paper. I got a C.

Dormitory life was fun. Much time was spent playing what we thought were pranks on others. A student of Chinese background, Zeppelin Wong, was a freshman in the same dorm the year I was. He was a nut about firecrackers. He frequently would throw a loud firecracker through your door transom in the late night hours. Carl Abercrombie, who was on the wrestling team, caught him one night and shook him over the third floor stairwell by the ankles until he promised to stop. Zeppelin later became a lawyer and city councilman for the City of San Francisco.

The room next door to ours in Encina Hall contained three very interesting people: Bob Fox, Jack Abouchar and Lawrence Gordon. Fox and Abouchar were Jewish, and a little ashamed of it. As I recall, at that time there was some social stigma attached if you were Jewish. I remember that they would sometimes get hard salami from their parents and hang it behind their door, thinking no one would see it there. I loved salami, and its smell came through their door into our room. I think I broke the ice with them by asking about the salami and pleading for a piece. Lawrence Gordon was a very homesick young pre-med student from Honolulu, Hawaii. He craved ethnic Hawaiian food and frequently shared care packages from home.

After becoming ineligible to compete in swimming, my next physical education class was tennis, which I did not particularly enjoy at the time. The third quarter of my freshman year, I signed up for polo. Stanford had a very good polo team during the 1940s. Because I had loved horses, I thought that would be an easy sport for me. Wrong. I had never ridden an English saddle before and it was required for the sport. In a western saddle, the rider balances himself with his weight in his feet in the stirrups and moves with every move of the horse. With English tack, you have a very small, narrow saddle with no horn to hold on to. You grip the horse with your knees and have little if any weight in the stirrups. To test your riding technique, the coach puts strips of paper between your knees and the saddle, and if the strips fall, he knows you were not gripping the horse properly. Also, you "posted" when you ride — lifting yourself up on every second or third step of the horse.

The theory is that this took much of the shock of the horse's movements away from our body. I did not find that to be true. I had much to learn. A classmate, Tom Shartle, had his two "ponies" flown to Stanford from Australia so he could participate in Beginning Polo. He was no beginner, believe me. I had to rent a horse from the school. She must have been hurt by some errant swings of mallets because she shied frequently when I tried some shots while moving fast. One time she turned so abruptly I kept on going straight as she turned right. I hit the dirt with a thump and the horse ran off. I walked back with my helmet and mallet in my hands, to be greeted by my coach with a sly "Where is your horse, Mr. Gordon?" I said I hoped she had come back on her own, which she had. Although I learned a lot about the sport, I did not do well in polo.

After your first year in college in a dormitory, you had some living choices to make. You could rent your own apartment off campus, an expensive choice; move in to a men's eating club such as Toyon Hall; or join a fraternity. Contrary to the bad reputations fraternities now seem to have, fraternities at Stanford were well-respected and desirable associations. Most national fraternities were represented at Stanford, and each had their own private living quarters, served by their own kitchens.

The fraternities in those days sought out good students, as well as promising athletes. They strived to keep their members academically sound and bragged about their grade point standings. But even jocks at Stanford had to take serious courses and keep their grades up. Some of the finest athletes in school while I was there went on to graduate schools and became doctors, engineers and lawyers. Because of its strict academic standards for student athletes, Stanford isn't very often the Pacific Coast Conference champion in football or basketball. It seems, however, to do well in tennis and swimming.

Stanford did not allow sororities on campus, although some of the living facilities for girls so closely resembled sororities that you could not tell the difference.

Fraternities provided an opportunity to become associated with some interesting leadership-type people on campus, have fun as "brothers" in a living facility close to classrooms, learn some keen fraternity songs, and play intramural sports such as volleyball, football and basketball. It gave you a feeling of belonging to a support group of people who cared and were willing to help you if you needed it.

I was rushed by and joined the Sigma Alpha Epsilon National Fraternity (SAE). I moved into the fraternity house my second year at Stanford, and became friends with some of the most wonderful people I have ever met, and with some of whom I still keep in contact. I wouldn't have traded that experience for the world, although I understand fraternities now may not be the same.

The site of the university was originally a huge farm owned by Leland Stanford, who later became a very influential millionaire involved in developing California and transcontinental railroads. The farm, I believe, initially was a wide strip of land bounded by the Pacific Ocean on the west and the San Francisco Bay on the east, and was several miles in width. Stanford deeded the land for the city of Palo Alto to the city. As a part of the sale, Stanford required that alcoholic beverages not be

135

sold in the city. There were no liquor stores or bars in the area to purchase alcohol, nor could restaurants serve liquor with meals. The nearest liquor establishment was Menlo Park on the north, and the next city to the south, which I think was Mountain View. There was a beer bar named "Rosotti's" up in the foothills to the west of the campus.

Of course, as most students enjoyed socializing over a pitcher of beer, it seemed to me that it was more dangerous to require students to drive somewhere to drink than to be served beer on campus. As I understand it, the rules are not the same today on the campus and in Palo Alto. How the change came about, I don't know.

Once a year, Stanford celebrated "Back to the Farm Day." One of the popular events was a parade featuring the oldest cars and wagons that could be found. While I was a pledge, the SAE house located a large horse-drawn hay wagon in a barn down the peninsula and rented it and two farm horses to pull it. This was a difficult task as there were few farm horses around in 1947-1948. The horses we rented had not pulled a wagon for a very long time, nor had they been shod. So, we had to find a farrier (one who shoes horses) in a modern residential community to shoe the horses. That being done, there was one last problem.

No one in the fraternity house knew how to drive a team of horses. I was probably the only one in the house who had any knowledge about horses, but none at all in driving a team. The brothers insisted it was my chore to bring the wagon and a two-horse team from East Palo Alto to the campus for the parade. Another brother came along with me. I did not know anything about handling this type of horse, but neither the owners nor my brothers seemed concerned. Luckily, the two horses were gentle and didn't mind going down busy city streets, being passed by cars with cheering passengers. (At least I think they were cheering. I was too scared and tense to notice.) The only problem I had was when we had to go under a four lane underpass on University Drive coming up to the stoplight on El Camino Real, a large highway that parallels the university campus. Some joker honked his horn in the underpass spooking the team, which then took off at a dead run right through the stoplight against the red light. The Good Lord must have been watching after me as cars took notice and stopped to let us through the intersection. When the wagon safely cleared the intersection and the horses calmed down, I looked to see how my buddy was, and discovered that he wasn't there. He had jumped from the wagon before we got to the stoplight to let me and the horses fend for ourselves. The rest of the parade was dull after that. However, I refused to drive the team back to the barn. I think the fraternity house had to have the farmer who owned the wagon come and take the rig back.

Fraternity life was fun. The SAE house had a wonderful singing chorus. Most of the members belonged. We learned many college and fraternity songs in harmony and serenaded girls' dormitories in the evenings. The various fraternity choruses competed for honors in the annual Spring Sing held on campus in April or May. Joan and I still sing some of those old songs together in moments of nostalgia. Jamo Wharton, a fraternity brother, even taught me a few songs on the ukulele.

Each year I had a different roommate in the fraternity house. One was Jay Niblo, who was captain and stroke oar on the Stanford varsity eight-man crew team. Crew at Stanford then was not even a university accredited sport. The crew members hired and paid for their own coach, shells, and rental on the boat house that stored them.

Jay suggested that I ought to try out for the team, and in a weak moment, I agreed. I was unaware of the many hardships a crew member must endure to make it to the first varsity boat, but I found out soon enough.

Every morning at about 4:30 a.m., we would go to the Palo Alto boat harbor on south San Francisco Bay and row four five-mile races — two up toward San Francisco, under the Dumbarton Bridge, and two back to the home yacht harbor. By the time we got back to the fraternity house after our workout, we were starved. On one occasion I ate 16 hot cakes, six eggs and a turkey neck for breakfast. But were we in wonderful physical shape! I was 170 pounds and rowed number two position in the second varsity shell. That was the port oar (I think) 12 feet long. There is no sport where team effort has to be so precise and in exact unison. When all eight oars pull through the water in a perfect stroke, the shell literally lifts and sings through the water, a distance of over twice its length which would be over 120 feet. It was grueling, everyday training.

We were not even allowed to go home on Easter vacation. One Easter, Jay and I were the only brothers left in the fraternity house – even our cook was on vacation. Because we were left on our own for meals, we had to find something to eat each day. We both loved cold cracked Dungeness crab, and which could be procured easily enough at the store.

I think between us that evening, we had about five pounds of crab that we devoured with mayonnaise, leaving a pile of empty crab shells. What to do with all those shells? So, we played one of what we believed to be our most humorous pranks on our brothers. We knew how badly the shells would smell if we didn't get them to a proper garbage facility. But why not give our brothers a little surprise? We wrapped the shells in the paper they came in and put them in the back of a drawer in a chest of drawers in an unoccupied room in the fraternity house on the second floor near the stairs. Easter week passed and the brothers returned. After about seven days there was this very strong odor in the hallway of the second floor. For some reason, as hard as they tried, no one could find the cause. The house president called a special meeting and pleaded for whoever was causing this problem to solve it. Jay and I relented and late one night secretly removed what was left of the shells which by then had turned from red and white to a green colored mold. It still took several days for the smell to abate. Many years passed until we confessed at a reunion.

One Thanksgiving, several brothers went to Reno, Nevada. Lee Auchumpah, the father of our brothers, was a professor at the University of Nevada. One cold evening, about five of us visited some casino bars, singing college fight songs. We knew that if we sang enough of those, some bystander would would join in and pay for a beer. At Harrah's Club, we were joined by a small college graduate who told us that he had always wanted to play football, but couldn't because of his small stature. He asked if we would play football with him. We consented, and moved enough empty tables and chairs from the dance floor to run about three plays with him as fullback before the police came.

The head officer, who was very nice, asked us whether football wasn't normally played outside, and of course we answered that it was. He also asked whether it wouldn't be more appropriate if we took the game outside. We agreed that would be so. And then he asked as we began to move outside, wouldn't it be nice if we replaced the chairs and tables that we had so carefully set aside. Of course, we said and did. The officers thanked us and we went outside. How different law enforcement was back then, and this is one example of how law enforcement can be achieved with honor and humor.

After we went outside, we discovered that about four to six inches of snow had fallen and we could not find my car which had been parked at the curb several blocks away. All cars looked alike with that amount of snow on them. Undaunted, we hailed a cab and went to our friend's home and reported the car stolen. The next morning the car was found.

Another thing. I am told (perhaps in jest) that Harrah's Club made an offer to sponsor the crew team if Stanford would allow it. All that the Club would require is that the word "Harrah" be painted on each oar, to show as it came out of the water. A fun idea, but I don't think Stanford would have agreed.

Now, for the rest of the story. Were it not for being a member of the SAE fraternity, I would not have met and married the love of my life, Joan Gipe. One of my roommates was Wilson Hanna, who was All Pacific Coast End on his high school football team in Fresno, California. He was a big jovial man, who unsuccessfully tried out for the Stanford football team. Joan, who I had not yet met, was then dating Wilson. In the meantime, when I had time off from my studies, I was casually dating girls from Mills College in Oakland and San Jose State in San Jose, California.

Wilson's car was frequently mechanically challenged, and one fateful day, he asked me for a ride to Fresno on my way back to Kingman. I agreed, as I had to go through Fresno anyway on the way home. As we entered Fresno, Wilson asked if on the way to his parents' home, where I was to stay overnight, we could stop off at Joan's house to say hello, and we did. We were introduced and I was immediately stricken by her charm and beauty. I was a little embarrassed because Joan was paying more attention to me than to Wilson, and I did not want to get into trouble with my roommate. I may have pro-

141

voked Joan's attention with my inimitable line to her, "How would you like to learn to play the ukulele?" Being a little uncomfortable about the feelings I had about Joan, I decided to drive right on to Kingman and not stay overnight with Wilson. I did not see Joan again for some time.

After he and Joan had broken up, Wilson, who was dating another girl in Fresno, again needed a ride for a date. He asked if I would like to double date with him in Fresno. I agreed. He asked who I would like to go out with, and I said Joan. That wasn't a problem for him, and we had a nice time that weekend. In my opinion, I felt it was just a nice uncomplicated date. Not in Joan's mind, however. I learned later that immediately after that date, Joan told her mother that she had found the person she was going to marry, (me) and that she would be married in the Stanford Chapel. She even had her attendants and color scheme picked out.

I continued to date a few other girls, some at Stanford and some at other schools, but I had no idea how captured I was at the time. Joan played me like a hooked trout, however, giving me slack, but ultimately reeling me in. We carried on a long-distance romance by correspondence and weekend dating. The distance was 150 miles over a road that my Chevy came to know by heart. Joan would sometimes come to Stanford by bus for SAE functions and go home by bus. It was not long before we knew we were seriously in love.

During our dating period, I was impressed with Joan's step-father, Birre Gipe. He was employed as a field warehouse

manager for a company that financed farm products. He traveled a lot, but when we got together, we had a lot of fun. An
avid golfer, he got a huge kick out of beating me at that game.
One of my other physical education classes for a quarter was
golf. I hit a pretty long ball at the time, but as now, the ball
rarely went where I wanted it to. As big and strong as I was, I
could not seem to beat Birre, and that delighted him. I have
never met a more affable fun-loving man. I enjoyed my time
with him almost as much as with Joan. Birre frequently got
his favorite dinner entre by asking his wife Grace to make
something that he wanted, saying that he thought that I would
really like that. Fried chicken and apple pie was always something he thought I would be especially happy with, and I was.

I took a job as a service station attendant in Fresno in the
summer between my junior and senior year at school. I lived
in the SAE house at Fresno State College, but would eat at
Joan's house almost every night. Joan and her mother would
cook me wonderful meals. We were convinced that my working in Fresno was a good idea, because we thought it important to find out what each of us was like on other than party
occasions. That was our rationale, anyway. Really, we just did
not want to be apart from each other from that time forward.

When a fraternity brother became serious about a girl it
was customary for him to give her his fraternity pin. Then
the couple was "pinned." When that happened, if time and
location were available, the brothers in the house arranged
for the couple to be serenaded by the group, singing beauti-

ful fraternity songs. The house serenaded Joan in the Quadrangle of the University, as a surprise, one beautiful evening. The Quad was a large square park-like area within classrooms on the main campus. About twenty of the brothers came out from behind some trees and bushes to serenade us in the moonlight.

My parents were aware that things were really getting serious between Joan and me, and I finally broke the news that we wanted to get married. My father would rather have had us wait until after I graduated, but he was a realist, and knew that if he insisted that we not marry until after law school, I might not stay on course with his plans. He agreed that we could marry and that they would help us financially through school. I know this must have been a worrisome time for them, as they were making a huge financial sacrifice already to keep me in school at an expensive private school like Stanford as a single person, and they were wondering what additional cost there would be to support a married couple.

Plans were made, just as Joan had made them, and we were married just before my senior year began in the beautiful Stanford Chapel on September 17, 1950, with the same color scheme Joan had chosen. My parents gave us a reception in Kingman at the country club a week before our wedding for the people that could not make the long trip to Stanford for our ceremony.

Bill Street, my freshman roommate in Encina Hall, was my best man. Bill Rideout and Jay Niblo, fraternity brothers, filled out the roster of my groomsmen. The wedding itself at the Chapel was beautiful. The only hitch was that in all his efficiency as best man, Bill had forgotten to make arrangements to get Joan to the Chapel in her wedding gown. Joan ended up on the street corner in front of the Cardinal Hotel in Palo Alto all by herself, dressed in her beautiful wedding finery, with no one to take her to the church. Luckily, one of our friends saw her there and after learning her predicament, drove her to the church with Joan sitting on someone's lap in time for the ceremony.

We spent the first few days of our honeymoon at the Highlands Inn in Carmel, California, and then a few days in San Francisco, before returning to school. We had a wonderful time together then and still do today. I think we are even more deeply in love now than when we first started going together. We are extremely fortunate.

When school started, we found a small efficiency apartment in East Palo Alto that fit our budget. Joan got a job as a secretary in the engineering department at Stanford, where she met some fascinating professors from all over the world. She was required to have a United States security clearance because she was typing some classified reports on nuclear energy experiments. Even though I did not have the necessary clearance,sSometimes I would help Joan with her typing. Joan's salary as secretary was enough to cover our apartment rent and most of our groceries, so I don't believe we were much of a financial burden on my parents at that time.

Joan and me on our honeymoon in San Francisco, 1950

Life during my senior year was wonderful. We were young, happy and enjoying life in the Bay Area. We frequently went to San Francisco to movies, plays and operas, and enjoyed the excitement of the city on long cable car rides. I found after marriage that I didn't care for getting up at four in the morning to row a shell with Jay Niblo, so I quit crew. I think there was a special waiver of physical education for married students.

With marriage, I had more time to spend on my school-work, and my grades improved. My major was sociology with a minor in psychology. By that time, I had completed my required courses so that I had my first chance to take some electives. Being from Arizona, I had always been curious about geology so I took a beginning course in Historical Geology — telling the history of the earth's formation through layers. It was interesting to me and I did well in the course, so the next quarter I took a more advanced class, which interested me even more. The last quarter of my senior year, I took the most advanced course in geology undergraduate work and did so well that I was offered a fellowship to teach at Stanford if I would agree to spend a year in the bottom of the Grand Canyon and do research on trilobites -- tiny primitive crustaceans whose physical evolution was thought to be a good indicator of historical time periods. This offer was a great honor. It indicated that I had a potential teaching career job at one of the most prestigious learning institutions in the world. What a tough decision! For the first time in my college career, I

147

was confused. I had been so carefully guided down my career path to a future in law that I had never given any thought to any other. It was a tough time for us, because I already had been accepted to the University Of Arizona College Of Law, and Joan and I were already making inquiries as to housing in Tucson. As flattering as the offer was, I turned it down, as a future in law seemed more secure than in teaching. Occasionally, though, I have since wondered what our lives would have been if that temptation had prevailed.

After our marriage, I kept up some ties with some SAE fraternity on campus, attending meetings, parties, and having some of the brothers over to our apartment. Being the only married couple in the fraternity at the time, on a couple of occasions we acted as the official chaperones for fraternity parties in San Francisco. Now that I look back on it, I can visualize the assurances the brothers would give school officials and fraternity parents that the student brothers and their dates would be all right on an overnight party because Joan and I were overseeing their activities. I'll bet parents and school authorities had the impression that chaperones would be considerably older and more authoritarian than we were. Luckily the brothers did not embarrass us because nothing bad happened on those occasions that we were aware of. It was neat because as chaperones we had our room expenses paid. I remember one overnight was at the Fairmont Hotel on Nob Hill in San Francisco, and another was at the Silverado Lodge in the wine country north of San Francisco. Beautiful places, both. A couple of years ago Joan and I trailered to the wine country and went to see the old Silverado Lodge. It had changed somewhat, but still had the old charm we remembered.

My senior year went quickly and happily. I graduated about in the middle of my class academically, which I thought was pretty good at Stanford for a kid from Kingman. We moved to Kingman for the summer, awaiting the start of law school in Tucson in September. Joan was pregnant with Trey by that time.

5

LAW SCHOOL,
1951 - 1954

After leaving Stanford, Joan and I spent most of the summer of 1951 in Kingman, living at the home of my parents on Spring Street. I did some work as a law clerk doing research and helping my father draft an appeal brief in the Arizona Supreme Court in the Regaldo Estate. Joan was growing bigger each day with a child we later found was Trey -- formally, Frank X. Gordon, III. At that time, they did not have ultrasound or any other medical device to predetermine the sex of your unborn child. I remember trying things like seeing how a metal object swinging on a string above Joan's navel moved, whether in a line or in a circle. That was supposed to be a clue as to the child's gender. I don't remember how accurate it was.

Because most of our kitchen appliances were packed in boxes ready to be transported to Tucson, Joan had to accept food my mother cooked, which although good, was hearty and heavy. Without good diet control, Joan ballooned. We packed up and started for Tucson in early August. All our household furniture and kitchen wares were sent by a moving company. The car was crammed full with all our clothes and a few cooking utensils Joan wisely kept out of the moving van. It was very hot and my old Chevrolet sedan had no air conditioner. The trip was most uncomfortable for Joan, who was about eight months pregnant at the time.

When we got to Phoenix, we stopped at a gas station to ask which of two highways to take to Tucson, either through Florence or Casa Grande. It was before there were freeways, and both highways at that time were two lane, paved roads each about the same distance. We didn't know which would be the easier. The gas station attendant took one look at Joan in her condition, and said not to go through Florence as the road had a lot more dips and curves than the other one. We were glad for the advice, but even the better of the two roads was a miserable experience for Joan. We arrived in Tucson in late afternoon. I think we stayed with Dick and Ruby Whitlow in Tucson for a day or two before we could move into our little rental home on South Twenty-Second Street. Dick was a patrolman on the Arizona Highway Patrol based in Tucson at the time, and helped us find important places in our new community, like a hospital, good but reasonably priced restaurants, and the law school. The Whitlows introduced us to authentic Sonoran Mexican food, which we still enjoy to this day.

Our first home in Tucson was a little three-room army-type dwelling in Pueblo Gardens in the southeastern part of town near the airbase. A lot of military personnel lived in the neighborhood. We leased it for a year and moved in. The problem was that our furniture did not arrive for several weeks and so we had to eat out most of the time. That again made it difficult for Joan to control her diet, and she continued to gain weight. I think she gained a total of 45 or 50 pounds during her pregnancy with Trey.

Trey was born September 1, 1951, at Tucson Medical Center Hospital. A week before he was born I took a picture of Joan bending over touching her toes with a big smile and a huge belly. If I ever can find it, I want to enlarge that picture. She was then, and still is, the most beautiful woman in the world to me.

Joan's water broke in the early morning hours of Trey's birthday. She had prudently packed her bag days before, and I rushed her to the hospital, which was clear across town. The roads had dips full of water in them, as it had rained that night. Apparently I was driving faster than Joan felt was safe, and she complained. I said that the hospital was far better equipped to take care of the birth than I was, and I would rather be early. In those days, fathers were not trained about the birthing process and how to be helpful -- and I sure wasn't. Joan's labor with Trey was a long one, and after several hours of waiting, Dick Whitlow and I left the hospital to get some breakfast. Trey was born before we got back. He was a beautiful baby, who soon became a handful.

Joan was unable to work with a new baby on her hands, so my parents had to support us fully. I had just started law school and the studies were hard for me. I was, and still am, a slow reader. I felt I didn't have time to take on a job after school. I don't know what was so hard about the casework teaching method, but I never had to study so hard before. I studied all the time, after class at school, at home and sometimes in the law library at night.

Most of the law students at the University of Arizona were returned veterans of World War II in school on the G.I. Bill of Rights. They were several years older than I, more mature, and several in my class were successful business people already. I felt quite inadequate.

The first year in law school consisted of required introductory courses: Common Law Pleading; Criminal Law, Equity, Torts, and Law Library Research methods. The faculty consisted of some nationally known and respected scholars in their fields who had written extensively about their subjects. I found out soon that being a recognized scholar does not make a person an effective teacher.

My father was of the opinion that it would be better for me to attend the University of Arizona College of Law than Stanford Law School. He was convinced that Stanford Law School was geared more to teach students to be law professors, rather than to be down-to-earth, in-the-trenches-type trial lawyers. He also felt that it would be better to go to a law school in the state in which you intended to practice because there were differences in substantive and procedural law between the states. Further, he felt that it was important for business referrals to get to know students who would be practicing in your own state, rather than another. I think my father was probably right on the latter two opinions, but maybe not so right on the first one. If I had remained at Stanford for law school, perhaps my name would have been considered for the United States Supreme Court, as were my classmates at Stanford, Sandra Day O'Connor and William Rehnquist, and even a later graduate Justice Anthony Kennedy. But who knows.

One of our teachers, Professor Thomas, was a colonel in the army in World War II, having served in Italy. We later learned that he was instrumental during the Allied invasion of Italy during the war in negotiating a pact with the subordinates to Adolph Hitler that the city of Rome would be spared from bombing if neither army garrisoned troops there. Colonel Thomas was very proud of his military rank and insisted on being referred to as "Colonel" Thomas, rather than "Professor Thomas." At one of our first classes with him in Common Law Pleading, Thomas so advised us. In a moment which I am sure the student wished he could relive, a first year student in our class announced to Thomas that he too had been a Colonel in the army and that he would appreciate being addressed similarly. That did

155

not go over well with Professor Thomas and it may only have been coincidence that the student did not get a passing grade in that class.

Professor William Spate Barnes (we called him "Curly Bill" privately) was a tall, lanky bald-headed gentleman who spoke with a southern accent, and also as though he had marbles in his mouth. Barnes was very difficult to understand. He taught Criminal Law. There is an ancient rule about criminal causation called the "But for Rule." When he said it, it came out "the Buffalo Rule." It promoted some giggles at first, but we learned to suppress them.

Byron McCormick taught Contracts. He was a friend of my father, but that did not help me when he awarded me my first and only "D" in law school for that course. That was my first and only D grade for the three years in law school. I think I learned a lot about how to write law school exams from taking McCormick's class.

Chester H. Smith taught Real Property, Personal Property, Mining Law and Water Law, all extremely important subjects. He was not a nationally known scholar, but, in my opinion, he was by far the best and most effective teacher in law school.

Some professors seemed to enjoy embarrassing students when they didn't get the main point of a particular case being studied. Smith did not. In fact he paid particular attention to the students that seemed to have the hardest time in school, both academically and financially. Years later we found that he had financially supported many students through law school.

After we graduated and he died, several of his students, including me, established a scholarship fund in Chester Smith's name in lieu of sending flowers to his funeral. There are nearly one hundred students that are now practicing law that would not have been able to complete law school without the financial help of the Chester H. Smith Scholarship Fund.

Our next-door neighbors in my first year of law school were really funny people — Dan and Laurie Sammons. Dan had just graduated from law school, had taken the bar examination and was awaiting the results when we moved into our house next to them in September 1951. Joan and Laurie got along famously together. Dan was working at the County Attorney's office in Tucson, and Laurie worked in the bookstore at the University. I have never met another couple who enjoyed bickering between themselves so. They would argue and shout at each other about anything, and have a good time doing it. Joan and I used to take our coffee over to their house in the morning and listen to them argue.

One time I needed to borrow Dan's deer rifle to go whitetail deer hunting near Sonoita, Arizona. My rifle had mysteriously become lost when my father mailed it to me from Kingman. Dan brought out his old rifle and handed it to me, and I noticed that the bolt, or firing mechanism, was missing. I asked him about it, and he had forgotten that he had hidden it from Laurie because he was afraid she might shoot him with the rifle some time during one of their arguments. I think he was kidding, but maybe he wasn't.

The Sammonses had a little spotted terrier dog they called "Clearly", a term one of our law professors, Claude Brown, used incessantly in class. One day when Dan was carrying out his garbage to a can on the street with Clearly at his side, a large white German Shepherd dog came walking up the street minding his own business. Without provocation, Clearly viciously attacked the Shepherd, who was at least five times his size. The Shepherd finally grabbed Clearly by the neck and shook him like a rag doll. Dan bravely tried to save Clearly by shouting at and banging the Shepherd on the head with the metal garbage can lid. When he didn't release Clearly, Dan banged him again. At that, the Shepherd released Clearly and turned his attention to Dan. Dan (and Clearly) retreated slowly backward toward their house with Dan using the garbage can lid as a shield all the way. When they finally made it safely into the house and closed the door, the Shepherd circled the house several times before he gave up the chase. Dan did not come out for some time after.

Dan didn't find out he had passed the bar examination until October. In the meantime he got pleasure out of starting false rumors that a large portion of his class had failed the exam. Each time the rumor came back to him, the number of failures got bigger, and Dan believed them, even though he had started the rumor. He worried himself sick.

One of the most interesting people in my first year law class was David Burr Udall, one of the last of the continuous line of the famous Arizona Udall clan to go to law school. He was from a small town in northern Arizona, St. Johns. His father was Levi Udall, once Chief Justice of the Arizona Supreme Court. His brothers, Stewart and Morris Udall were lawyers who graduated just before he entered law school. Stewart became Secretary of the Interior of the United States and Mo (Morris) became a U. S. Congressman who made an unsuccessful run for the presidency of the U. S. in 1964. Burr worked his way through law school doing orderly work at the University Health Clinic mopping floors, cleaning bathrooms, anything in return for free rent of a room in the basement of the Clinic. He was one of the most serious students in our class, and I attribute my being able to pass my first year's classes to him teaching me how to study. I give him this credit, even though he openly claims it himself.

Burr took very complete handwritten notes in each class each day, then in the evening typed these notes up verbatim. Then he made a typed outline of his daily notes. At the end of each week, he reviewed thoroughly all of his notes and outlines taken up to that point in each course. He didn't need to study for exams at the end of the semester as he was ready at any time. If someone missed a day of classes, when he or she returned to class the next day, on his or her desk would be a carbon copy of Burr's notes of the previous day's class. The notes were so good that they were better and more complete than mine. I would have done better to miss more of the classes and get Burr's notes.

Burr had a personality trait that I noticed immediately and

159

always admired him for. Law students then, and I imagine now, were intensely competitive. There always were some cliques of friends formed in each class. With that came the natural tendency to be catty or critical of other students' study methods or attitudes. During the hundreds of times that I heard remarks about other students, I do not believe I ever heard Burr Udall make a single negative comment about another person. You literally could not force him by direct questions to say something bad about anyone else. He would just smile and either change the subject or find something, regardless of how small, nice to say about that person. What a wonderful trait. Wouldn't it be nice if all people followed that practice?

Burr's brother Morris wrote a classic textbook on Evidence in Arizona which was for several decades the "Bible" for any lawyer or judge in Arizona on questions of whether any evidentiary objection made during trial was good or not. No matter that several new evidence handbooks have been written since, Morris' work is still one of the best, in my opinion. It went through several revisions and updates after Mo became a Congressman by other university professors. Morris was a prodigious note-taker in class also. Someone got a copy of his class outline in the course on Evidence and it was copied and sold to law students for many years. Claude Brown (the one who said "Clearly" all the time) was the professor who for many years taught the course on Evidence. He taught the course the same way each year, so Mo's outline was current for at least a decade. It even contained all the questions that Brown asked students in class, and even all the jokes he would tell.

Lester Penterman, a big jovial freshman from Phoenix, was also in my class. We became good friends. Les was single at the time, and we both rode bicycles to school. He had been a semi-professional boxer between college and law school, and at 6' 8" tall, had never been hit on the nose in boxing. Les was an ardent snow skier and member of the National Ski Patrol, which rescues injured skiers on the slopes. Les almost lost his leg in a ski competition at Snowbowl near Flagstaff during his first year in law school. His leg was broken so severely in so many pieces that he was put together several different times with wires, screws and metal plates. In retrospect, the leg never totally healed and was finally amputated some forty years later. Les missed quite a few weeks of classes in his first year because of his injury, and was told that he should drop out of law school and come back the following year. Not having the money to do so, we found a law professor, Lester Feezer, who taught Negotiable Instruments, who volunteered to tutor Les after school hours if I brought my notes on all the classes Les missed. Most of these were courses that Feezer had not been the teacher. We did that for several weeks and Les squeaked through, barely passing, but saving himself a year of school.

Les made slim finances stretch by eating horsemeat instead of beef. There was a market in south Tucson that sold nothing but horsemeat at prices ridiculously cheaper than beef. He convinced me to try some, and I found it was very good, once I got over the idea of eating one of my favorite animals. Sometimes Les would invite himself over for dinner and bring beautiful filet mignon horsemeat steaks for grilling. Joan would not eat it and would have a hamburger instead.

Les and another friend, Neal Roberts, another 6'7", first-year law student, made a good portion of their law school tuition playing contract bridge and gin rummy for money. Neal and Les were Assistant Attorneys General for Arizona for some time together. Neal was a brilliant lawyer, but always hung around with shady characters. Ultimately he became entangled in a dispute in which one of his clients was convicted of murder. Neal later in life drank too much and died quite a few years ago a crippled old man.

Timeouts from study at the law library were spent out in front of the law school, with students pitching pennies to see who could come closest to a certain crack in the pavement. Closest took the pennies. Law school then was just across the street from Old Main, the original wooden building that was the entire school when it was first built. There was a huge multi-level water fountain on the west side of Old Main where newly pinned fraternity men and others for similar minor infractions were unceremoniously thrown into the fountain. The law school has moved twice since then, and is now in its own freestanding facility on the north side of Speedway north of the University Campus.

Maynard P. Goudy, "Hank", also was a close friend. He was a single student in law school. Our friendship was mainly in studying until after law school and his marriage. Some years later we became very good friends with him and his second wife, Mary Alice. We had many fun times together. He died in 1985 from pancreatic cancer.

Another first year student friend was Peter Kiewit, son and eventual heir of Kiewit Construction Co., a world-wide heavy construction business. He and I played golf occasionally, he being a much better golfer than I was. Today he heads a large philanthropic foundation giving charitably to many causes.

We moved into a nicer home on North Third Street in Tucson during my second year in law school. That year we got our first station wagon automobile, a 1953 Ford. It was great to have so much more room for hauling kid's things. Now we could take Trey to a drive-in movie in a playpen in the back of the station wagon.

Trey was about a year and a half old then, and very active. He was amazing. He could unscrew and take apart his crib with his bare little fingers. Not only that, but he would escape out the window of his bedroom. How he raised the window and let himself down several feet to the ground without hurting himself was impossible to understand. We finally had to nail his bedroom windows shut from the outside and put a hook on his bedroom door about five feet off the floor to keep him in his room.

By then we had acquired a purebred German Shepherd

dog named Agueda, who became Trey's constant companion and protector. If we let the two play outside in the fenced yard, Trey would climb over the gate and Agueda would jump the gate and follow him. If we hadn't noticed him leave, Agueda would walk down the street next to Trey and let no one near him. Not even some policemen who once saw this diapered youngster walking down the street without his parents. The police drove along next to the sidewalk in their cruiser, talking to Trey, trying to find out who he was and where his home was. When asked what his name was, Trey would say anything, like "George" or "Bill." Agueda would not allow even the policemen to get near Trey. We would finally catch up to the two of them, and take them home.

In February, 1953, our son Scott Kenneth was born. He was diagnosed soon after as having several types of congenital heart disease and other health problems. At that time, little was known about how to treat heart defects as surgery on hearts was experimental and rudimentary at the time. So our little baby Scotty needed special care. This was a very tough time for both Joan and me. I was working hard at my law classes and Joan had to spend much more time with Scotty because of his illness.

One time, just before Scotty was born, Trey took off while I was gone and Joan had just finished her bath. She was in her bath robe when she discovered Trey missing. It was in winter and Joan ran out in the street, looking for Trey. Our house was one block north of Speedway Boulevard. The street was aptly named. I believe it was the largest and busiest street in Tucson at the time -- four lanes and infrequent stop lights. Joan looked toward Speedway and saw Trey and Agueda standing on the corner of Third Street and Speedway, a block away. Just as Joan called to them, Trey walked right out into traffic. Agueda saw what was happening, and went ahead of him and toward traffic. The dog stopped the two oncoming lanes of cars on one side, and as Trey went to the other side, she ran in front of him toward the oncoming cars and stopped them in that direction, so that the child could safely cross to the park on the other side of the street. Joan said she almost delivered Scotty right there on the street corner. Trey did indeed keep us at attention.

Usually, when Trey ran away, we could find him by calling Agueda. The dog would come out of whatever yard she and Trey were in and then we could go after him. Trey figured that Agueda was giving him away, so one day he went into a strange yard with a high fence and when Agueda followed him in, Trey closed the gate on her and left her alone in the yard. I think her barking luckily gave us some clue, however, and we found him.

In my third year of law school I was elected Student Body President. My grades got better in my last two years of law school, and I believe I graduated "with honors" with an LLB, or Bachelor of Laws. I know I made the Dean's list in most of the semesters. Only about two-thirds of the students that started law school in my class graduated. My class included only two women.

My father and mother came to Tucson for my graduation ceremonies. Father took a picture of me in my cap and gown in front of our house under a palm tree in Tucson, with Joan, Trey and Scotty. As my father was getting ready to take the picture, I said, "Dad, now I would like to go to medical school." I thought my father would drop the camera, as I am sure he was celebrating that day as the last day that he and my mother would be financially subsidizing my education. The shock of my statement gave my parents pause, but not Joan. She said, "Like heck you will. It is time for you to get a job and start making a living." I guess I am just a student at

Joan and me at my law school graduation from the University of Arizona

heart, as by that time I genuinely enjoyed the learning process, and would have gladly gone on to seven more years of medical school and internship if it were possible. But it wasn't.

The rest of my law studying was for Chester H. Smith's Bar Exam Law Review course, which he held at his home on Cherry Street in Tucson. He lectured from three large-typed, bound and copyrighted outlines that had to be returned at the end of the course. The course covered everything taught in law school, and included outlines on even elective courses some students had not taken.

The tuition for the Bar Review course seemed large at the time, but it was well worth it. We found out later that Smith never turned anyone away from the course who could not afford it. He made a "loan" to them of the tuition. I don't know if he was repaid those loans later. I hope he was. Smith was a great instructor, not only in the bar review course, but in his law college courses. He would preface an important point by saying: "This is a gem. Remember it. If you haven't been paying attention before now, listen to this, because it is important and truly a legal gem. I will repeat it over and over again until you get it." Many students disliked Smith's teaching methods, but they were the best for me. To this day I can remember many of his "gems" and even as a judge they would pop into my mind after more than fifty years.

There were several weeks between the Bar Review course and the Bar Examination. These were weeks of intense study for the students, because that examination was the most important one of a law student's life, with all three years of law school in the balance. Although you could take it again if you did not pass, (some students did several times) there was some negative social stigma attached to those who had to retake the exam. Those students did not get the plush job offers others did. I know one trust officer for a bank who had been in business as a financial adviser for many years, who took the exam three times and never could pass it. When they handed out the first day's questions, I was told of at least two students who went into the bathroom and threw up. Talk about pressure!

During these three weeks, I sent my family away so I could concentrate fully on studying for the Bar Exam. One of our classmates was Jack Greenway, whose parents owned the Arizona Inn in Tucson. The Inn was an historical vacation resort built far outside of town in the 1920s. Today, it is right in the center of the city, across from the University of Arizona Hospital. The Inn is still a very elegant, plush resort with small rooms and a wonderful restaurant. Joan and I frequently stay there when we go to Tucson. Early in its history, many celebrities came to stay at the Inn, riding horseback in the desert, swimming in the heated pool in the winter. The Greenways also owned a large cattle ranch in northern Arizona, near Williams. They were Democrats and very politically connected.

President Roosevelt made his northern Arizona campaign speech at the Greenway Ranch in 1932. My father said I was the opening speaker at that event. I was three years old and my father placed me on a chair on a platform in front of all

168

those people waiting to hear President Roosevelt. I became so frightened that forgot the things that my father had primed me to say. All I could say was "Ladies and Gentlemen. My father and I are here." Whereupon I jumped down from the chair and ran to my mother.

The reason for the digression about Greenways is that Jack Greenway, a student in my law class, invited me and one other student friend of his, Ferris Bellamak, to live with him at the Inn for a week or so, to all study together without interruption. That sounded so good to me that I felt no guilt in asking Joan to take Trey and Scotty to Fresno to be with her parents during my "Bar Exam Cram Week." We had wonderful rooms at the Inn, with elegant formal meals prepared by Jack Greenway's private cook. There were more hours per day of quiet uninterrupted study than I had ever experienced before. In fact it was so quiet and boring to study that hard that I couldn't stand it. After about a week, I called Joan and asked her to bring my noisy, interruptive family back, so that I could study as usual.

After having taken the three-day exam, we moved back to Kingman to await the results. Like most of the others, I was sure I had not passed. In October, 1954, the names of those who had passed the exam were printed in the Arizona Republic, with formal letters sent that day to those who passed. Those whose names did not appear in the paper, about 15% of those taking the exam, had not passed. The letters took two or three days to get to the out-of-town applicants, so the first notice those who passed got was in the newspaper. I passed and was very relieved. About a week later there was a formal swearing in held in the Arizona Supreme Court Chambers, where my parents and family witnessed me taking my oath as a newly admitted member of the State Bar of Arizona. Then-Chief Justice R. C. Stanford administered the Oath. It was a proud day. All of my friends in my class that I have mentioned passed also.

6

LAW PRACTICE IN
KINGMAN, 1954 - 1962

As I had scored among the five highest of those who took the Bar Exam that year, I was offered a great honor — to serve for a year as a law clerk to Justice Levi Udall of the Arizona Supreme Court, who later became Chief Justice. Because I felt a strong obligation to my father, who very much wanted me to come back to Kingman to be his partner in his law practice, I refused Justice Udall's offer, and our family found a place to rent and live in Kingman. It was an old frame house on Gold Street. It had been the residence of a family that had run the property as the "Kingman Rose Garden." It was on a very large lot, with a huge glass greenhouse in the back. Although it was no longer cultivated, the greenhouse and also the residence had a lot of living things in them — big cockroaches that came out at night after you turned out the lights. There were so many of them and they were so big that you could hear them running

171

around on the linoleum floors at night after the lights were turned off.

My father's law office in 1954 was the front right office of the Masonic Temple on North Fourth Street as it exists today. Coincidentally, it was in almost the exact location that it had been in our old bedroom-office in the home that we had lived on that lot before the Masonic Temple was built. After you entered the double door main entrance to the building, the entrance to the office was the first wooden door to the right. This lead into the office reception room where Lucy Tapia, my father's secretary for many years, would greet clients. The office consisted of three rooms with the reception area in the middle. The room to the east of the reception area was a storage room filled with filing cases and supplies. Father rearranged the office for my return. He allowed me to have his office on the west end, which had a one-room air conditioner. Father removed the contents of the store room and made that his office. At the time, the one and only post office in operation in Kingman was the building just to the north of the Masonic Temple, which was built in the 1930s.

As I mentioned before, my father did not believe in requiring clients to make appointments to see him. They just came into the office whenever they pleased, and father would stop whatever he was doing and handle their matter. Fresh out of law school, I thought I could make the office more modern and professional by changing the drop-in practice. That would, in my thinking, make it more efficient, as we could reserve the mornings to do our drafting and trial preparation, and reserve the rest of the day for client intake and consultations. When I made this suggestion to him, my father listened, but did not agree. He patiently explained to me that because everyone had to come to the post office to get their mail every day, they would have to walk right past our office. He had encouraged friends and clients on their way to their mailbox to stop by and visit, even if they didn't have any legal work. And if it were in the summer, they might want to come into my office just to be refreshed by the air conditioner, and that was fine too. I had the only air conditioned law office in town.

My father really enjoyed people and liked to talk with them. He told me he did not want to change the feel of the office from what it had become. And we didn't. The office remained a place for friends and clients to stop by and visit, and occasionally to bring in legal business. If a regular client came in and asked a legal question that could be answered out of hand, without research or drafting, I was not to charge them for our service.

At first, I resented this informal office procedure, but as the years went by, I came to realize that this type of relationship between the attorney and his clients is what made the practice of law more than just a business. The office was a friendly place where we got to know our clients better in times other than stressful ones. As a down side, however, this practice did make it necessary to work late or in the evenings to do the things that required quiet and concentration. But in looking back, it was worth it and I believe that if more lawyers were able to use this office procedure, they would become closer to their clients socially. If they did, I believe the legal profession would not have the negative image it does today.

My father explained to me that I had a lot to be thankful for, having been raised in this small town. Many people had paid taxes that built the schools I had attended in Kingman. Others in years past had formed the organizations in the community that gave it its social and cultural framework. I had a great debt to repay. To do so, my father wanted me to join and participate in every social and civic organization that I could, and do their legal work without charge. My father was sure, and correctly so, that in the end because of these community services, they would ultimately bring in legal business.

I formed many corporations for organizations like the Elks for Dig-N-Dogie Days rodeo; the Mohave Museum of History and Art; the Mohave County Chamber of Commerce, and many others. I became active in Rotary, Elks Lodge, the Chamber of Commerce, the Kingman Area Boy Scout Council, Arizona Heart Association and the Kingman Country Club. Being usually the only lawyer-member in organizations, hardly a meeting went by that I wasn't called upon to give free legal advice or draft some document. Father was right. People, especially professionals, who do not get involved in civic activities, remain strangers in their communities and their names do not come to mind when members have legal problems. They are forced to look through the gaudy, boastful and sometimes deceiving ads that lawyers today put in the yellow pages of the telephone directory, in newspapers or on TV. The best advertisement a lawyer can get is by word-of-mouth from a satisfied client.

Candy was born in 1956 in the old hospital next to Metcalf Park, across from where the old railroad steam engine rests. Dr. Brazie, our family physician for many years, delivered. By this time, we bought our first home at 2644 East Ricca Drive, built by Emil Zancanaro, a Phoenix builder. The Ricca Drive houses became the first multi-housing development built in Kingman. We paid $11,000 for the home, $1,000 down and an FHA mortgage for the balance at 4.25% interest. I think our payments were $45 per month at first. We were so poor that we lived in that house for over a year with bed sheets for window curtains. The house had linoleum tile floors and was constantly dusty because of construction going on around us. I think our house was the third or fourth house completed in the subdivision.

Roy and Peggy Dunton lived across the street from us, as did Mayor Alex Thomson. Howard and Betty Grounds were our neighbors to the north. The subdivision was several blocks north of any existing houses in Kingman. The houses were all three-bedroom homes, so almost all were purchased by people with small children. Ricca Drive was a friendly, tight-knit community, where it was not uncommon to see a large group of children from different families going through suc-

175

Dinner party for Mohave County attorneys, 1955. Third couple from right,
my mother and father; fourth couple from right, Joan and me

cessive houses, receiving cookies, cake, soft drinks and other
goodies from surrogate parents. Our friends during those
days were Ernie and Shirley Scott, Ivan and Lorene Wilson,
Roy and Mary Jo Hoover, and Claude and Rita Neal. Those
friendships have remained close and warm to this day, and are
very important to us. Joan and I have developed many other
friendships since moving to Phoenix, but none have been as
special to us as the old ones.

Working late and being active in civic organizations took
time away from my family and made it more difficult for Joan,
who had three little ones at home, one chronically ill, and no
transportation, as I had to take our only car to the office.

My father was the first City Attorney for the City of King-man after its incorporation in 1952. He gave up the job in 1955 and I was appointed his successor. I acted in that position for two years. The City paid our firm $100 per month for my services. That was the same wage that had been paid my father for the three previous years. That sum was intended to cover the additional secretarial services that our office incurred as a result of our work for the City. It was a small amount for the hours that I spent in attending City Council meetings, zoning hearings, drafting ordinances, and being in court collecting fines for traffic or other ordinance violations. But there were many other benefits. I became good friends with many wonderful City Council persons, and attended several City Attorneys' conferences in different parts of the state. The job of City Attorney was considered a part-time employment. Now, as I understand it, the job is full-time and pays handsomely.

The firm of "Gordon & Gordon" was in 1954, the only multi-person law firm in Mohave County. Our law practice consisted primarily of handling commercial transactions — creating corporations and partnerships, drafting documents for the sale or lease of ranches, homes, raw land, and mining claims. One of my earliest jobs was to create a mortgage on several hives of honeybees to secure a loan made to the bee-keeper. They didn't teach me how to do that in law school. My first thought was who was going to put a little identification collar on each bee so it could be identified as being subjected to a lien. As I remember, the value of each bee was five cents at that time. I have forgotten how that question was resolved, but it had something to do with the queen bee determining where all the rest of the hive would stay.

Dealing with sales of ranching land and mining claims, I had to learn how to legally describe them. Using terms of "metes and bounds" and "section, township and range" was a new experience to me. That was another thing at that time not adequately explained in law school. I sought and obtained the help of a very fine civil engineer in Kingman, John T. Jordan. He was about ten years older than me, and took a liking to me. He let me accompany him on surveying trips and when he inspected old mines, for purposes of evaluating them. Joan and I became fast friends with John and "Jimmy", his wife. John died after heart surgery before we moved to Phoenix. We still keep in touch with Jimmy, who lives in Phoenix now.

One of my most interesting mining clients was a man named John Sherman Bagg, who had prospected almost all of Mohave County on foot and by jeep. He was a dapper little man, a little stout, but wiry. He dressed in a suit and usually had a rose in his lapel. John's father was at one time the owner and publisher of the Tombstone Epitaph, a very famous pioneer Arizona newspaper important during the heyday of the mining days near Tombstone in southeastern Arizona. His father at one time owned the mine whose tailings are just east of Lake Mohave Marina on Lake Mohave. John, being raised

178

in the publishing business, became aware of the importance of properly copywriting all important documents to secure them for sale. Having learned the ins and outs of copyright law, John discovered that if it were not done correctly, someone else could take over the publication and sell it as his own. He found some technical error in the copyright process of Winnie the Pooh, a very famous children's book in the early part of the 1900s. John published his own version in paperback, forcing the original publisher to buy him out in order to save its publishing rights.

Having learned how to jump publishing copyrights, John became an expert in jumping mining claims. Mining claims in the early days were located on U. S. land by "staking it out." That was accomplished by digging a location hole deep enough in the ground to discover and "expose mineral in place." Then the locator was required to build monuments of rock or wood at the corners of the claims, which as I recall were 600 feet wide by 1500 feet long. This staking of the claim was supposed to give notice to the world that the locator had found a mineral deposit on government land and that he was claiming it as his own as against all others except the U.S. government. A copy of his location notice was usually placed in a Prince Albert tobacco can and put into a cairn of rocks near the discovery hole so others could know who the locator was. A copy also was to be recorded in the County Recorder's office. The government would then allow the claim owner to keep possession of the claim and all mineral that he extracted from the land without paying anything to the government, except that each year he had to do at least $100 worth of work on the claim in improving it. This was called "assessment work" or "annual labor." If the claim owner did not do his assessment work each year and file his proof of annual labor with the County Recorder, or if it wasn't filed or recorded properly, the mine and all the improvements thereon became open for relocation by someone else.

Bagg became an expert on critical evaluation of proper locations of minerals and of annual labor, and if he found these weren't done correctly, he would over-locate the claim and take it for his own. Imagine the prior claim owner's consternation when he went out to his mine, maybe with buildings and machinery on it, and found that Bagg now claimed that it was all his. This was dangerous business as these old miners were tough customers. The mines were in very remote parts of the county, usually in the mountains. John could have disappeared into a mineshaft somewhere with no one knowing about it for months, or even ever. How he stayed alive I often wondered.

In the 1950s, the most respected legal authority concerning mining law was a three-volume work called "Morrison on Mining Rights." I honestly believed that John Sherman Bagg had memorized everything in those books. He bragged that he knew more mining law that any lawyer in Arizona, and he was probably right.

There used to be tall rose vines in front of the fence

around the Mohave County Courthouse in Kingman. They bore beautiful roses most of the summer. About once each month, John would pick a bouquet of these roses and put one in his suit coat lapel. He would then go into the courthouse to visit Peggy B. Smith, who was the County Recorder, where all the mining claim documents were recorded. John would give Peggy the bouquet of roses and ask if there were any new mining claims recorded that week. If there had been, Peggy would give him the information and he would go out, find the location and check to be sure it was properly located. If it wasn't, John would over-locate the claim and go to the claimant and advise him he was the property's new owner, but he would sell it back to him for a certain sum.

I was curious as a young lawyer about mining claims. John offered to take me on a tour one day in his jeep in the Chloride, Arizona area. He showed me many claims that day. He showed me which ones were properly located and which ones weren't and why. He showed me how to do annual labor properly. I learned a lot from John, and have fond memories of him. With my help, he filed his own lawsuit against a large mining company for rights he felt were taken from him. The case went to the Arizona Supreme Court and he prepared and filed his own briefs. Not surprisingly, he was successful and the mining company paid him. I don't remember the company's name, but the Supreme Court's index would show the case name under John Sherman Bagg's name.

John was also a thorn in the side of the Atchison, Topeka

and Santa Fe Railroad. Early in America's history, as an inducement for the railroads to build lines across the country, the U. S. Government gave the railroads a great deal of land within, I believe, 20 miles of either side of the roadway. But the lands granted to the railroad were supposed to be non-mineral, other than coal, which was intended to go to the railroad for their steam engines. If the land had substantial other mineral content, it was not to be granted to the railroad but be reserved for development by mining people. Evidently in those early days the government did not do much investigation before the land was granted to the railroads, as many of the sections that were granted to the railroads were very valuable in their mineral content. Because it was then the owner of the land, the railroad would charge the miners for exploration rights and a royalty on any minerals removed. This really burned John Sherman, who considered the railroads as illegally holding the mineral lands. He caused the railroads a lot of consternation by refusing to pay Santa Fe for exploration on their land. He consulted me once on a potential class action lawsuit that would attempt to recapture any mineral lands that the railroad had obtained from the government all the way from Chicago to Los Angeles. His theory was that the mineral land had been obtained through fraud. It was an interesting idea, but after we considered the costs that would have to be fronted to investigate and prove which lands were and were not mineral properly granted, I think John reluctantly gave up the idea.

Some of our main clients in the ranching field were John and Amy Neal, the parents of Claude and Leonard Neal. The firm of Gordon & Gordon represented the elder Neals in the sale of what was their ranch to their sons. At one time in the late 1800's, the Neal family ran cattle from Bagdad, Arizona, west to the Colorado River, and north to where the Pierce Ferry crossed the Colorado River in northern Mohave County. That was most of the area of Mohave County. The Neals had first established a cattle operation in Hillside, near Baghdad, west of Prescott around 1900, I believe. Amy came to that camp, she said, with Leonard, the oldest, riding behind her saddle on horseback, and Claude, the youngest, riding in front of her saddle at the same time. What portion of the ranch they had left when I first dealt with them was a ranch that comprised all the land north of Kingman and west of U. S. Highway 66 almost to Hackberry, including everything between Stockton Hill Road to Highway 66, and north to the Music Mountains. It was a big spread, perhaps over 90,000 acres. Joan and I became good friends with Claude and Rita Neal, and to a lesser extent with Leonard and Grace Neal.

The Grounds family was also our clients. W.F. (Bill) Grounds was the father of Howard and John Grounds. Their main ranch was in the Hackberry Valley. Their headquarters was at the old Crozier ranch, near Valentine, Arizona. During the boom days of Highway 66 that ranch had a nice "motor court" and swimming pool, which was fed by the icy waters of springs nearby. It was the only swimming pool in Mohave

County for many years until Goodwin's pool south of Kingman opened in the 1930s. In the late 1800s, the Grounds
family had shootouts with the Hualapai Indians who felt the
Grounds had taken their land. Howard told me a story about
how early one day about daybreak, the family awoke thinking
it was either raining or hailing. They looked outside and saw
a clear sky. What was happening was the Indians were shooting at the house from a great distance above them on a mesa
and the rifle balls were hitting the roof and rolling off. The
story is that Bill Grounds and his hired hands sneaked out
of the house and went around the back side of the mesa and
caught the Hualapais still shooting at the house. According to
the story, the Grounds group shot and killed several before
the Hualapais escaped. Over the years, however, the Grounds
family became good neighbors and friends with the people of
the Hualapai tribe. Some of the tribe members who worked
for the Grounds even took the Grounds name.

Clyde and Irene Cofer were also clients. They had a
large ranch on the east side of the Cerbat Mountains north
on Stockton Hill Road. He was a tough old horseman and
miner who smoked a tiny little crooked pipe. I drew many
mining leases for him on manganese mining claims that he
had located in the Buckskin Mountains between what is now
Lake Havasu City and Parker. Clyde never paid his legal bills
until the evening of New Year's Eve, so he could claim his tax
deduction for legal expenses that year. He usually came to
our home on the afternoon of New Year's Eve. When he paid,

he also expected my father to give him a drink of whiskey and they would toast the New Year. Trey and Candy learned about turkeys and goats on Clyde and Irene's ranch. John and Jimmie Jordan later bought that ranch. There are still wild horses in the Cerbat Mountains behind the ranch house. We sometimes went there when the Jordans owned the place to cut Christmas trees. It was also good deer and quail hunting country then.

My father and I were local counsel for the Santa Fe Railroad. We were not on a retainer, but were given a few perks. One was that we could have passes on the passenger trains between Kingman and Los Angeles. The trouble with that was that the only train we could travel on had no Pullman cars and stopped in Kingman about two in the morning. The other perk, which was much more fun, came every two years. At that time, Santa Fe would put together a special train starting in Chicago, and pick up all the local Santa Fe lawyers and their spouses along the way to California, and wine and dine them for a weekend at some marvelous resort in California. All the costs were on Santa Fe. You didn't even need to bring your wallet. Anything you needed you could charge to your room. The one time Joan and I attended was held at Hotel Del Coronado in San Diego, California. We missed some others because of other commitments, problems with our son Scotty's health, and because I left the law firm to become a judge.

If our law firm became involved in a lawsuit on behalf of

a client, I was the one that handled the litigation or the trial proceeding. We had some mining claim disputes, divorces, will contests, water rights disputes, and some others. We were associated as local co-counsel in personal injury matters when insurance companies were involved. I was sometimes appointed by the Court to represent clients who could not afford counsel in criminal cases. For these cases you were paid little or nothing, but handling these kinds of cases was part of your duty as a lawyer and one that you acknowledged when you took your oath as a newly admitted lawyer.

My very first jury trial was a court appointment in a criminal case. I was sworn in as a lawyer in October, 1954. I think the trial came up the very next month. My client was John Graham, who was accused of pistol-whipping an old friend over a money dispute. The charge was aggravated assault and burglary, I believe. Carl Hammond was the County Attorney at the time, and because jury trials were a rarity, he was going to try this case to develop some notoriety for the next election. He was the one and only lawyer in the County Attorney's office at the time. I believe they have nearly thirty now. Carl had been the County Attorney for about twenty years then.

In those days in criminal cases, there were no pre-trial disclosure rules where the prosecutor had to disclose his evidence to the defense. Also, there were no rules requiring the police or sheriff to even talk with the defendant's lawyer. Lawyers now look back at those days and call that type of practice "trial by ambush." I remember trying to get the city police to show me their files, but they wouldn't. I was considered a "friendly enemy."

Because Kingman was a small town and my family was well known, there was a lot of curiosity about what kind of lawyer "Young Frank" or "Junior" would be. Several of the people who ended up on the jury panel in that case had known me since I was an infant.

I did not know it at the time, but John Graham claimed to be the son of a very famous family in Arizona history. For those of you who have heard about the feud between the Hatfields and the McCoys in Appalachia, there was an Arizona equivalent: the Graham-Tewksbury feud. This occurred before Arizona became a state in an area just below the Mogollon Rim in central Arizona called the Bloody Basin. The Grahams were cattle people who grazed their cattle in the rim country. The Tewksburys were sheep people who moved their sheep from the valley south of the rim up on the rim in the spring as the grass grew better there in the summer. The typical grazing land and water disputes resulted, and many people of both clans were killed. Some wonderful accounts of the feud and about early Arizona justice were written. One by Zane Grey, "To the Last Man"; one by Earl Forrest, "Arizona's Dark and Bloody Ground"; and another, by far the best in my opinion, written by Don Dedera called "A Little War of Our Own: The Pleasant Valley War Revisited". I have copies of these books. My children and grandchildren should read all of them.

The Graham-Tewksbury feud, which killed over twenty

people, spanned several years, and the last of the adult Grahams, Tom Graham, was assassinated, allegedly by two members of the Tewksbury clan in Mesa while he was driving a wagon of wheat to the mill in Tempe. The widow of the last of the Grahams attempted to kill one of the two accused murderers at a preliminary hearing in a courtroom in Mesa. She had hidden a .45 caliber revolver, a huge weapon, in her shawl when she came to court, and walked up behind one of the accused in the courtroom, put the pistol to one of their heads, and pulled the trigger. The gun did not go off, and she was kept from trying again. There were several theories about why the gun did not fire. One was that the bullets had been removed from the gun by the person at whose home the widow had stayed the night before. The other was that the pistol was loaded, but that her shawl had become entangled with the hammer of the pistol so the firing pin could not reach the bullet to fire it. Having handled that pistol myself, and knowing the strength of the hammer, I doubt that this version is correct.

This long preface concerning the Graham-Tewksbury feud is important to my telling about my first jury case because John Graham claimed to be the son of the last of the Grahams, and the pistol that he used to hit the victim in my case was supposedly the one that his mother had used in attempting to kill one of the murderers of his father. Thus, the pistol was perhaps of historical importance and perhaps very valuable. I didn't know anything about either the Graham-Tewksbury feud or this pistol until the trial was over.

John Graham was a very large, tough man in his sixties at the time. He worked in a mine in Searchlight, Nevada. His story was that he went to the victim's house on west Oak Street in Kingman to inquire why the victim had not repaid a loan John had made to him. They met at the front door, words were exchanged, John said the victim swung at him, so he hit the victim on the side of the head with the barrel of the gun. John was charged with burglary. I guess John proceeded to collect the debt from the victim's wallet after he was knocked unconscious.

Not many criminal cases went to trial then, as the presiding judge, Judge Elmer, had ways of encouraging defense lawyers who were appointed to represent indigents to get them to plead guilty. The disincentive to take a case to trial was that the appointed defense attorney would be paid a total of $50 dollars if his client pleaded guilty and waived trial, but the defense attorney would be paid only the same amount if he represented his client clear through trial. Most attorneys at that time would rather make some sort of deal with the County Attorney, rather than risk a trial, with the additional time necessary to prepare and present a defense.

But John Graham insisted he was innocent, and would not agree to plead guilty to any lesser charge. I needed the jury trial experience, so it was to be my first great jury trial.

Carl Hammond was running for re-election as County Attorney, and the election was to be the same month, so he had an incentive to push for conviction as it would be good publicity for him, especially when the opposition lawyer was a young kid just fresh out of law school. Carl was very pleasant to me in all the proceedings in the case. Perhaps condescending would be a better way of describing it. He told me it was a shame that my first case was such a tough one, as he had a convincing witness-victim who still had a scar with stitches to show the jury. Carl was also happy to tell me that he had not lost a case in years. Of course he hadn't. He only tried the ones that were lead pipe cinches.

My father sat in the back of the courtroom on the day of trial. I wonder now what his thoughts were. He was a very experienced and effective trial lawyer. He knew most of the jurors, and most of them were close friends. Here was his protected, innocent only child, about to receive his baptism by fire. I think he only stayed through the selection of the jurors and perhaps part of the state's case. Maybe he just couldn't bear to see me lose.

The end result was that the jury must have believed John Graham's story that he was only defending himself, and only justly trying to gain the return of money owed to him. The jury deliberated only about twenty minutes, and returned a verdict of "not guilty." My victory in that case was not because of my brilliant defense of Graham, but more likely because one of the jurors had been my babysitter when I was an infant, and also because Bill Freiday was on the panel, and he was my friend, and besides, it was his birthday and he did not want to miss his birthday party that evening.

That day, after the trial, John Graham asked if he could get the pistol out of evidence, and he explained its background. I told him it would be some time before the court would release the pistol. I really didn't want him to have it for a while, as he might go after the victim for filing charges against him. John gave me a copy of the book "Arizona's Dark and Bloody Ground" and I read it with great interest, now knowing John's background.

Quite a few years later, the court released the pistol to me and I kept it for a while, not knowing how to contact John. In the meantime, Ford Proving Ground was having its formal dedication of its facility in Yucca, Arizona. This was a large economic event for Mohave County, and statewide publicity was given to it. A large party was held at the Elks' Hall in Kingman for the media people attending the dedication. One of the displays at the Hall was a collection of old pistols, some owned by Carl Hammond. The manager of the Chamber of Commerce asked if the historic pistol that I had in my custody could be shown. I agreed, as I was assured that it would be carefully protected. The pistol display board was put up on the back board of the bar at the Elks. Someone stole the Graham pistol off the board during an absence of the bartender, who had been regaling his patrons with the story behind the pistol. Ford Motor Company tried unsuccessfully for years to locate the pistol. Luckily I had taken pictures of the pistol for a keepsake after John would come to reclaim it. It had white bone handles on it that John had said were made from the bones of a Tewksbury the gun had killed. Dr. Brazie told me that a human pelvis bone would be large enough to provide bones for a gun handle. I don't really know if that claim was true.

Some years later, John Graham returned to inquire about the pistol. I was embarrassed to tell him that it had been stolen and had not been recovered. Surprisingly, John was very understanding, and forgave me for allowing the pistol to be shown and ultimately lost. He probably could have held me liable for the loss of the pistol. I never saw him again after that. Ford Motor Company spent a lot of time and money trying to locate the pistol; however, it was never recovered. I have my own suspicion of who has the pistol, but I don't think I will ever be able to reclaim it.

Because Mohave County was small in population, there were relatively few civil cases that went to trial in the 1950s. I tried my share of them, however. I handled a case involving a water rights dispute on the Sandy River, several mining claim disputes, a will contest, a few personal injury claims, quite a few divorce cases. Besides the Neals and John Sherman Bagg, some of our firm's clients were: Peter Bartmus who owned a large ranch east of Wickieup; Dick Banegas, who we represented in a water dispute on the Sandy River; and the Valley National Bank.

Another case that I handled might be of interest. During World War II, fatigued air force pilots were given a little rest and recreation at a place provided for them on the eastern

192

shore of Lake Havasu. It was called "Site Six." The Air Force provided a landing field for these pilots where the Lake Havasu City airport is now. It also built three or four barracks next to the airfield, and got a state liquor license for use at this site. Pilots would come there for a week or two and spend their time fishing on the lake and partying. In the late 1940s, after the war ended, the site and its improvements were leased to a couple from Bullhead City, who ran a little fishing camp and boat rental facility there. The only things there were the barracks buildings, about a dozen aluminum boats with small outboard motors, a diesel generator for electricity, and the liquor license, which was very valuable.

In the early 1950s, about six Continental Airline Pilots thought they saw some potential for Site Six, and negotiated a transfer of the government lease, as well as a transfer of the liquor license from the Bullhead City couple to the site with the hopes that they would renovate the army barracks and make them into a resort-type fishing camp. They spent many weekends flying from Los Angeles in their private planes, painting and fixing the barracks up to make them presentable. The pilots ended up needing some capital, however, to complete their plans. They met a wealthy man named John Smith from Los Angeles, who loaned them $5,000. The promissory note they signed was a form Smith got from a bank. It was a "demand note" which meant that at any time Smith wanted to call the loan, he could, with interest, and if not paid, he could also get attorney's fees for his efforts to recover. For

193

reasons beyond my knowledge, the airline pilots' dreams were not realized, and they stopped working on the site. Mr. Smith asked me to act as his lawyer to collect the debt. Mind you, there was nothing else anywhere on the shores of Lake Havasu at the time but the airport landing strip and this semi-resort called Site Six. The area later became the hub of Lake Havasu City.

There were several substantial legal problems involved in the case. First, the barracks were located on leased government land, and were considered improvements to the land and could not be levied upon. Next, the lease from the United States was for a term of years and not much to levy upon. Another problem was that the pilots signed the promissory note in their individual capacities, and they all lived in California and were not subject to being sued in Arizona unless I could obtain service of process in Arizona. My father knew the Bullhead City couple who owned the liquor license, the Merrills, who had leased the license to the airline pilots. I contacted them and they agreed to honor a levy upon the license if I could get a proper judgment against the pilots. I contacted the Bureau of Land Management of the government and it agreed to honor a levy on the land lease.

With this as a base, I filed a lawsuit seeking a judgment against the airline pilots for $5,000, plus interest and attorney's fees. Mr. Smith had a friend near Site Six who tipped us off when the six airline pilots were at Site

TO A MAN WITH A GAVEL

Six and we had a sheriff serve them with the Summons and
Complaint. Because the pilots felt they were judgment-proof
not being Arizona residents and thinking that there was
nothing at Site Six which could be levied upon, they did
not contest the lawsuit. I got the judgment entered and
then set up a sheriff's sale of the property. There were
not even any telephones at Site Six at the time, so the Sheriff
(Floyd Cisney) drove down at the designated time in a
county jeep with a radio for the sheriff's sale, which was
to be at 10:00 a.m. on a certain day. Mr. Smith
flew me down to Site Six in his four-passenger private plane. Two sheriff's officers and the two of us were
the only ones present for the sale. I was levying on
the liquor license, the government land lease, the 12
aluminum boats and motors and the diesel generator.

When the pilots discovered what arrangements I had made,
they called the sheriff's office in Kingman, which relayed by
radio that they would present a check for the full amount by
10:00 a.m. I told the Sheriff my client would not accept a
personal check, but would accept a Western Union telegraph
money order to be delivered to the Sheriff's office payable to
me and Mr. Smith by 11:00 a.m. They complied. The point of
this long story is that on that date, Mr. Smith and I could have
owned everything that was of any value on Lake Havasu at
that time for less than $10,000. Now think what Lake Havasu
City is at present.

During those years of community involvement, I served

195

as president of the Mohave County Chamber of Commerce. During my tenure, two things came up that affected the County drastically. One was that the Metropolitan Water District of Los Angeles exercised its legal right to use a portion of the electricity generated by both Hoover and Davis Dams, which portion had been used by residents of Mohave County with Metropolitan's permission for many years at very reasonable rates. Most of the homes in Kingman were electrically heated at the time. There was no natural gas line then. The Metropolitan recapture of that portion of the generating capacity of the dams would cause a tripling of the costs of heating homes in Kingman, and would be a great financial hardship to many people.

The other event was that the Bureau of Land Management of the federal government announced it would be re-routing the Colorado River by dredging in such a way that Mohave County would lose about three miles of river frontage on which there were already homes and resorts near Bullhead City. These events would be great blows to the economy of Mohave County, which at that time probably had a total of five or six thousand residents, almost all registered as Democrats. The City of Kingman and County of Mohave, together with Citizens Utility Company, our electric utility, all decided that the best thing to do was have the Chamber of Commerce and residents of the City of Kingman deliver their collective plea to the Bureau of Land Management in Washington, D.C. Secretary of the Interior Andahl was the person to be petitioned.

Being the president of the Chamber of Commerce, I was to lead a delegation consisting of the Mayor of Kingman, Charley McCarthy, the Chairman of the Board of Supervisors, George C. Ricca, and Ennis Vaughn, a member of the Board of Supervisors, to make the plea. We contacted our congressional representatives asking for their help in presenting our plea to the Secretary of the Interior. Those in the House of Representatives were Stewart Udall (Democrat) and John Rhodes (Republican). In the Senate were: Carl Hayden (Democrat) and Barry Goldwater (Republican). Udall promised to help and was present during our presentation, but did nothing to follow up that I am aware of.

John Rhodes told us Mohave County was not in his district, so he would not do anything. Hayden was in his late eighties at the time and not competent to help in any way. His administrative assistant helped arrange the appointment with the Secretary, but otherwise was of no assistance that I know of. Barry Goldwater did help, and was a man whom I came to admire and respect greatly, even though he had almost no Republicans to please in Mohave County at that time. He provided us with two administrative assistants in the hearing and had obviously made our positions known personally to the Secretary before we arrived. Picture this delegation from the tiny city of Kingman arriving in Washington D.C., where none of us had ever been, and appearing before the most powerful person in our government pertaining to public

Washington D.C. delegation: Me, Kingman Mayor Charley McCarthy,
Barry Goldwater, Ennis Vaughn

lands. I was a pink-cheeked 27- or 28-year-old lawyer who had practiced only two or three years, appearing to present an important case to an administrative leader who was used to presentations from only the most influential and expensive law firms in the country.

With the help of Barry Goldwater's administrative assistants, one of which I had been in law school with, we prepared well enough in advance that after our presentation we were granted relief from both of the hardships we had come to complain about. I am sure the reason was only because of the behind-the-scenes help of Barry Goldwater, who used his influence to sway the Secretary to find some other source of power for us, and to re-route the dredging program so that it didn't leave the Mohave County real property high and dry.

This victory was sweet, but not as sweet as what Barry Goldwater did for me personally just afterwards. Our plane to leave Washington D.C. was several hours after we met with Andahl, so we had a little time to be tourists in that marvelous city. Goldwater arranged for the rest of the delegation to be given guided personal tours of the Library of Congress, the U. S. Supreme Court, and other Washington sites. But for me he reserved the greatest treat. He asked me if I would be interested in sitting in on a Senate Hearing regarding an investigation of racketeering in the hotel unions. I was thrilled. I went with Barry to a Senate hearing room and sat at counsel table, if you can believe it, between him and John F. Kennedy, later to become President of the United States, as they questioned witnesses in the hotel union. Some of these witnesses looked like characters in a Mafia movie. They answered most of the senators' questions with "I refuse to answer the question." I will never forget that afternoon, or the honor of becoming acquainted with two of the greatest statesmen in the modern history of our country.

My friendship with Barry Goldwater continued throughout the remainder of his life, although we didn't meet often. When we did, it was as though we had been warm friends for years.

Whatever trials there were in Mohave County, I handled my share of them, and became a fairly competent and well-known trial lawyer for the region. Our family became good friends with most of the prominent citizens of Kingman and we enjoyed a favorable reputation. Times were good while I practiced law with my father, although we had differing views of how the office should be run. I started my practice as a partner with my father with a monthly draw of $500 a month. At the end of the year if there were any profits above the draws of my father and me, and the costs of operating the office, they would be equally divided. As I remember, the largest surplus was $7,000 to each partner in any of the eight years I practiced with my father. That was not a large sum for a lawyer at the time, but it covered our living expenses, with Joan running a tight ship. Joan also worked several years as a secretary for William Welch, an investment counselor, which helped out a lot.

Joan carried a heavy burden during those years that I practiced with my father. She cared for three children in a small home with no car for quite a few years. Our son Scotty, who was chronically ill with several heart defects, needed a great amount of care. I am sure that Candy and Trey felt that they were slighted in the amount of attention we were able to give them, because of Scotty's demands for time. They didn't complain, however. They were wonderful children. Despite dire predictions by doctors to the contrary, Scotty was finally able to walk and got around pretty well. He could not run or play hard, but the other children were mostly good with him and played things he could participate in. He attended school and even rode the bus to school. If he had to walk more than a block or so, his coloring turned a light blue and his lips were almost purple. He would be very short of breath. I am sure there were times when some children were mean to him, but he didn't complain. Scotty was a very intelligent and humorous child. There were times, though, when he played his illness to its fullest extent.

On the few evenings that Joan and I could get away by ourselves, we were very social in the Kingman Country Club activities. The Club had once-a-month dinner dances, where the members took turns decorating the club and cooking the food. We developed close friendships with the Duntons, Scotts, Gilpins, Wilsons, Hoovers and Claude and Rita Neal.

For a time, Joan and I would arrange for a sitter on Saturday, and go to Lake Mead all by ourselves to fish, promising

201

the children that we would take them to Lake Mohave on Sunday. This was great time alone for Joan and me. On those days fishing we had some time to discuss family matters and also to enjoy each other. Joan loved to fish. She caught more bass than I did, and that was without really trying. She would lay back and read a book while we trolled near the shoreline. I have never heard anyone laugh and giggle as much at catching a fish.

Joan and I are blessed with strong love for each other. So much love doesn't mean that we did not have our personal disagreements. One time I thoughtlessly spent too much time playing golf with some friends on a day that Joan had a very trying day. I had promised Joan that I would come home to take her to the Club when I finished playing, but I forgot. When I got home, Joan was furious. The next thing I knew she had packed a bag. I asked where she was going. She told me she didn't know, but she was leaving me. The only problem was that neither she nor I had enough money for her to buy a train or bus ticket to go to her mother in Fresno, California, or even to buy gasoline for the car. There were no credit cards then. When we realized that, Joan's sense of humor came to the surface and we started to laugh at our plight. She was so upset she wanted to leave me, and we could not afford it. We had a great laugh, and do even now every time we think about that evening. By the way, I became a lot more sensitive toward her needs thereafter, or at least I think I did. Somehow, we were able to buy a second car for her use.

During these early years of my law practice and our rais-
ing of our children, we were fortunate to belong to St. John's
Methodist Church in Kingman, where our first minister was
DeWayne Zimmerman. The Kingman church was also De-
Wayne's first pastorate. He later rose to great heights in the
Methodist Church, and was in our opinion the greatest pulpit
minister we have heard. He was a great help to us during our
family's stressful periods of Scotty's illness.

Our backyard at our Ricca Drive house was huge. We had
prolific trees, yielding apricots, peaches and almonds. Our
dog, "Risa," a young German Shepherd, was a perfect companion to our children. Her name means "laughter" in Spanish and it fit her beautifully. She was a happy clown all the
time. Her first view of snow falling caused her to jump up and
try to catch as many snowflakes as she could. She could jump
over the 6' wooden fence that surrounded our house to go
visit her friends in the neighborhood. She would jump up and
eat the peaches and apricots, and even the almonds as soon as
they were ripe. Risa would join in the children's games in the
back yard. She could intercept a football pass in midair, and
then have a wonderful time keeping the ball from the children.
When a child had the ball, she could block the ball carrier just
as well as any high school half-back. Risa would get in line
with the children as they ran and slid through a large plastic
play pool full of water, taking her turn jumping into the water
and out with the kids. Once she decided she would just stay in
the pool and kept the kids out for a while.

Clockwise from top left: Frank X. Gordon III (Trey), Scott Kenneth (Scotty), Me, Joan, Candace Lee (Candy)

When our apricot and peach trees had ripe fruit, our children helped harvest what Risa had not taken, and crushed the fruit with 2 x 4's in 30-gallon plastic garbage cans so that I could start the annual batch of homemade wine. That was an annual affair for the family which we all enjoyed. We lived in that house for almost 20 years before we moved to Phoenix.

Our station wagon held the whole family as we went to a movie at our local drive-in movie theater. When the almonds were harvested, the children's job was to shuck husks and shells from the nuts during the movies. They even left some for us to eat.

Many warm memories come to mind when we think of our years on Ricca Drive in Kingman. Roy Dunton and I spent several Christmas Eves late, after the children were in bed, assembling doll houses, trains sets and other goodies while having eggnog by our fireplace. Also, on New Years' Day, Charlie Lum, another neighbor, would go door-to-door with champagne and orange juice to toast in the New Year.

7

THE BENCH – SUPERIOR COURT, 1962 - 1975

In May 1962, while I was still practicing with my father in the firm of Gordon & Gordon, Judge Charles P. Elmer, of the Superior Court in Mohave County, resigned because of ill health. He was not very old, but had been gassed by the Germans in World War I. It affected him greatly. He had emphysema. It got so bad that he could not climb the stairs in the old county courthouse. Besides the two retired judges, Faulkner and Elmer, there were only five lawyers in Kingman: O. Ellis Everett, Carl D. Hammond, Louis L. Wallace, my father, and me -- all Democrats. The governor of Arizona was Paul Fannin, a Republican, who would appoint Judge Elmer's successor. Of course, Governor Fannin would have liked to appoint a Republican, but there were not any Republican lawyers in Mohave County at the time. He even had former Attorney General Ross Jones, a fellow Republican, come up from Phoenix in his new motor home to visit the County to see if he and his wife would be happy living in Kingman. After about a week living in his motor home plugged into the old county jail, Jones decided Kingman wasn't to his liking and was later appointed by Fannin to the Superior Court in Maricopa County.

Governor Fannin's dilemma was great. He was forced to pick a Democrat to fill Judge Elmer's vacancy, although he had not appointed a single Democrat to the bench before or after, to my knowledge.

Fannin's choice was narrowed by the fact that my father did not want the job, and other than Carl Hammond, the rest were too old to be considered. I was not really interested in becoming a judge at first, although the handsome salary of $12,500 per year was somewhat appealing. I felt somewhat beholden to stay in practice with my father because he had financially supported Joan and me for the years in law school and in our partnership during all of my education and the first few years of my practice. My father made the choice easy for me by encouraging me to seek the job as judge. It didn't take too much urging, as a judgeship is the ultimate goal of almost every serious lawyer.

I was sworn in as Judge of the Superior Court in May 1962. The swearing in ceremony was special because four of the five members of the Arizona Supreme Court came to Kingman to hold the investiture ceremony in the courtroom of the old Courthouse. Also, the president of the State Bar of Arizona presented me with my first gavel, a traditional but seldom used symbol of the office of judge. A great many of

Swearing in at Superior Court with Justice Charles Bernstein

my law school friends came to Kingman to be present at the installation ceremony. The old courtroom, which held over one hundred spectators, was packed, including the two jury boxes. It was a very happy day for my father and mother, as well as our many old friends in Kingman.

I inherited Judge Elmer's staff when I took the bench, some of which were very good and some caused me much anguish. The one good staff member was Dick Brock, the Chief Juvenile and Adult Probation officer who also acted as jury bailiff under Judge Elmer. Dick was a former rancher who, although he had some college education, had no formal training to be a probation officer. That office is very important to the judge.

The person holding it must be able to evaluate all people that the judge may sentence after they are convicted of crimes, or children who have been adjudicated delinquent, neglected or incorrigible.

These evaluations precede the probation officer's recommendations to the judge as to whether the person should be placed on probation rather than being incarcerated. They also assist in determining what the conditions of the probation should be, such as not only fully obeying the law during the time the sentence is suspended, but also whether they are to undergo various treatment programs for alcoholism, drug addiction, psychiatric treatment, counseling, or even going back to school for literacy training. If the probation officer feels that one or more of these programs would turn the person's life away from one of crime, and the crime he had committed was not a serious one, he would recommend that the judge order the person serve the probation on his specifically recommended terms and conditions. If he felt there was little if any hope that the person could be salvaged, he would recommend incarceration and the length of time to be served under the statutes involved. The person making these evaluations and recommendations has to be very intuitive and perhaps even clairvoyant. It is a very important job now sometimes requiring graduate college degrees.

Back in 1962, that was not required, and very few probation officers were as good as Dick at predicting the future of the people he had to make recommendations about. How

Swearing in as Superior Court Judge

Dick acquired these skills I am not sure. I have a suspicion that his background in dealing with horses, cattle and humans in general gave him certain hunches about people and their instincts. However he acquired his skills, he was very good at his work. His predictions about future human behavior were almost always correct. I followed Dick's recommendations most of the time, especially after I disagreed with him once and put a person on probation when he had recommended against it. Dick proved to be correct. The person re-violated the law and had to be sentenced to prison. Luckily, no one was hurt by my mistake in judgment.

Many times when I visited other courts and dealt with their

probation officers, I found that the highly educated ones were not nearly as insightful as Dick. He was a gem.

My inherited secretary, court reporter and elected court clerk caused me real problems. Within six months after being sworn in, I developed the beginning of a peptic stomach ulcer in my stomach, which I attributed to their insufficiencies. It was not until after I fired the court reporter and replaced my secretary that my ulcer symptoms disappeared.

Let my preface my remarks about my court reporter by saying that even though I was the only judge presiding, the Superior Court calendar in Mohave County was very light. There were very few criminal cases to try, as most were bargained out by the county attorney, and the civil cases mostly settled before trial. So, most of the matters I was to handle were defaults, meaning that there was no need for a trial – the parties did not object to the requested relief being granted. These were mostly uncontested divorces, will probates, guardianships, or mental illness petitions. If I could organize the hearings in such a way that they could be heard one after another, including actual trials, I would guess that during the first year or two of my judgeship, I could have handled all the matters to be heard in my court in two or three days of each week. Also, some of the matters being defaults did not require a court reporter's presence unless requested by an attorney. I had one of the lightest court calendars in the state, other than some of the even lesser populated counties in Arizona.

James T. O'Day was the only and official court reporter

for Mohave County, having been appointed by Judge Elmer. Although machines were just becoming popular for court reporters to use in verbatim reporting, most reporters at that time used shorthand, handwritten notes on note pads. Mr. O'Day was a very proficient pen writer whose notes I later found could be read by other reporters. Mr. O'Day's proficiency, however, was overshadowed by his laziness and excessive time spent in bars around Kingman. I didn't realize it before I took office, but he was behind in furnishing transcripts of testimony in five or six cases that were on appeal to the Arizona Supreme Court which had been decided before I became judge. I started receiving calls and letters from the lawyers that represented the appellants in those cases, asking what could be done to hurry up the filing of the transcripts, as the time was running out. If they were not filed within the time allowed or extended, the appellant's case could be dismissed, thus leaving the person who had lost his or her case in the court below without review by the appellate court.

When Mr. O'Day came in one day I asked him about the transcripts, and he told me that they would be filed soon as he had turned his notes over to a typist for transcribing. I found later he was lying, but at the time gave him the benefit of the doubt. Later, after more calls by the appellants' attorneys, I asked him again, saying the attorneys had obtained all the extensions they thought they could get. He gave me the same answer. I asked him for the name of the transcriber or transcribers and he refused to give them to me. He said it was none of my business. He would take care of it. I told him I wanted him to come to his office every work day and start work on typing those transcripts. He said he had an agreement with Judge Elmer that he did not have to come to the office unless there was a trial or hearing scheduled to happen in court where a reporter was needed. I told him I expected him every day until those transcripts were completed. He told me I could not make him do that.

O'Day was a short fair-skinned Irishman who was brash and temperamental. He had a black mustache and eyebrows that appeared to be colored with mascara or some other coloring. When he did not come to work the next day, I went looking for him. I found him right after lunch. He was in a little bar on Second Street, just south of Beale Street, called the "The Office," sitting at the counter with a few of his buddies, drinking. I told him I wanted to speak with him and asked if he would step outside so we could talk. He refused, saying anything I wanted to say to him, I could say right there in front of his friends. So challenged, I told him I expected him to come to work in his office at the courthouse the next morning, or else I would have to enter an order that he do so. He said I could do what I wanted, but I had no right or authority to make him come to the office if there was not a trial or hearing requiring his presence. I said, "Try me." He did, and didn't show up the next morning.

I spent that day calling some court reporters in other courts of the state to find out how many pages of typewritten transcript (or folios as they were called) would be reasonable for a court reporter to prepare in a day if he were not in court. The very minimum I was told would be 50 pages per day. Then I drafted an order to Mr. O'Day, saying that beginning the following day, I expected him to file with the Clerk of the Court at least 50 pages of transcript in the first of several cases that I cited to him, or else the Sheriff of Mohave County would come and get him and put him in jail until he provided 50 typewritten pages per day using a court-provided typewriter, paper and carbon paper. After I had the Sheriff serve O'Day with the order, he ignored it, and was furious when the Sheriff made him spend that night in jail. Thereafter he was allowed to type in an office the Sheriff had, where the typewriter and supplies were provided. If he did not hand over 50 additional pages each day, he would bunk at the jail that night.

I think I had the sole distinction in the history of Arizona at that time of having put a court reporter in jail for failing to provide transcripts. I know other court reporters in Arizona were well aware of it. This procedure worked, however, as O'Day reported to the Sheriff every day for a few weeks and completed the transcripts in three of the five or six cases that were needed. The Supreme Court, being advised about my tactics, was patient in waiting for the transcripts. O'Day had not given the notes to a transcriber at all. He had them all the time and just would not do his work.

One day I got a call at the office from O'Day's wife that O'Day was furious about my treatment of him, was drunk, had a gun and was going to kill me. She called late in the afternoon. When I drove home that evening, I saw O'Day's car parked across the street from our house. I pulled into our driveway, got out of the car and went inside the house. I told Joan what had happened. We looked out the front window and O'Day was still out there in his car. I thought about calling the police, but that might cause further problems. So I walked out the front door, across the street and spoke with O'Day through his open car window. I said, "Your wife called and said you have a gun and are going to kill me. I have a deer rifle in my house. If I have to, I will get that rifle and shoot you." Then I turned, walked across the street with my back to O'Day, and re-entered my front door. On each of the 30 or 40 steps that I took to get to the house, I expected to be shot. O'Day did not shoot, however, and drove home. He evidently then kidnapped his youngest daughter and left town, with not even his wife knowing where he was going. I was glad to get rid of him, but was left with the problem of two of his cases not having been transcribed. He had left his notes on the cases in his office. As I mentioned, his handwriting was so good that the attorneys in the cases were able to hire transcribers that made acceptable transcripts for the appellate court.

Months later, I got a call from a trial judge in Oklahoma who said O'Day had applied for a reporter's position in his court, and did I have anything I would like to tell him about O'Day. If you can believe it, O'Day had listed me as a reference about his previous work experience. I gave the Oklahoma judge an earful about Mr. O'Day, and as a result of the call the Sheriff of Mohave County was able to retrieve O'Day's young daughter. I have no idea what happened to O'Day after that. I never heard from him or about him since.

My next problem was my inherited secretary, whom I shall not name, as she may still be alive and I do not wish to hurt her feelings or reputation. She was a single mom, with a small pre-school child who she said was frequently sick. She would arrive late almost every day and spend the next half hour or more putting on her makeup and fixing her hair at her desk. She was undependable and incompetent. She was a bad typist and could not file. I had to re-do almost everything she did, and when she was not there I couldn't locate documents in files. Judge Elmer must have been saintly in his patience with her and keeping her on. I could not get anything done, so I had to let her go. Both O'Day's disappearance and my secretary's leaving occurred within about six months of my taking office.

My next secretary, Marguerite Lamb, was a very competent and loyal helper, who was a blessing. Marguerite was happy and upbeat about life and her family. She brought happiness wherever she went. She not only liked the office part of the work, but loved being the court bailiff in trials. Marguerite stayed with me until I left Kingman to become a Supreme Court Justice in 1975. I do not know how I could have handled a lot of my problems as a trial judge if Marguerite had not come along when she did. She still lives in Kingman and we keep in touch by way of Christmas cards and an occasional email message.

Once I got my personnel problems ironed out, I found that the work as Judge of the Superior Court in Mohave County was enjoyable and challenging. I liked trying cases and I wanted to update our local rules of civil and criminal procedure. In those days, new judges were not given the administrative education they are now required to take before taking on a full calendar. Judges then had to learn by solving problems one by one as they came to his or her attention. At my swearing in, I was given one little book dealing mostly with matters of judicial ethics. Nothing was given to me about dealing with practical problems that would come up almost daily in my new role. I was the only judge in Mohave County at the time, and would be for almost ten more years. I had no one to discuss matters with, as Judge Faulkner was too feeble to get around, and Judge Elmer was too ill even to help me with budget matters. Larger counties, like Maricopa and Pima, had many Superior Court Judges. Maricopa County had about 13 and Pima County about 5. Those judges could consult with each other about cases they had, or problems they encountered, to pick each other's brains for past experience.

With my light calendar, I consented to go to Maricopa and Pima Counties at the request of judges there to handle matters in which local judges felt uncomfortable trying, either because the issues were hot political ones, or involved local officials with whom they would have future dealings.

There were several judges in the northern counties of Arizona that served as visiting judges in Maricopa County. Judges Larry Wren from Coconino County, Judge Shelley from Navajo County, Judge Jack Ogg from Yavapai County, and Judge Greer from Apache County and I were frequent visitors. Judges in Phoenix were very busy. They had so many cases to try that they would set several for trial on the same day, hoping that all but one of them would settle before trial date arrived, leaving only one to be tried that day. If those they hoped to did not settle, then these double or triple set cases were assigned to some other judge there, if available. If no judge were available, the Presiding Judge would call one of the smaller county judges to see if they were able to handle the excess trials.

Even if a judge in Maricopa County were available to handle a last day case, he or she had to cram other hearings in during morning, noon or afternoon recesses of that trial, thus shortening the amount of hours available for the trial. A visiting judge brought in from another county usually was only assigned one case to hear, and could give it his or her full attention for up to eight hours a day, compared to four or five hours from a local judge. So visiting judges got the cases completed quicker, and had advance notice of the case so they could do more complete research of the file in the case, as well as looking up some of the law on problems that the judge could foresee would come up in the trial. The unintended result was that visiting judges were more highly thought of by local lawyers than most local judges. The visiting judges seem more focused, better prepared, and even appeared smarter on the law at issue than their local judges, although the latter part was rarely true. Invited judges had more time to spend on the case and prepared ourselves more in advance of the trial than the local judges could. Each of the judges I mentioned were so well thought of that they were later appointed to the Court of Appeals of Arizona. We were referred to as "Have gavel, will travel."

I served as a visiting judge in many cases, both civil and criminal, in all but two counties in Arizona -- Graham and Santa Cruz. La Paz County had not been formed at that time. Judges Ogg, Wren, Greer and I frequently exchanged courtrooms on cases in which we each had to step aside because of former associations with litigants in previous cases. We became close fishing and golfing buddies. At this writing, all of these judges have passed away. I miss them all, and have great memories of fun times together.

The first murder case I tried as a judge was State v. Raymond Hudgens. Hudgens had shot and killed his young wife, her mother and her father in Kingman in the winter of 1963. I had been a judge less than a year at the time, and the case had received a great deal of publicity in local and state media. As background, Hudgens was a young man, probably around twenty years of age. Born into a wealthy family living in the Oakland, California area, he lived with his parents and a brother and sister. The children had all the luxuries upper middle class children have, but Raymond in his early teens developed a personality problem. He was later diagnosed as a true sociopath. That means he was not a delusional psychopath, had nothing wrong with his nerve connections, but just obsessively believed he did not have to comply with any rules, either of his family or of society, and would become aggressive and violent if his demands were not met.

At 14 or 15, he threatened his brother with a broken milk bottle because the brother would not give him $100 to pay a debt Raymond owed. When he was 16 he choked his sister nearly to death because she would not loan him her car. At this point Raymond's parents knew he was out of control, and were desperate to find some way to manage him. They came to the conclusion that if he spent some time in the military he would learn discipline and to obey rules. So they convinced Raymond to join the army and lied about his age. Raymond made it through basic training and even married a young woman from California before he was shipped out to Korea to be an infantryman. Not long after, Raymond was given a dishonorable discharge from the U. S. Army for having attacked his corporal with a bayonet. Raymond returned to the U. S. and held a few menial jobs in California at stores as a clerk or gas station attendant. His wife left him, taking their child, and came to Kingman to live with her parents who lived in the Elmer Butler addition.

Raymond tried to get his wife to return by following her to Kingman. His wife's parents did not like Raymond, so he called his wife and arranged for her to come with him to a local Kingman café to have a cup of coffee one morning and talk about reconciling. She said she would. He went to pick her up at her parents' home at the appointed time. She came outside the front door still in her nightgown and robe, with her hair up in curlers. He asked why she was not ready to go for coffee and she said she had decided not to go with him. They argued. At that time her father came outside and told Raymond to leave. They argued.

Raymond then pulled out a pistol and shot and killed the father. His wife ran back inside the house and closed the front door. Raymond called for her to open the door, tried to force it open, and then emptied his pistol through the door. He then pushed the door open, finding his wife and mother-in-law lying on the floor, wounded. Raymond went back to his car, got another pistol and fired more rounds into his wife and mother in law, killing them. He then heard a sound in the living room, turned his gun towards it, and trained it on his 18-month-old son, standing in a crib. Realizing it was his child, Raymond put the pistol away, picked up his child, calmed it, changed its diaper and returned him to his crib. He then pulled his father-in-law's corpse into the house and left, driving back to California.

Raymond stopped in Ludlow, California, just east of Barstow, and called the Sheriff of Mohave County and reported that there was a baby alone with three dead bodies at the parents' address in Kingman and hung up the phone without identifying himself. The Sheriff went to the address and found the child in good health only four or five hours after Raymond had left, along with the bodies of his wife and in-laws. The heat had been left on in the house.

Within hours of the Sheriff having received the call from Raymond and finding the bodies, almost all the people in Kingman had heard about the murders. Hudgens drove on into Los Angeles and tried to contact his sister, who was not at home. He left her a note at her home and went to a motel. After some time, he tried to commit suicide by turning the unburned gas on in the kitchen and sealing the windows and doors of the motel room. Somehow the police found out where he was. Maybe he had told his sister where he would be staying. They forced their way into the motel room and found Hudgens unconscious. The police took him to the hospital where he was revived. At the police station Hudgens, without being warned of his rights, which was not required at that time, began confessing what he had done. The police had him writing out his own confession on a legal pad in handwriting. As he finished a page, the police read it and handed each page to a local newspaper reporter, until all was confessed and in the newspaper. He was sent back to Kingman to answer to three first-degree murder charges filed against him.

When Hudgens appeared before me for arraignment, I was amazed at how young he looked. My wife Joan said he looked like any clean cut college kid you could picture. He had no money and wanted counsel, so it was my job to find an attorney who would take this type of case. Mohave County did not have a public defender's office then. The attorney I was to obtain had to be someone who was experienced in capital cases and who would be satisfied with the low pay that court appointed counsel would be paid. This was really a tough assignment. None of the lawyers in Kingman were competent in my opinion to handle this type of case. I contacted several experienced lawyers in other cities who were either already too busy or felt that they could not adequately represent Hudgens. Finally I called Eino Jacobson, a lawyer in Prescott, who reluctantly accepted the assignment after I pleaded with him as a friend, to do so.

So many people in the community had heard so much about the case from the media and had formed an opinion about Hudgen's guilt that it was very difficult to select an impartial jury. It took three days of my questioning over 120 prospective jurors to satisfy myself and counsel that we had a panel that, although they may have heard things about the case, had not formed an opinion about Hudgens' guilt and could be fair and impartial in his trial.

From a prosecutor's standpoint, the case against Hudgens was an easy one. He had all the elements necessary: motive, opportunity and a confession which could be corroborated. Eino Jacobsen had a tough defense decision. If he pleaded Hudgens not guilty by reason of insanity, it opened the door

226

to the prosecutor's bringing in all of Hudgens' prior bizarre and aggressive background. But there was no other practical defense. If the rulings of the United States Supreme Court on improper police questioning and Miranda warnings had been in place before the murders, it is unlikely that Hudgens' confession would have been admitted in evidence. I am not sure how the case would have come out under those circumstances.

In preparation for trial, the prosecution obtained an order to have Raymond Hudgens examined by a noted Phoenix psychiatrist, Otto Bendheim, who gave his opinion that Hudgens was not mentally ill to the extent that he did not understand the charges against him, or could not assist in his defense. That only meant that he was competent to stand trial. Bendheim also stated that Hudgens was not acting under an irresistible impulse, and that he understood that what he was doing was wrong. These fulfilled the definition of legal sanity of the day. He did come to the conclusion that Hudgens was a pure sociopath, which was not a mental illness, but a personality defect, in which Hudgens believed he did not have to comply with rules, regulations or laws if he didn't want to, and that he would become aggressive or violent if someone attempted to require him to do so. He also said Hudgens was dangerous, and if provoked would kill again, without remorse. He also told the jury that there was no known medical treatment to change Hudgens' behavior.

The trial of the Hudgens case was fraught with difficulties. The selection of the jury was the first one. But the one that gave me most anguish was caused by my official court reporter, a competent although emotional reporter who used a stenographic machine. After the state, through the County Attorney Clark Kennedy, put on its witnesses, Eino Jacobsen put the defendant himself on the stand to establish his main defense – insanity. Under oath, he gave his version of his troubled life (spoiled brat), and then described his turbulent marriage. He went on to describe his trip to Kingman to attempt to reconcile his marriage. Hudgens then, on the witness stand, described in detail the argument he had with his wife, her father, and the subsequent shootings of all three victims.

Somewhere in the hush of the courtroom during this lurid description of three murders out of the mouth of the murderer himself, a spectator in the audience stood up and shouted, "Judge. Look!" pointing to the court reporter! When I looked down at her, she was looking at the Hudgens, intently and rapidly depressing the keys of her reporting machine, but she had run out of paper in the machine and nothing was getting put on paper. As I looked at the reporter, she looked at her machine, and became hysterical. She cried out, jumped up and ran out of the courtroom. Everyone in the courtroom was shocked. I called a recess and called counsel into my chambers for a discussion. I knew at this point that if defense counsel were to request it, I would be forced to declare a mistrial and have the prosecution start trying the case all over again to a new jury, which might be impossible to obtain in Mohave County, considering the daily publicity state-wide the trial was getting. The attorneys were as shocked as I when they came into my office. It took several minutes for all of us to gather our thoughts.

After my telling Jacobsen that he would get a mistrial if he requested it, and without objection by Clark Kennedy, Jacobsen suggested that before he consulted with his client as to what their decision would be, that we should find out from the court reporter at what point in Hudgens' testimony she had run out of paper. I asked my secretary to have the reporter look at her notes and let us know. Marguerite Lamb, my secretary, came back with the distressing news that the reporter was not in her office and was nowhere to be found. She had gone home, I think, in embarrassment. It took two hours to find her, and get her calmed down enough to read the last notes on her paper to tell enough for us to realize that she had missed Hudgens' account of two of the three murders. Having discussed this with his client, Jacobsen told me that his client and he had decided not to ask for a mistrial, but to have Hudgens go over the same testimony again, beginning where the reporter's notes left off. I had to recess the jury from that afternoon until the next morning when the reporter got herself composed enough to continue.

When the trial resumed the next morning, Hudgens recounted his testimony, and the defense put on Hudgens' parents and a doctor who opined that Hudgens was in a psychopathic rage at the time, and did not know that what he was doing was wrong.

The jury did not buy the insanity defense and found Hudgens guilty on all three counts of first-degree murder. At that time, the law required the judge, rather than the jury, to decide the sentence to be imposed on the defendant – either life imprisonment or death by gas. This was a difficult thing for me as a sentencing judge to do, not only because it was my first time to sentence a first-degree murderer, but because I had some religious scruples against the death penalty. But I had taken an oath as a judge to support and defend not only the constitution and laws of the United States, but the constitution and laws of the State of Arizona, which at that time mandated my imposing either life or death. If ever a death penalty was called for, in my opinion, this was the case for it.

I steeled myself for the occasion of sentencing. The courtroom was filled with spectators at the day of sentencing. Joan was there, knowing how I felt. Because I had never had occasion to impose a death penalty, I obtained a form from a very good friend and trial judge from Phoenix, Henry Stevens. The form required that I remand Hudgens to the custody of the Sheriff for delivery to the Arizona State Prison, and that the warden of the state prison execute Hudgens by the administration of lethal gas on a day certain, which I had to set, within 60 days from the day of sentencing. That got to me also, picking the very day that I had to order a person be killed. I was depressed and unsure of myself as a judge. At times I even wished that the jury had found Hudgens not guilty by reason of insanity, so I could lock him up in a mental institution.

It did not occur to me at that time that it might be several years at least that this death date would be postponed until Hudgens' various appellate and habeas corpus remedies would be pursued and decided. He might even have his judgment of guilt set aside for some error in the trial caused by me or his attorney, and a new trial awarded. Erroneously, I felt at the time that my decision was an ominous and final one, which would be quickly followed.

Because Hudgens had been found guilty by the jury of killing three people, I was required to read the order of sentence on each count separately. I was nervous as I entered the judgment of guilt on each count, and then started to read the first order of execution. As I was reading it, I faltered on a word or two, and apologized to Hudgens for my miscue, saying that it was the first time I had to administer the death penalty to anyone. With a smile and chuckle, Hudgens said, "Don't worry about it, Judge. It's the first time for me too."

As it turned out a few years later, because the United States Supreme Court found fault in another case with the way Arizona juries were selected in death penalty cases, the Arizona Supreme Court ordered that I vacate my previous orders, and re-sentence Hudgens to life imprisonment, instead of the death penalty. I did so, but imposed three staggered life imprisonment terms, the second commencing 20 years after the first was served, and the third 20 years after the second was served. It was my feeling that he should not be released for at least 60 years as there was, at that time, no cure for Hudgens' mental problems.

Before the re-sentencing, when Hudgens was originally delivered to the Arizona State Prison in Florence, Arizona, as a triple murderer, he was perceived by the prison authorities much as Joan had felt about him – he was just a young man who had killed in a rage and who was probably of no particular danger to anyone in the future. Warden Eyman, the warden of the only prison in Arizona, or someone in his command, put Hudgens in a dormitory with about thirty other prisoners, where they lived and slept together, and not in individual cells or on death row. That was a mistake, and it later proved the prosecution psychiatrist correct. Hudgens still was dangerous. One night when a detention officer was making a bed check in the dormitory, he was grabbed by Hudgens and beaten almost to death in the presence of the other prisoners in the ward. Warden Eyman evidently knew how to handle him then. I was told that Hudgens was placed in an individual cell, and three burly detention officers went in with him. Two of the officers held Hudgens while the other beat him with his fists until Hudgens was almost unconscious. Then they put Hudgens' hands down on the cement floor and stomped on his fingers with their boots until all his fingers were broken.

Although this treatment may seem today excessive and inhumane, Eyman either accidently or knowingly prescribed the right medicine to cure a sociopath – the one thing a sociopath understands is that he can do what he wants until he meets someone else bigger, stronger, and meaner than he is who will beat him to a pulp or kill him. From that point on, Hudgens never exhibited any of the symptoms of sociopathy he had in the past. He was a model prisoner from that beating forward. In fact, he appeared many times before the Board of Pardons and Paroles of Arizona and bragged about his good record in prison.

I believe it was about eight or nine years after re-sentencing that Hudgens escaped from prison, along with another triple murderer, Schmidt, who had killed several people in Tucson, and was also serving several life sentences. Hudgens supposedly told others in prison that if he could escape he was going to "get" me, the County Attorney and the jurors. I somehow got word of the escape, and our local law enforcement agencies all banded together to provide safety for my family.

In 1962 or 1963, the law enforcement agencies individually in Mohave County did not have sufficient manpower to provide full-time protection for anyone under those conditions, but they made a cooperative effort that at times was humorous. First, I believe it was the City of Kingman Police Department that arranged for "panic buttons" to be installed in several places in our home on Ricca Drive. These were silent alarms that went off at the police department when pushed, and would bring help as soon as possible. Also, an officer would be with me, Joan and the children whenever we were at home or away from home. These officers would be provided on rotation by the City of Kingman, Mohave County Sheriff's Office, Department of Public Safety and the Arizona Game and Fish Department. An officer from one of those agencies would stay at our home at night and supposedly stay awake while we were sleeping. They usually stayed in the playroom, which was our enclosed carport at the north end of the house on Ricca Drive. Most of the time, those on duty just watched television.

The children, all three of them, went to school in caged police cruisers each day. They were mortified. I think later on Scotty began to like it. Joan had to go shopping with police officers.

One sheriff's officer who was specially trained, appeared at our home each morning to check whether our car, which was parked outside all night, had been rigged with a bomb. He would go over the car carefully, and then make me wait on the other side of the house while he started the engine.

Sometimes that summer, our alarm system would go off without an apparent reason other than possibly a thunderstorm had vibrated the windows or doors. One time, on a false alarm, the police came to the Grounds' house next door by mistake and made them come outside while the police searched their entire house. The officers did not know they were at the wrong address. The officers would not take your word for it at the door that everything was all right. They tried hard to be efficient.

The first time a City of Kingman officer went with us to
church, he was in full uniform and carrying a riot shotgun. We
sat in the last pew of the church and the minister kept a wary
eye on us and the church doors.

Once when I went to Prescott to try a case, a DPS officer,
Roscoe Baker, whom I had gone to high school with, stayed
with the family. The officers would answer the phone and were
not supposed to say where I was. When my trial in Prescott
lasted late in the day, I wanted to tell Joan I would be late and
not to worry. I called my home and Roscoe answered. I said,
"This is Judge Gordon and I want to tell Joan –". Roscoe said,
"No, Judge Gordon isn't here. He is trying a case in Prescott
and should be home soon." I told Roscoe he wasn't supposed
to tell where I was, and he said he was sorry.

When the officers were setting up our family's security, the
Sheriff said I should always be armed. So I was provided with a
snub-nosed .38 caliber revolver in an under-arm upside down
holster for me to wear wherever I went. Because the prison
had not taken a picture of Hudgens since he was put in prison
nine years before, no one could give me a good description of
what he looked like now. So my instructions were that if I saw
anyone that even vaguely looked like Hudgens, I was to shoot
first and ask questions later.

One of the Sheriff's officer's duties was to see to it that I
knew how to handle the .38 revolver I was carrying. He took
me to a target range and set up a profile target of a man. I
was told that shootouts occurred usually within 25 feet, so

there was no use practicing at a greater distance. The officer didn't know that I was familiar with most kinds of firearms. He paced me off 25 feet from the target, told me to reach under my coat, pull the pistol, drop to my knee, empty the pistol at the target and then he would give me further instructions. I did what he told me, rapidly firing six shots, which entered the target in the subject's mid-section all in a space that could be covered with a small dinner plate. The officer was very surprised. He said, "Well, I guess we would be wasting ammunition to do anything more."

The admonition to shoot first and ask questions later worried me. The officers could not be with me all the time at work, so I reluctantly agreed to wear the pistol.

One time I was trying a civil jury case in the courthouse, and during a recess I was going to use the restroom, which was one flight down the marble stairs to a mezzanine floor on the way to the ground floor of the courthouse. It was the same men's restroom that all men in the building used. A lot of jurors were standing around the mezzanine smoking, or waiting to use the restroom. I started down the stairs. I had only made one or two stairs when the pistol under my arm came out of the holster, which was under my jacket, and fell on the marble stairs.

At that point, everything seemed to be happening in slow motion. I instantly reached for the falling gun, seeing the jurors were backed against the wall watching. I missed catching the pistol on the first bounce, but caught it on the second bounce. With that I crammed it back into its holster, looked up at the shocked and terrified jurors, smiled, and went into the restroom. I went into a stall and stayed there a long time, hoping all the people on the floor would have returned to the jury room. No such luck. They all waited outside the restroom for me and chided me about being so clumsy. I was embarrassed. I later went down to the Sheriff's office and told them what had happened and that I was afraid to wear the pistol because of the danger to others. The Sheriff showed me that the pistol could not go off if dropped, but I still was skeptical.

Another case provided some humor. This was a civil case wherein the State of Arizona was condemning or taking some highway frontage in Yucca, Arizona. It was a jury case, with two very prominent attorneys. One was Karl Mangum of Flagstaff who was the Dean of Northern Arizona Lawyers. Karl was one of the most admired and respected lawyers in the north, and also an excellent trial lawyer. The property owner's lawyer was a friend and law classmate of mine, Jay Dushoff, from Phoenix. He was a specialist in eminent domain cases. He also was an exceptional trial lawyer, but was an intense dark, almost sinister looking person. His eyes seemed to burn through you. If a man ever fit the description of "meaner than a junkyard dog," he was it.

At one point in the trial, during a recess, I was hearing an argument in chambers between the attorneys as to some evidentiary matter. Suddenly my court reporter came banging on my office door, shouting, "Judge! Judge! Cut her finger off! Juror cut her finger off!" I left the two lawyers and followed the reporter to the rest room landing, where one of the lady jurors was holding her hand up at shoulder height, with blood spurting from her middle finger of her left hand. She had put her hand on the ladies' rest room door, just when someone was coming out and opened the door. When the door closed, it caught the lady's finger in the door and cleanly pulled the cap of her first digit off her finger. The cap of the finger fell on the floor, where a Native American juror saw it and picked it up with a Kleenex. The wounded juror was very calm, but bleeding badly. I took her to the jury room on the top floor of the courthouse, had her lay down on a bench, got a blanket to put over her, and went in my office to call a doctor. I asked the tough bulldog lawyers to help me with the juror, but both refused and stayed in my chambers because neither could stand the sight of blood. I was surprised to see how deceiving even lawyers' looks can be.

Dr. Jack Standifer came looking very doctor-like in his white coat and carrying his black bag. While he was coming up the stairs, the Native American juror handed him the finger cap in the Kleenex and told him what it was. He put it in his bag and proceeded to tend to the wounded juror. After cleansing the wound and splinting the finger with a tongue depressor, the doctor started looking through the bag. I asked him what he was looking for and he told me jokingly to "shut up, you know what I am looking for."

The doctor took the patient to his office, which was only two or three blocks away, and I returned to my office to discuss with the queasy lawyers what we should do about proceeding without this juror. After the lawyers could not agree on what number of the remaining jurors would be sufficient to render a verdict, I suggested that I talk to the doctor about what we could expect as to the juror's condition the next day. So, I recessed the case until the next day, and went to the doctor's office. The receptionist recognized me and directed me to one of the doctor's treatment rooms, where I found the doctor stitching the juror's finger cap back on. As the juror was talking to me, I called the doctor's attention to the fact that he was stitching the finger cap on backwards, with the hole for the fingernail facing inward. Without explanation, the doctor removed his stitches and turned the finger around for proper alignment. The juror insisted she would be all right and wanted to continue to serve the next morning. I made her promise to call me at home early the next day and let me know how she was feeling, which she did. She said she had very little pain and wanted to continue to serve.

The next day the juror arrived with a huge bandage on her middle finger. She sat in the first row of the jury box, with her arm propped up on the jury rail, hand and finger pointing skyward. You can guess the impression this made on the lawyers, witnesses, and spectators, as she intently observed the rest of the trial in that position. When the verdict of the jury was rendered and the case was over, my secretary Marguerite

Lamb, presented the injured juror with a hand-lettered citation, framed and all, awarding her a Purple Heart for service
above and beyond the call of duty. Everyone in the courtroom
responded with applause.

I truly enjoyed the trial bench. Every case a judge hears
is different from the others. There almost always is some
unique twist to the case making it exciting, sometimes
amusing. People and their priorities are vastly different and
always surprising.

In a small county with only one judge, I was looked to
as the ultimate legal authority on everything. Almost every
morning I would have two or three people waiting for me at
the office, looking for some free legal advice, which I was not
supposed to give. Before you could tell them that, however,
you had to patiently listen to the whole problem, usually cast
in the third person: "I have this friend who had this happen to
him." It was really their own problem, but they wouldn't say it.
After listening to them, I would politely advise that this was a
serious problem that should be analyzed by a lawyer who was
expert in that field and who would be available to follow up
with the right procedure, whether that would be a lawsuit or
just a letter. Occasionally, I would refer them to some agency
that could take care of the matter without charge. This not
only assured you of a vote next election, but made you feel
good that you were able to help.

Being the local judge did have some perks. Joan and I,
and even our children, were looked up to as important

people in the community. I think there were times when our children's questionable conduct was somehow overlooked. I also feel that it must have been hard on the children to know that they were always being watched, sometimes enviously, and perhaps with disdain.

Trey, being the eldest of our children, was the first to ask to drive the family car. Because his driving would increase our liability insurance several hundred dollars, Trey was required to get summer employment to pay us for the insurance. He did the first year, and he made it through the year without any accidents or tickets as I recall. The next summer, he didn't get around to looking for a job until late. I had warned him, no insurance money, no keys to the car. By the time he got around to searching for a job, the summer was upon him and no jobs were available. He handed over the keys without complaint. Being a junior or senior in high school, I am sure that was a big blow to his social status, but he did not complain.

One evening, after a day in juvenile court, where I felt the anguish brought upon a pair of parents that I knew well because of the thoughtlessness of their son who had been arrested for marijuana possession, I came home feeling good about Trey. I told him that I was going to forgo his paying for the insurance difference because he had been a good son, hadn't embarrassed us by bad conduct, etc. He gladly accepted the return of the keys to the car, and said that the fact that he had not been involved with marijuana wasn't always because he hadn't wanted to. Trey said a judge's son is not normally

241

invited to marijuana parties. He said that when he went away to college, though, he was going to try it.

At this point, a parent is put to a test. Should the parent show great resistance, threaten sanctions, or what? My tactic was to tell him that if he did, to make sure he was not with a group of people who might get him in trouble with the law, and make sure he was not going to be driving a vehicle. He promised to follow this advice. When he returned for Christmas vacation during his first year in college at Bethany Bible School near Oakland, California, I asked him if he had tried marijuana. He said he had, but that he didn't like it because it made his throat sore. He also said that he had not even smoked a cigarette before that. I had no idea how "square" Trey had been throughout high school. It pleased me greatly that he had been so pure as compared to some of our friends' children.

One of my favorite memories of being a judge in Mohave County was having some of my judge friends from different levels of the court system join me to go fishing. It wasn't until I became one that I came to realize how much a judge's life changed when he or she put on that black robe. They could no longer go out and party with friends in public or couldn't let his or her hair down to become a just plain person. They could not continue close relationships with lawyer friends or organizations that might have cases that would come before them. Judges had to hold themselves above some strong friendships you previously enjoyed. Your friendship circle became smaller than before, and usually consisted of only other judges, which could be rather boring.

I knew quite a few judges that loved the outdoors and either went hunting or fishing when they could get away. In my mind, I figured the outback of Mohave County would provide the privacy needed for my friends to let their hair down (what we had left) and enjoy each other in the faraway canyons of the Colorado River chain.

It started out in the mid 1960s with just a few judges at a time. Only one or two had boats big enough for long trips on our large lakes. My friends Ernie Scott, Roy Hoover and Ivan Wilson had good fishing boats and agreed to help out with transportation. The first judges to come on a "Highline Judicial Conference" were: Judges Jack Ogg from Prescott (later to be appointed to serve on the Arizona Court of Appeals), Jack D. H. Hays (later to serve on the Arizona Supreme Court), and Judge Tom Tang, (later to be appointed to the U.S. Court of Appeals from the 9th Circuit). We were the founders of what became a rather large and prestigious group that met once a year, usually on Presidents' Day in February. The "Highline Judicial Conference" was a title that had no official status, but looked good when it appeared on a judge's calendar to keep it free for the judge to take off a day or two to enjoy a rest from the great pressures of their office and to relax in fun and good fellowship.

Judge Larry Wren of the Superior Court of Coconino County, later to serve on the Court of Appeals, came on the

243

register of the Highline Conference, as did Ray Haire, and Eino Jacobson, Court of Appeals Judges. Wren then asked that his friend and Coconino County Attorney, Jerry Smith, be allowed to attend, which was granted. That was the first non-judge to join the group. Then came Mohave County Attorney, Dan Schimmelpfennig. Down the road, Paul Beer, a Phoenix attorney, and his partner Jerry Kalyna, joined the group. I forget the order of the next additions, such as Jack Anderson, a Phoenix attorney, Doug Wall, attorney from Flagstaff, Paul LaPrade, and Howard Thompson, judges on the Maricopa County Superior Court, Art Johnson, Phoenix attorney and perhaps some others who I cannot now remember.

The Highline Judicial Conference got together each year in our home in Kingman on the Friday of President's Day weekend. All would arrive in the evening in time for dinner and to camp out overnight at our house. Sometimes our children would have to step over men sleeping in sleeping bags on the floor wherever they could find space. Joan usually had a huge pot of spaghetti and meat sauce ready for the group who arrived at different hours of the evening. Judges Haire and Jacobson usually arrived early with the beer and wine the attendees had paid for. After dinner, and some drinks, Paul Beer sang songs and played his guitar accompanied by my court reporter, Keith Welch, on the piano. The group singing that followed late into the evening sounded great to us, but probably didn't to the neighbors on both sides of our house. I

My campaign photo, approximately 1963

had pre-warned our neighbors of what would occur that night, and promised that any disruption to their evening would be kept to a minimum and would quit before midnight.

My career as a trial judge lasted thirteen years in Mohave County, during which time I had to run for election, successfully four times, twice with opposition. The most I had to spend for my campaigns was about $500 which covered the cost of my three colored posters, bumper strips, matchbooks and radio and newspaper ads. Things are certainly different now. Judges in the rural counties of Arizona where judges are still elected rather than appointed have to spend many thousands of dollars, sometimes more than their first year's salary, to carry on a campaign for election.

I was first appointed to the Superior Court bench in May, 1962, and had to run for election in September of that first year. I knew nothing about political campaigning and had to learn the hard way. I had a campaign committee, chaired by Ernie Scott, who raised the money for my campaign materials. Because I did not want to know which of my friends did or did not like me enough to contribute to my campaign, I told Ernie not to tell me who gave and how much. He had to file a campaign report with the county, showing who and how much, but I never looked at it and never knew.

I got around to my first campaign by passing out campaign literature with the help of my children and making speeches in Kingman, Oatman, Bullhead City, Chloride, Yucca, Peach Springs, and Wickiup. Those were the only population centers in the county at the time. Lake Havasu City did not exist then.

At this point, I realized that there was a big part of Mohave County in my district that was north of the Grand Canyon. That area was called "the Strip." I had heard about that area being populated by polygamists and outlaws from the old days and about the raid made by the State of Arizona on the community of Short Creek in 1953. Until the raid, the Grand Canyon effectively cut those people off from law enforcement from Mohave County, as to get there from Kingman, you had to drive through three states, Nevada, Utah and back into Arizona, about 250 miles to Colorado City, or "Short Creek." There were no bridges across the canyon then.

The area intrigued me, but my campaign advisors told me not to bother going there, as the people there were mostly polygamists who were originally Mormons and who refused to give up polygamy when it was made illegal in Utah. As I mentioned, Arizona officials had raided the community in 1953, and they would not vote for anyone running for office in Mohave County as they believed that was where their troubles had come from. There were lots of people there, perhaps over a thousand adults, but only about 500 registered to vote, as doing so might reveal several polygamous marriages. But my curiosity got the best of me. I had to go to Colorado City, put up my signs and introduce myself to the people there. After all, it was almost 10 years after the raid that caused the people there to be so unhappy with the rest of the state who refused to tolerate their form of marriage. Surely by this time they would have forgotten, or at least forgiven, the people in the rest of the county for this transgression. Was I ever wrong.

I drove to Colorado City in late August or early September 1962. I did not take Joan or the children as I felt that her appearance might make the women there envious of her style, dress and apparent freedom. Besides, I knew it would be difficult for Joan to keep her opinions about the subservient status of the women in that community to herself. I was told that there was only one place on the strip that I could post one of my election signs, and that was at the local community store in Colorado City. If I posted them on telephone, power poles or fence posts other than that, they would be torn down. I was told that because Arizona license plates showed by a letter preceding the numbers what county your vehicle was registered in, if they saw your car coming, the people there would run in their houses, pull the blinds and refuse to answer the door. Still, undaunted, I made the trip for one poster with the hope of being able to reach as many of the townspeople as possible.

After driving through Las Vegas to Saint George, Utah, you had to go south back into Arizona on a dirt road for almost 100 miles, passing through small communities like Wolf Hole and Mount Trumbull before arriving at Colorado City. When I arrived at what I considered the first farm home in Colorado City, I saw an elderly man and a young boy out in a cornfield. I pulled into a driveway between this man and his house, and as I did I saw five or six young girls in the yard picking pears from the trees surrounding the very large home. As I pulled in, the girls, dressed in ankle-length gingham dresses with their hair in braids around their heads, ran into the house, pulled the blinds and stayed there.

I got out of my car and approached the man in the field, who did not move away or toward me. I had the man cut off from the house. I am guessing he was either in his late sixties or early seventies, and had a young boy maybe three or four with him, holding onto his leg. I introduced myself to him by saying who I was and that I was running for Judge of the Superior Court in Mohave County, and would appreciate his vote. He responded that his name was Mr. Black. I don't remember his first name. I then naively asked if the five or six young girls in the front yard were his daughters, and he said no they were not. He sensed my surprise and puzzlement. Mr. Black introduced me to his son who was pulling on his leg, and said that he had seven pre-school children, six or seven in grade school, and seven in high school. He added that none of them were on welfare, and most would go to their local "Academy" which was their private college. Then it came to me that the five or six young girls were in fact his "wives". I finished with what I wanted to talk to Mr. Black about, but he was not through with me. He told me that it happened that there was going to be a meeting of the elders of his church that evening, and he would like me to come and tell them all how I would treat them if I were elected judge of the county. Sensing the type of questions I would be asked, I had to make some excuse to leave soon. I told him that I was sorry, but that I had commitments in Tuweep and Moccasin just down the road, and had to leave.

After leaving my only poster in the community store and meeting a few people there, I went on my way through the remaining communities without stopping and stayed overnight in Fredonia before coming back to Kingman by way of Flagstaff. It is beautiful country, especially Pipe Springs National Monument northwest of Fredonia. Also, the Toroweap overlook of the Grand Canyon, which is almost 5,000 feet below you, is the most spectacular view of the Colorado River that I have seen. I can see why the Mormon Church chose this area as the summer grazing area for their tithing cattle herd given by the faithful for their 10% tithe each year.

Somewhere along the line, I was privileged to meet Mr. Jessop, who was the leader of the church in Colorado City and who was the only person I needed to visit each four years when I came to campaign again. After he saw that it was not my job to rid the country of their clan, he became a good friend and dutifully saw that I got all but a few of the 500 votes from that precinct.

The area of the strip near the Grand Canyon was the scene of the "Mormon Massacre" written about by Zane Gray. It is said that for some reason the Mormons there had massacred

a whole wagon train of people – men, women and children —
passing through. My father-in-law and Joan's stepfather, Birre
Gipe, was an avid Zane Gray fan and had read all his books,
some more than once. He had read about the massacre and
when he found that I was going to the strip to campaign one
time, he begged to go along as he wanted to see the area where
the massacre had occurred. I was reluctant to take Birre, as
he was a very outspoken man who drank, smoked and might
make some remark that would offend Mr. Jessop. He promised
to be good, so after a few specific assurances, I took him. After
the hot, 100-mile trip by dirt road, we arrived in Colorado
City at Mr. Jessop's home. I had pre-warned Birre not to ask
questions or make any comments about the young pregnant
girls that might be seen at Jessop's home, as Mrs. Jessop #1
was the head midwife in the community.

When we arrived, Mr. Jessop warmly invited us inside his
huge home where Mrs. Jessop #1, in her ankle-length gingham dress and braided hair, presented us with some Kool-Aid
in small cheese glasses with an ice cube in each of them. This
cool repast was much appreciated, as it was over 100 degrees
outside. I was surprised when Birre smacked his lips and said
to Mr. Jessop, "Mr. Jessop, that was fine, but after this long
hot journey, do you happen to have something with a little
more 'snap' to it?"

I was mortified when Birre asked the question, as I was sure
this teetotaling, religious man would be offended and I would
instantly lose 500 votes. Instead, Mr. Jessop said, "Birre, I am

glad you asked. "With that, Jessop reached behind a curtain
and brought out a gallon jug of homemade wine, and proceeded to pour a glass for each of us and himself. When Jessop
said he made the wine, I replied that I was a licensed home
wine maker myself, and would appreciate his recipe. That was
the start of a friendly relationship between us. I don't know
anything else that Birre could have done that would have
made the trip better.

Whenever a person from Colorado City was summoned
to act as a juror in a case in Kingman, Jessop would personally drive that person the 250 miles and wait for them until
their service was over to return them back to the community.
I knew each time when that occurred, on my desk that morning, would be a paper bag with a mason jar full of Jessop's
newest batch of wine for me to taste.

I know very little of Mr. Jessop's religious beliefs, but I
understand that the elders of the church are given first prefer-
ence to pick which of the young girls for their brides. Therefore, the younger men in the community are forced to take
for their wives the girls who are not chosen by the elder men.

One time in the late 1960s, Mr. Jessop made an appointment to talk to me in my office in Kingman. It was a serious matter for him and he needed my advice. It was not a
legal matter, but one he needed advice on and he trusted me
enough to give him that advice. I felt honored that Jessop, the
highest moral authority in his community, considered me a
trusted advisor. The subject of the conference meeting was

that Mohave County was offering him, without cost, to bring into Colorado City a translator for the first television channel to be shown to the residents of his community. Jessop asked me if I thought he should accept the offer by the county. Although it was an honor to be asked for my advice, I felt torn.

Surely the residents of Colorado City should have the same privileges all the other residents of Mohave County had. Still, I had to look at this from Jessop's viewpoint. I asked him what TV channel would be broadcast and he told me it would be Las Vegas Channel 2. I felt that if he accepted the County's offer it would seriously erode his control over both the male and the female population in his community. I felt it would be difficult for Jessop to make the young males wait their turn to marry and stay in the community when they started seeing the nearly nude chorus girls in the TV shows. I felt it might also have the same effect on the female community members when they saw the privileges afforded to women in society outside their community. So, this is what I told him.

Jessop followed my advice for some time until a new regime allowed the translator to be installed. My advice to Mr. Jessop proved prescient, as the sect has started falling apart from secessions and public views of his community brought about by some of the people who left the area unhappy with their forced marriages. Also, the recent leader of the clan, Mr. Warren Jeffs, has been convicted in Texas of sexual assault on several juvenile females, supposedly his "wives", and has been sentenced to life imprisonment plus some additional years for these crimes.

In all, my service as Superior Court judge was a happy and rewarding one, both for me and my family. I shall never forget the help and support that I got from officials and friends in Mohave County. I still feel like Mohave County and northern Arizona are my home.

8

APPOINTMENT TO THE SUPREME COURT, 1975

D uring the 13 years from 1962 to 1975 that I served as a Superior Court judge in Mohave County, many important events happened in Joan's and my lives. According to some, I had become a well-known and respected trial judge, we had raised our children through their teenage years and both Trey and Candy had been to college. My father died of an apparent heart attack in 1968, my mother died in 1971, of congestive heart failure, and our son Scotty had died in 1973. In the same year Scotty died, a massive propane explosion occurred in Kingman. A propane-filled railroad car was parked at a siding in northeast Kingman and was being off-loaded into a propane company's tank farm. Something went wrong with the unloading process and the car developed a large gas leak which turned into a huge, roaring sheet of fire blowing out of the car and parallel to the ground. It burned for over 1/2 hour. Our local volunteer fire department was called and they were following appropriate procedures by spraying fire hoses of water on the car to cool it. It was over 100 degrees in Kingman that summer day. Unfortunately, this procedure was not enough to forestall disaster. The railroad car exploded, killing and injuring many of the firefighters and some spectators who were watching from across the highway to the west.

The firefighters closest to the tank car were horribly burned and ultimately 13 died. These were men of high stature in our community – Lee Williams, the high school principal, several school teachers, store clerks -- all people we knew well. Those killed were members of the Rotary, Lions and Elks Clubs in town, and one Highway Patrol officer that was directing traffic around the fire area. One fireman, Nolan Davis, was spared, as he was in Bullhead City selling insurance and was not able to respond to the call for the fire.

Some spectators who were across the highway over 100 yards away from the explosion were burned seriously. The local hospital and medical facilities in Kingman were not sufficient at that time to cope with this disaster. There were not enough ambulances to get the injured to the hospital, and the hospital did not have enough staff or ice to treat the burn victims. Our local radio put out an emergency call for anyone with a pickup truck to go to the various convenience stores and gas stations to bring ice to the hospital. The burn victims were transported by passenger car or truck to the hospital. All you could hear outside your home was the blaring of sirens. The

Swearing in at Supreme Court with Justice James "Duke" Cameron

sky had turned orange with smoke and dust.

That day was the first day Scotty had been able to come home from one of his frequent hospital stays dealing with an infection of the tissues around his heart. I hurried home from the barbershop near where the explosion occurred and as calmly as I could, told Joan and the children to pack up whatever they thought was important, and that we had to leave the house immediately. The radio announced that most of the north part of Kingman was being evacuated due to the possibility of further and larger explosions of the tank facility at the propane plant. If that went up, perhaps all of north Kingman would be destroyed.

In near panic, and within minutes, we each grabbed what personal property we individually thought was important, which was little, and jumped into our car. (What we did take, and what was left behind, was somewhat humorous: remembering our sleeping bags, for example, but forgetting Scotty's medicine and the family dog.) Discussing it afterward, we each came to the conclusion that most things we possessed were really not important. Our family's safety was all that mattered. We drove the back way around north Kingman and took shelter with the Hoovers in their home in central Kingman where we waited, listening to the radio, to be advised when we could return to our home. In our haste, we forgot to take our dog, Risa, who stayed at our home and I am sure was as terrified as we were because of the loud explosion.

The deaths of our friends in the fire department were agonizing and slow. These men were strong and vital, in the prime of their lives. Most were still conscious when they arrived at the hospital. The bandages placed on their arms, legs and bodies pulled flesh with them when they were changed. Fingers fell off their hands. Still most of them were in good spirits and encouraged each other as they lay on gurneys in the hospital's halls, awaiting rooms and medical attention.

What they did not know was that they had inhaled flames from the massive fireball that engulfed them, and the fire had burned the delicate linings of their lungs. They would die slowly of congestion, eventually drowning in fluids in their lungs. That process took days, and even weeks, however.

Within three or four weeks, all who had answered the fire call had died. There were several funerals a week to attend, and many families to console. Each funeral required the fireman's tradition that the body of the victim and his casket be carried on a fire truck through town, reminding all of his bravery and sacrifice. Dick Waters, the publisher and editor of the Mohave Miner newspaper, was called upon to speak at most of the funerals of the victims who were members of the local Elks Lodge. It must have been a miserable experience for him to do this so many times.

The emotional impact of the deaths and burials of so many of the community's leaders was devastating. A pall was cast over the entire city that did not lift for almost a year. Many community events were cancelled because no one felt like participating in anything that might be fun while everyone was still grieving.

As Superior Court judge, I was required to officiate over estate matters of the dead firemen, such as probates of wills, guardianships of children and settlements made between the insurance companies and the victim and their families. Day after day, for months after the explosion, I was reminded of the tragedy that had befallen our community. I was depressed, as was the whole community.

It was only months after the explosion in 1973 that Scotty died. His heart infection had worsened and he returned to the hospital. One day he called me at the office from his hospital bed and told me about a dream he had the night before; I forget the details, but it was a dream that frightened him. I tried to console him. Luckily, I was able to leave the office and go to the hospital. Joan joined me there. He had lost so much weight. He tried to be brave, but I think he knew he was dying. Joan and I both were holding his hands when he died that very afternoon. He was only 19 years old. I have found that no one ever gets over losing a child.

Scotty had a great many friends, not only school friends, but Citizen Band Radio buddies that he conversed with over his CB radio from his home bed. In his last months he was mostly confined to bed, so the CB radio was his primary source of friendly contact. Many police and sheriff's officers, as well as others in the town, knew this and would contact him by radio frequently, cheering him up. However far a CB radio signal would travel, he had people he knew well and loved. Almost all came to his funeral at the Methodist church.

Joan was the biggest source of strength in our family at that time. She comforted all of us during our time of grief. It was in this period of my depression over the loss of my father, mother, son and so many friends that Lorna Lockwood, a Justice on the Arizona Supreme Court, gave notice that she was going to retire from the bench. It was suggested that I might be appointed to fill her vacancy.

At this time, life in Kingman was not a happy one, and the offer of a chance to be appointed to the Arizona Supreme Court and moving to Phoenix sounded interesting. Ours was basically a small-town family. We loved to hunt, fish, water ski, and do all the outdoor things that would most likely no longer be available to us if we moved to the big city. We had so many close friends in Kingman that until that time, moving away to the big city of Phoenix would never have occurred to us. In 1959, before becoming a judge, I had turned down a very impressive offer from the Phoenix law firm of Snell & Wilmer, one of the most prestigious firms in Arizona, to become one of their trial lawyers. The firm had even found out about Scotty's illness and had located a good school and doctors to help him if I were to come to work with them. If I had joined the firm at that time, it is possible that I would have become a very wealthy senior partner by now.

Lorna Lockwood was a revered associate justice of the Arizona Supreme Court. She had been on the court for many years, and was the first woman to serve on the Supreme Court in Arizona. She had also served as Chief Justice of that court for a couple of years.

Joan and I discussed the matter. She agreed that it was time for us to make a change. Trey and Candy were already married. With that in mind, I went over my options. Politically it would be extremely difficult for a lawyer or judge from a small outlying county in Arizona to be appointed to the Arizona Supreme Court.

All of the sitting justices at that time were from Phoenix, except James Duke Cameron, with whom I had gone to law school. He was from Yuma and got to the court the old-fashioned way – he ran for the job and won the election. Since

Duke's successful election, the Constitution of Arizona had been amended in such a way to remove politics as much as possible from the elections and appointments of judges to the Arizona Supreme Court, the Court of Appeals and the Superior Courts of Maricopa and Pima Counties. There were to be no contested elections thereafter for those courts. This amendment was made in 1974 by a vote of the people in Arizona, and was called the "Modern Courts Act."

Under this new system, judges in the courts mentioned could only get there by appointment by the Governor of Arizona, who could only appoint someone who had been nominated by a special commission appointed for that purpose for each level of the court. When there was a vacancy on one of those courts, the existing commission would put out a notice that there was a vacancy and for candidates to apply. The applications to be filled out and submitted were very detailed and lengthy, requiring a great deal of background and the experience of the applicant. The commission would then decide who amongst the applicants it wished to interview, conduct the interviews, and decide which three or five of the applicants they would submit to the Governor.

The list, by law, could not be overloaded with candidates from any one political party. This procedure is still the law in Arizona, except the commissions are much larger for each of the three levels of the courts than was the case in 1975. The Governor is bound to accept and appoint one of the members of the list submitted by the selection committee. If the

262

Governor does not do so within a short period of time, (30 days I think), the then Chief Justice of the Supreme Court is to appoint from the list submitted to the Governor. Once appointed, the judge would run unopposed in the next election, with the public voting simply "yes" or " no" as to whether that judge should be retained in office or not.

Under this new system, the Superior Courts in counties other than Maricopa and Pima still retain the old contested election system, where aspiring candidates run for election in party primaries and then against others in the general election, until those counties' populations reach a certain number, and then if the Board of Supervisors' choose to, that county can transfer to the merit selection non-political system. Until now, none of the counties which have reached that population qualifier have chosen to do so.

The old system of electing judges had been in place since Arizona was admitted as a state in 1912. It required incumbent judges to take time off from their calendars to campaign for re-election. They would have to travel around their counties or the whole state, just like all other county officers, although technically the county superior court judges are actually state officers. Also, if they had opposition, they might be forced to raise a lot of money to pay for political ads on television, in newspapers, and on radios, and also attend public meetings, making speeches, asking for elector's votes. In the larger counties, the old system had proven inefficient, expensive and consumed considerable time for the incumbent judges which would have been better spent handling cases on his or her calendar.

It also created potential conflicts of interest for the judges who had to campaign for election and had solicited donations from large law firms or individual attorneys who might appear in their court in the future. First, if the potential donor refused to contribute, and the judge was successful in winning election, there was the potential for the judge to hold it against that firm or its clients in the future. Second, from the judge's viewpoint, if a donor made a considerable campaign donation, the judge might feel uncomfortable ruling against that firm even if the facts and law supported an unfavorable ruling. This was a bad system all around, but it took over 60 years for Arizona to get rid of it in the state's most populous counties and most important courts. Now, over 37 of the 50 states in the United States have some sort of merit selection in some levels of their courts.

As an example of how unreal the old system can be, I relate what Justice Stanley Feldman told me happened while he was Vice-Chief Justice of the Arizona Supreme Court, while I was still the Chief Justice. He was in Texas at some judicial meeting, and attended a cocktail party wherein many judges from different states were present. Feldman was talking to the Chief Justice of the Texas Supreme Court, Tom Phillips, who was running for election with opposition. As they were talking, a lawyer for either Standard or Exxon Oil Company came up and presented Judge Phillips with a check for many thousands of dollars and wished him well in the upcoming election. Feldman knew that that company was appealing a judgment against another oil company for many millions of dollars to the Texas Supreme Court. Evidently sensing Feldman's shock at witnessing the transaction, the Judge Phillips remarked that this might seem unfair to someone who was not used to their system. He assured Feldman that if one party to an appeal to the Texas Court made a large campaign contribution to a judge, he would see to it that it wasn't unfair. Judge Phillips said he would simply contact counsel on the other side and advise him of the size of his opponent's donation and give him the opportunity to make a similar contribution. This shocked Feldman, and also me. Our system is much less political and gives judges a great deal more autonomy in their decision making.

This is a long way of telling what obstacles confronted me, a judge from a very small and politically unimportant county, in attempting to become a Supreme Court justice in Arizona. If the system in place had been the old elective system, I would not have stood a chance to be elected to that court, as almost any candidate from a larger county would poll more votes than I could statewide. However, under the Modern Courts Act, I had a unique advantage.

Governor Raul Castro was in office at that time. He was a very remarkable man who I was proud to call my friend. His parents were immigrants from Mexico and he was raised in mining towns in southeastern Arizona. He paid his way through school at University of Arizona by being a professional prize fighter. At county fair time, he would travel around Arizona's mining towns and challenge anyone to fight him for an entry fee of about $50, winner take all. He even fought in Oatman, Arizona, in Mohave County, during that town's heyday. As you can expect, he came up against some of the toughest miners in Arizona, and according to him, never lost a fight. He also taught Spanish part-time at the University of Arizona. Castro knew politicians in all small counties and was very popular with the Mexican-Americans statewide. Tough and fair, he was a good judge.

One time, he ordered a big Mexican youth be sent to jail or detention. The young man cursed Castro in court and said that if Castro would take off that black robe he would beat him up. Castro calmly said to him that he did not think the young man could do that, but if he wanted to try, he would have to wait, because there was a long list of young men who were waiting in line in jail to try the same thing. I would imagine that when the young man found out what a fighter Castro was, he gave up on his challenge. Castro, after being elected as Governor, was appointed ambassador to El Salvador and to Argentina under Presidents Johnson and Carter.

Given my acquaintance with Governor Castro, I felt I had a chance to be appointed to fill Justice Lockwood's vacancy, assuming I was successful in getting my name submitted to him by the Supreme Court Selection Commission. At that time, the Supreme Court Selection Commission was a nine-

Governor Raul Castro

person bipartisan body consisting of four lawyers and five non-lawyers. John P. Frank, senior partner in Lewis & Roca, another preeminent law firm in Phoenix, was very helpful in giving me contacts on that commission. Frank also advised me on how best to draft my application. Having done this, I awaited the commission's call if they decided I was to be one of the fortunate ones to be interviewed for the job.

The call came when I was in Denver taking part as a presenter at an educational seminar for trial lawyers from all over the west. I explained to whoever called that this was not a inconvenient time to come to Phoenix because of my commitment to teach in Denver. The caller merely said that if I was interested in the job I should be at the Capitol building in Phoenix two days hence. I made arrangements with the seminar leaders to be gone for one day, returning to the program after my interview the same day. I left Joan in Denver and flew to Phoenix on the appointed day.

When I arrived in Phoenix, I went to the Capitol building, to the office of my friend Eino Jacobson, who by then was serving as a Court of Appeals judge. I asked Eino if I could use his office to change clothes before my interview. He agreed and told me for the first time that the only two other persons to be interviewed for the job were himself and another good friend of mine, L. Ray Haire, also a Court of Appeals judge, and also a former fishing buddy. Both of them were Republicans and I was a Democrat. Judge Castro was a Democrat.

My interview by the nine-member commission was to

be the first interview of the day, and it was to be held in the
Supreme Court conference room. As it was summertime
in Phoenix, I was wearing a cool blue and white pinstripe
seersucker sport jacket. When I returned to Jacobsen's office
after my interview, he asked me what questions the commission members had asked and I told him. His interview for
appointment to the same Supreme Court position was to be
next. Eino said he had forgotten to bring a sport coat, and
asked if I would I loan him mine. I agreed, and he put it on.
Although Eino was about my height, he was quite a bit larger
in the middle than I was at the time, and so he had a several
inch gap in the front that could not be covered. Eino proceeded to the interview, armed with helpful knowledge of the
questions to be asked, and my sport coat. After the interview,
Eino came back and thanked me for preparing him for the
questions, and returned my jacket. Ray Haire, also a Court
of Appeals judge who was the third person seeking the same
position, said he didn't have a sport jacket either that day,
and asked if he could use mine. I agreed, but it looked
even odder on him than it did on Jacobson, as he was considerably shorter and smaller than I was, and the sleeves of
the jacket came down over his hands. Also, on him the
shoulders of the jacket looked like they had football pads
under them. At any rate, Ray Haire went to his interview also
armed with the questions the commission asked and my sport
jacket. I have always wondered what the selection commission thought when they saw three successive applicants come

in wearing the same type of jacket, although it only fit one of them.

That afternoon I flew back to Denver and completed my teaching obligation. I was called the next day by a member of the Selection Commission. The Governor had received the three names and had advised the Selection Commission that I would be appointed to the Arizona Supreme Court to fill Justice Lockwood's vacancy. Joan and I were thrilled and honored that I would be selected for such an important position. The vacancy would not begin for some two months thereafter, in September. This left time for me to finish all of the cases on my docket that were under advisement, allow us time to put our home on the market and begin our search for suitable housing in Phoenix.

Joan went to Phoenix to begin house hunting. She met with a realtor whose father we knew from Yuma, and within a day found one she liked. She called me at the office. I was on the bench, but the call was important enough to interrupt the proceedings for a few minutes. Joan's first words after my "hello" were: "How much higher than the amount we agreed on can we afford to pay for our new home?" I asked why, and she told me she had found one she liked, and that it was in a nice area with citrus groves all around the subdivision, and it had a pool. It was a very comfortable three-bedroom, Spanish-style home at 321 East Marlette in Phoenix, north of Bethany Home Road. We lived in that home for 25 years thereafter.

Before we moved to Phoenix, I was officially sworn in as an Associate Justice of the Supreme Court in a ceremony held in Kingman in my own old courtroom. Chief Justice James "Duke" Cameron, Vice-Chief Justice Fred Struckmeyer and Associate Justice Jack D. H. Hays came to Kingman to participate in the ceremony. Also present was Governor Raul Castro. To have these great men take the time to come to Kingman to be involved was indeed an honor.

Our son Trey and his wife Ruth had their infant daughter, Brandee, in their arms at the ceremony. Our daughter Candy and her husband Scott Lander, were there also. The courtroom was packed, even the jury boxes, with old friends from Kingman, as well as members of the State Bar who I had gone to law school with. Also attending were some of the local lawyers and public officials of the county. It was a grand day for the Gordon clan. On that day, my fondest wish was that my mother and father had been able to be there to enjoy it with me. I think they were watching, though, and were proud.

John Frank, who was instrumental in my appointment, sent me a framed quotation from Abraham Lincoln that he made when he left Illinois to become President of the United States. John must have felt my leaving my hometown to come to Phoenix and the Supreme Court was analogous. The quotation was:

"My friends: No one, not in my situation, can appreciate my feeling of sadness at this parting. To this place, and the kindness of these people, I owe everything. Here I have lived a quarter of a century, and have passed from a young to an old man. Here my children have been born, and one is buried. I now leave, not knowing when or whether ever I may return, with a task before me greater than that which rested upon Washington. Without the assistance of that Divine Being who ever attended him, I cannot succeed. With that assistance, I cannot fail. Trusting in Him who can go with me, and remain with you, and be everywhere for good, let us confidently hope that all will yet be well. To His care commending you, as I hope your cares will commend me, I bid you an affection-ate farewell."

I felt that quotation was extremely appropriate for our family at that time.

9

ASSOCIATE JUSTICE AND VICE CHIEF JUSTICE, 1975 - 1987

We arrived in Phoenix on Labor Day weekend in September 1975. The temperature that day was 110 degrees Fahrenheit. Although our friends in Kingman were not happy that we were moving to Phoenix, they were a huge help in moving us. Elmer Butler, a land developer and good friend, provided his tractor, semi-trailer and driver to move our furniture. John Conrad, manager of the Ford Proving Ground in Yucca, personally drove a company flatbed truck with a lift gate to haul our refrigerator, freezer, washing machine and dryer. We had hired some temporary employees from Manpower to help us move the furniture inside. When all of us arrived at the appointed time, the house was locked and we could not get in. One of the Manpower men said it was a shame his brother, who was doing time in prison for burglary, wasn't there, as he could get by any lock system on that house. Coming from

Kingman where we didn't even bother to lock our doors, this made us a little apprehensive about Phoenix.

Our neighbor to the west, Will Anderson, vice president of Arizona Bank, came out to greet us. When he saw my gas powered lawn mower come out of the trailer, he jokingly told me that no homeowner in the neighborhood was allowed to do yard work. Will, an ardent golfer, said garden tools didn't fit his hands. He said Mr. Garcia did the mowing of the lawns in the neighborhood and I should avail myself of his services. We did, and Mr. Garcia and his family cared for our yard for the entire 25 years we lived in the Marlette house.

The real estate lady finally came and opened up the house for us and we were able to get moved in that afternoon with wonderful assistance from friends. It was the beginning of a whole new way of life for Joan and me, as well as our German shepherd dog Risa, then over ten years old. We were excited and eager to get to know "our new city."

I was also eager to learn about my new job. Even though I was not expected to start work on the Supreme Court for about two weeks, and my paycheck would not start until then, I wanted to visit with my new colleagues and see the court- room and judges' chambers where I would be working for the foreseeable future. The judges' chambers and Supreme Courtroom were then on the second floor of the Executive Tower on the west side of the Capitol grounds, just west of 17th Avenue and between Adams and Jefferson Streets.

I went to the court's offices and located Justice Lockwood's chambers. I peeked into the chambers door from the hallway, and saw Ms. Matilda Gaio, Justice Lockwood's secretary. Tillie was an attractive, divorced, middle-aged woman of Italian heritage who had no children. She had been with Justice Lockwood for many years and had mothered all Justice Lockwood's law clerks for the years they were there and afterwards.

I had not met Tillie before, but I guess she recognized me from newspaper pictures. She quickly jumped up from behind her desk and met me at the door, barring my entry. She introduced herself and then proceeded to tell me that I could not come in to the office as Justice Lockwood was still in her chambers finishing her cases and should not be disturbed. Tillie evidently felt my coming to work early might make the Justice feel she was being pressured to leave early. Although I tried to assure her that I was only there to say hello and to wish her well, Tillie insisted that I not go in. Tillie was very loyal and protective toward Justice Lockwood and would not allow her to be embarrassed by anyone. She became just as protective and loyal toward me over the many years she served as my secretary. Over ten years later, she married a psychiatrist and left Phoenix to be with her husband in his career treating mentally ill patients in military hospitals in Wyoming, Texas, and even in Prescott.

When I was allowed to take possession of my office, I found a very touching handwritten note left by Justice Lockwood, wherein she congratulated me on my being ap-

275

pointed to the court and wished me well in my new job.

Before being appointed to the court while still a Superior Court judge, I had been asked to sit with the Supreme Court to help decide several cases in which one of the justices had disqualified himself or herself. Those occasions had been at a time before the intermediate Court of Appeals of Arizona was created, and appeals from the Superior Court went directly to the Supreme Court. It was a great honor for a Superior Court judge to be asked to serve on special cases such as these. One of these early cases that I remember most was In re Harber's Estate. This case established law in Arizona requiring postnuptial agreements between husband and wife to be treated with special care in Arizona so that fraud, deceit and nondisclosure of assets would not cause harm to a trusting wife.

On that occasion, former Justice Charles Bernstein had recused himself and I sat with Justices Cameron, Struckmeyer, Hays and Lockwood. Of all the Superior Court judges in Arizona who were available, I had been given that privilege. I was even trusted to draft the opinion of the Court when it was decided. Being on that case and several others before my appointment and having been allowed to be the author of those opinions probably gave me favorable consideration by the later selection panel which sent my name to Governor Castro. This showed that I already had appellate judicial experience.

Those occasions also gave me insight as to how cases were discussed by the justices in conference before decisions were made as to who would author the opinions, what the deciding issues of law were in the cases, and how the Chief Justice ran the court.

Although I had this small amount of background knowledge and experience before my appointment, Justice Hays was kind enough after my appointment to be my mentor on other, more important matters that dealt with everyday workings of the court. Soon after coming on the Court, Justice Hays and his wife Dorothy invited Joan and me to their home for dinner. After the meal, Jack took me aside and spent the rest of the evening acquainting me with the many political and ideological differences that existed between the justices. This included background information on each justice, hot-button issues that could divert his support, and past personal situations that had caused dissension and even ill will among certain justices.

This information was invaluable. It made my work on the court much easier, knowing which approaches to each justice would or would not be the most appropriate for me to take when seeking support for my position on a case. Before coming on the court, I thought, perhaps naively, that all there was to deciding a case was to write up a draft and circulate it to the other judges.

Tillie Gaio was also very helpful in my first year on the Court. Being the new guy on the court, the media and organizations all over the state were curious as to what I was like, what my experience was, and what my judicial philosophy would be. At that time, and even now, judges are classified by the public as either being "liberal" or "conservative." Being liberal by some people's definition meant that those judges felt they were not obligated to abide by prior decisions or precedent of the court, or felt that when there was no legislation to cover a situation, the court should MAKE laws. Being conservative was just the opposite of being liberal.

I had never thought of rating myself as either liberal or conservative, and when asked, I believed myself to be neither, but rather a "moderate," a somewhat new term at the time.

Tillie helped me avoid a lot of bumps in the road before I became aware of some of those things for myself.

One day, soon after I had my office straightened out and my law clerks hired for the first year, I sat in my comfortable high-backed chair looking out over the courtyard of the Capitol building, pondering some decision I was about to make. It was then that I noticed for the first time how very quiet and isolated my new job was, compared to the hectic life of a trial judge. There was no line of townspeople outside my door like in Kingman, seeking free legal advice. There were no lawyers dropping in to visit. Very few telephone calls. The silence was almost deafening. I had heard others refer to appellate judges as having "retired to the ivory tower." It seemed to me that they were right.

For the first time I had the luxury of taking any amount of time I felt necessary to search for what my answer to important questions would be, and not having to make quick decisions, or shoot from the hip as a trial judge must do. I also had at my disposal two very intelligent recent graduates of law schools, law clerks, who were there to help in research and recommendations. Another resource available to the justices was a cadre of staff attorneys who worked for the Supreme Court who did synopses of petitions for review and special actions for the court, and even made recommendations to the court as to disposition of cases. My, what wonderful tools appellate judges had, compared to the trial judges who acted as the front line troops in the battlefield who had little time or backup to rely on. The analogy occurred to me that my new job was like being the commander of a submarine, looking through his periscope in the safety and invisibility of his submerged ship as he watched the infantry fight their way up the beaches through machine gun and cannon fire while landing on the beaches of Normandy.

My working hours were luxurious compared to that of a trial judge. I came to the office about 9:00 a.m., had lunch downtown, and came home around 5:00 p.m. As an associate justice, I rarely had to bring work home. So Joan and I had time to explore our new city, savor its luxuries, and become acquainted with new friends.

Soon after we set up housekeeping in the fall of 1975, it was time for us to vote in the general election in November. We studied our voting pamphlet and found our polling place a few blocks from our home. As we came in, the ladies who were voting officials asked our names, looked up our registration, and asked us to sign the voting list. As we did, one of the

ladies said to us, "You are new here, aren't you?" I replied that
we were. She said, "I think I know you. Wait now, I am sure
I do." This prompted a little boost of ego in me, as there had
been considerable publicity about my coming on the court
in local newspapers, and it was nice to know that someone
in our neighborhood knew we were important additions to
the community. She stroked her chin for a moment. Her col-
league said, "Come on, now. You told us you knew everyone
in this precinct." The first lady thought a moment longer, and
finally said, "I know. You are the window washer at McDonald's down the street." Whereupon my ego was deflated like a
punctured balloon.

Joan and I were invited to quite a few dinner parties by
prominent lawyers, which gave us an opportunity to get to
know some of the really important lawyers and business
people in town. John Frank, the senior partner of Lewis and
Roca, saw to it that we were given complimentary memberships to the Heard Museum and the Phoenix Art Museum,
two of the most wonderful opportunities granted to us. We
have continued our memberships in those organizations ever
since. We loved it in Phoenix.

One time, Phillip Von Ammon, a senior partner in the prestigious law firm of Fennemore Craig, and whose wife Barbara,
who was the Mayor of the Town of Paradise Valley, invited us
to a dinner at their home. Joan took the call, answered that
we would be honored, and wrote it down in our appointment book. The only problem was she wrote it down for the

280

wrong week. On the day we thought we were to go, we were running late because we had attended the investiture ceremony of Mary Schroeder, a new U. S. Circuit Court of Appeals judge. We called to tell the Von Ammons we would be a few minutes late. Phil very coolly said to Joan, "No hurry, Joan, because that dinner was last week." Were we embarrassed! I wonder who the other guests were and what their opinion of us was after we didn't show up. Phil never mentioned it in the future, and neither did we.

Duke Cameron, my first Chief Justice, was an excellent administrator for the court. He not only took his share of the opinions to write, but he also felt that our court should play a more aggressive role in administering the lower courts in Arizona, which is specifically mandated by the Arizona constitution. Prior to the time I came on the court, the Supreme Court had been quite lax in enforcing rules of procedure on Superior Court judges throughout the state, and also on the recently created Court of Appeals. Duke was very active in committees of the American Bar Association's Judicial Administration Division, and in fact later became Chairman of that division. In that capacity, Duke became aware of many changes that had been made in rules of procedure and evidence that had been made by Supreme Courts in other states. He felt we should update our rules and delegated to each of us different rules to research and put before the court for consideration. This required our working with the State Bar of Arizona to make sure the changes proposed were appropriate for Arizona's law practice and courts. I was given considerable responsibility in that respect and in performing my duties became quite familiar with some of the most active trial lawyers in the state, as well as committee chairs of the State Bar.

The Arizona Supreme Court has discretionary jurisdiction over most appeals in Arizona. That means that once the Superior Court has ruled in a civil case and the Arizona Court of Appeals has reviewed the case and decided whether the Superior Court's decision was correct or not, the Arizona Supreme Court can refuse to hear a further appeal of the case to our court. The Supreme Court merely enters an order denying the Petition for Review in the case, without further comment. In fact, in civil cases, up until the time of my retirement, only five percent of the civil and criminal cases decided by the Court of Appeals are accepted for review by the Arizona Supreme Court. Denying petition for review merely meant that our court was satisfied that the matter had received an appropriate appellate review by the Court of Appeals and that we were leaving its decision as controlling in the case.

In the five percent of the cases we accepted for review, some were accepted because there were conflicting decisions between the two Courts of Appeals in Arizona on some point involved in the case, or the Supreme Court did accept the case for review because a majority of the Court felt either the Court of Appeals was wrong in its legal reasoning, or had not gone far enough in doing its duty of fully explaining the law

on the subject in the case at hand. The Supreme Court's decision then was meant to declare the correct law in the case.
On matters of pure interpretation of State law or Arizona
Constitution, the Arizona Supreme Court is the court of last
resort for the litigants in civil cases. There is no further appeal
to the federal courts on those decisions. A lot of people do
not know this.

As I recall, the Supreme Court is required to accept jurisdiction in only three types of cases: disputes between Arizona
counties, election contests and cases in which the death penalty has been imposed in a criminal case. Although death penalty cases were few in number compared to the other cases the
court is deciding, they are the ones the court spends the most
time in deciding. In civil cases, each justice normally does not
read the entire record from the courts below, which include
the pleadings of the parties, motions, preliminary decisions,
the depositions of the witnesses, or the court reporter's transcript of the evidence taken at trial. He or she relies on his or
her law clerks and the staff attorney assigned to the case to do
an analysis of these and tell him or her whether they do or do
not support the claims made by counsel for the appellant in
the appellate briefs.

In death penalty cases, however, at least when I was on the
court, each justice made it a practice to do a complete review
of all the record below. After all, each justice understands that
his or her vote in the case may very well determine whether
the defendant lives or dies. In my own practice, I spent two

or three times the number of hours on death penalty cases assigned to me as I did on civil cases.

That brings me to my thoughts on the death penalty. While a trial judge, in qualifying a jury in a murder case, it was my duty to excuse any potential juror from service in the case if he or she had a religious or other conscientious opinion against the death penalty and felt that he or she could not put that opinion aside and not be influenced by it in his or her deliberations as a juror in that case. I often wished I had the same option to excuse myself from hearing the case, because as a trial judge I heard several first degree murder cases in which I was called upon to impose the death penalty. In those days, the judge, not the jury, made the final decision whether the defendant would get life imprisonment or die in the gas chamber, not the jury as is now the case as required by the United States Supreme Court.

Very few murderers are serial murderers, or ones who would commit more than the one killing that he or she perpetrated. Usually, killers killed in what some call the "heat of passion" or on sudden provocation wherein the pressures weighing down upon him or her at the time were more than he or she could bear. Some studies have shown that after being paroled from prison for first-degree murder, most defendants do not commit any further crimes, much less additional killings. Also, putting a defendant to death for killing someone, in my opinion, does not have the effect of deterring others from killing. If it did, murders would cease. The state of Texas

284

executes more criminal defendants than any other state and murders still continue in that state.

If premeditated murderers were put away in prison for the rest of their natural lives, without possibility of parole, society would be adequately protected, and I believe fewer convicted killers would continue their expensive and time consuming appeals through both the state and federal courts for years and years after their conviction. In each case where the death penalty has been ordered, millions of dollars are spent in public funds to provide years of lawyers' services, judges and juries work, and repeated appeals in both state and federal courts in order to exhaust every state and federal potential constitutional hearing available to the defendant. In my opinion, life imprisonment without possibility of parole, would solve a lot of problems at much less cost and would relieve the court system of much of the congestion that it now suffers.

But at the time I was trying cases, I had taken an oath upon my being sworn in as a judge to "faithfully and impartially uphold the Constitution and laws of the United States and the Constitution and laws of the State of Arizona" in the performance of my duties. The death penalty was a part of the Constitution and laws of Arizona when I served, and I was bound to faithfully and impartially uphold and administer it. Now, most of the responsibility of whether the convicted first degree murderer lives or dies must be borne by the jury in the case. That disturbing decision is no longer the primary responsibility of the judge trying the case.

In Arizona, the ultimate decision as to the justness of each sentence imposed by judges in Arizona rests on the shoulders of the five members of the Arizona Supreme Court. Whether you are a trial judge or a judge on the highest court of the state, the type of sentence that should be imposed in criminal cases is one of the most agonizing and heart rending decisions a judge can make, as each judge knows the life prisoners live in our penal institutions.

Some people feel that a prison experience should be torturous and barbaric, as when a criminal commits a crime he or she "loses all his civil rights." "Lock 'em up and throw away the key" is their answer to everything. It would be wonderful if this philosophy was effective. The truth is, however, that it is not. 95% or more of people who serve time in prisons are ultimately "maxed out" or released at the end of their term. What has their prison experience done to change their criminal tendencies? Rarely do they come out better off than they were when they went in for several reasons: first, after the first few years in jail, they become hardened cynics, critical of all authority and looking for ways to get even with the system. Second, somewhere around 2/3rds of those in prison are functionally illiterate when they entered prison. That means they could not read above the 3rd or 4th grade level, and therefore could not get a job or hold one for more than a few weeks either before or after they had a prison experience. Third, over 80% of prisoners are there because the crime they were involved in was caused by their drug or alcohol addiction.

Some prisons are now trying to address prisoners' problems with programs to reduce drug and alcohol addiction, illiteracy and mental problems. I believe these are the most effective programs if pursued far enough. But it is my experience in Arizona that not enough of this is being done, and if done, not done long enough to be effective. More emphasis is placed on keeping the prisoners in secure surroundings than in promoting skills that will give them a fair chance to succeed once they are released from prison. On release from prison, a prisoner is given about $50 and a new suit of clothes. He is then dumped on the street, frequently at a homeless shelter. You can guess where that $50 goes in most cases – to the nearest bar or liquor store.

It is hard enough for an ex-con to find a job after release as employers have a choice not to hire a business risk when other applicants have clean records. Add to this an untreated addiction to drugs or alcohol, or an inability to read and you have an almost insurmountable barrier to becoming employed, especially when most released prisoners have no support group to take over upon release, such as a supportive functional family or affordable private treatment.

After years of sentencing defendants as a trial judge, and years of reviewing sentences imposed by others, I became convinced that our penal system with its focus being primarily on punishment rather than rehabilitation of its inmates has doomed our society to suffer the disgrace and expense of an ever increasing spiral of failure as our country's incarceration rate, as compared to those of other countries, has proven. I will get to my efforts in changing this focus later.

While Jack D. H. Hays was Chief Justice, sometime before I came on the court, he had a run-in with the Arizona legislature that caused him to refuse to have further communications with either the House or the Senate. Before that time, a "State of the Judiciary" address in written form was sent to each House explaining the programs and financial needs of the courts. Hays' attitude created a chasm between two of Arizona's branches of government that continued through Cameron's and Holohan's administrations as Chief Justices. I always felt that this caused problems, especially for the Court's budget, which had to be approved by the both Houses of the legislature. Because of the lack of the Supreme Court's input, both Houses became increasingly ignorant about what the courts in Arizona do and why, even though several of the court's programs, such as foster care for children, victims' rights, and probation in criminal cases, among others were legislatively created.

This lack of knowledge about the Supreme Court and its needs made members of the legislature more reluctant to fund the court's budget, which included not only the financial needs of the Supreme Court, but those of the two Courts of Appeals and half of the budget of all the Superior Courts in Arizona. In retaliation for some of the Arizona Supreme Court's decisions that the legislature felt was unfair to them, such as declaring some of their legislation as unconstitutional, the legislature sometimes would cut the budget of the court in significant ways, sometimes requiring the cutting of programs.

The National Center for State Courts commissioned a survey by the Yankelovich firm to determine what the public in the United States thought about the court system in our country. The results were delivered in 1977, and were shocking. The public had less confidence in the courts than almost all public institutions, below the media, Congress, and others, being rated somewhere around undertakers and used car salesmen. This was a wake-up call for me and for a lot of judges who felt that courts suffered this loss of confidence because most of the public was truly ignorant about what the courts were required to do and under what circumstances. I remember many times at meetings I attended, people commented, "why don't the courts make it a law that ***" when they should know that courts don't make laws; legislatures do. Somehow the course in civics given in our country has not been effective in teaching the public about the works of each of the separate branches of government established by the United States Constitution and the laws of the states.

This lack of understanding kindled a desire in me to try to improve the public's understanding of the work of the courts. I served on several committees of the American Bar Association designed to improve the image of the judiciary in the United States. I even wrote an article published in the American Bar Association Journal entitled "The Image of the Judiciary, Does It Need a Facelift?" I also wrote an article published in the Law Journal of the Law School at Arizona State University entitled "The Care and Feeding of Judges." These articles were designed to encourage lawyers to use their speaking opportunities to enlighten the public about the judiciary. Many other judges across our country started similar projects. One was a New York trial judge who formed a committee to make immediate response to unjust criticism of the courts published in the media. This was somewhat effective, but difficult to do within the time to properly answer the incorrect information published.

By the time I was Vice-Chief Justice of the Court, I had expressed an interest in mending some fences between the legislature and the courts. Chief Justice Holohan put me in charge of presenting the court's budget to the various legislative committees each year, such as the Judiciary Committee and the Finance Committee in both the Arizona House and Senate. Each of these committees gave us about an hour to present our request which had been presented previously in written form. The Supreme Court's Executive Director, Bill McDonald, made the factual presentation each time and I would be present to answer any questions the panel members had.

From the very first time, most of the members of the committees seemed to appreciate that one of the highest judicial officers in the state was taking the time to come to their House to be available to answer questions that they might have and had never received official answers before. In my naiveté,

I had not realized how dangerous a position this was for me: for example, it was possible that there may have been some committee members who were particularly peeved about some recent decisions of the Court. But in the years that I did this, even through the years as Chief Justice, I never received discourteous reception or comments from any of the legislative committee members. In fact, I think many future good relations came of it. During these meetings, however, I discovered how very little these committee members knew about Arizona's court system and found some ways in which to educate them, tactfully, and without publicly embarrassing them.

In the years while I was serving as Vice-Chief Justice, the early 1980s, the television media was pushing hard to be able to cover courtroom proceedings. At that time, and to the present, the federal courts do not allow video or even audio recording of their proceedings, at any level, and only one state, Colorado, under Chief Justice Pringle, allowed trial court coverage by live TV, and under strict supervision by the courts. To first test the water, at my suggestion, the court allowed a one-year trial period of TV in the appellate courts in Arizona. The TV media agreed to our rules that allowed only one stationary camera to be in the courtroom, with outside feed to any interested television channels. The media had to provide noiseless cameras, without flash, noiseless sound equipment, and the operators of the cameras had to wear business attire (white shirt, tie and at least a sport jacket). The dress code caused the greatest stir, but was reluctantly agreed to.

The live televising of appellate arguments was eagerly awaited and appreciated by the video media, and many arguments were filmed in the first few months. However, soon after, the TV industry gave up on filming appellate arguments as they considered them too dull and arcane. Not enough action. No witnesses or courtroom melodrama. What TV wanted was access to the juicy criminal trials or divorce cases.

The Arizona Supreme Court found that during the few filmings in our courtroom, the presence of the camera caused no disruption, or even exaggeration of counsel's actions. Therefore, we granted a one-year video and audio experiment in the trial courts in cases where the trial judge, in his or her discretion, felt that in any particular case being heard, it would not be detrimental to the presentation of the case or the jury's deliberations. Then after the experiment, our court did a survey of judges, lawyers, litigants, jurors, witnesses and courtroom personnel to find out their opinions as to the effect of the presence of the camera on the quality of justice rendered in their case.

Questionnaires crafted specifically to each group of participants in the trial were sent to them within two weeks of their experience in the trial. Then the results were collated and studied by a committee consisting of law professors, lawyers, media people, judges, and laymen, and their report was given to our court. The cost of this survey was surprisingly low, as we used volunteers from various industries to handle various phases of it. The results of the study was surprising to most trial judges, but not to me. Most of each group surveyed agreed that the presence of the camera did not affect the quality of justice rendered in the case. They saw no exaggerated conduct on the part of the lawyers, no intimidation of the witnesses, and no judges playing to the media. There were some objections, but most were minor and were handled by amending the rules. Jurors are not to be identified or visualized during the trial, for example. This reduced any feelings of intimidation on the part of a juror to serve or to render a strong verdict.

All in all, the "TV in the Courtroom" experiment had been successful, and the rule of the Supreme Court allowing it under its conditions has become permanent. Juvenile and divorce cases are excluded from the rule. Arizona's courts became one of the first in the nation to allow full, live coverage of trials in cases deemed appropriate by the presiding judge of the case. Therein lay the most important discretion -- the judge's. If any party feels that TV would interfere with the presentation of their case or prejudice them, the cameras do not come into court. I do not believe any judge in Arizona would have allowed the televising of the murder trial of O. J. Simpson, presided over by Judge Ito in Los Angeles, California. When a celebrity defendant who can afford five or six lawyers in court to defend him, and whose lawyers are intent on creating a circus in the court, the case should not be televised, and would not be in Arizona.

Another innovation in the administration of the Supreme Court that came about as a result of my leadership on the Court was in revising the rule-making powers of the court. The Supreme Court regulates procedure and appeals in most courts in Arizona, as well as admission to the State Bar and discipline of lawyers and judges. Before revision, rules of the Arizona Supreme Court were adopted without public input by two methods: the court on its own motion and for reasons of its own passed it and put it into effect; or the Court passed the rule at the request of the State Bar of Arizona. No one else, either private or corporate, had authority to propose a rule for consideration by the court. I thought to myself, why not allow any member of the public, the police, the legislature, lawyers outside of State Bar Committees, title companies, any business propose a rule or a modification of a rule of procedure of the Arizona Supreme Court? What would that hurt? It would certainly make all members of the public feel they had the power at least to suggest a change in the court's rules that would make the courts more accessible.

At my suggestion, the court adopted a rule that allowed anyone to petition to adopt a new rule of the Arizona Supreme Court, or to modify an existing one, setting forth the reasons for the rule change and the need therefor. The court then refers copies of the request to the State Bar, the legislature, other courts, and the general public for their comments, suggestions, objections, etc., to be filed within a certain time. If, after receiving all comments and suggestions, the court wishes to gain additional information, it may set a time for a hearing and allow suggestions or argument at that time for or against such rule or modification. Then the court will decide whether to adopt the rule or modify it. This change, in my opinion, has greatly increased the public's awareness of the rule making power of the court, and has perhaps increased its confidence in the process.

In the last year of his being Chief Justice, Bill Holohan graciously gave me permission to go a training conference with my court administrator, Bill McDonald, to learn how to work together when I became Chief Justice. The conference was put on by the National Center for the State Courts, in conjunction with the Conference of Chief Justices of the United States. It was a several day conference held in Phoenix. I learned the workings and needs of the Court Administrator's department and Bill learned more about me, my goals, and my personality. It was a very good conference, and resulted in a joint working agreement between Bill and me as to what we hoped I could achieve during the five years that I would be Chief Justice. I think Bill saw firsthand that I intended to be an innovative and pro-active Chief Justice, and that I wished to accomplish more than he knew was possible in five years, which was the normal term of a Chief Justice. But the two of us emerged from the seminar in agreement as to a working list of projects and directions that we wished to have become reality. I took that agreement and list to my colleagues on the court after I became Chief Justice and had them approve all the items before I began. They readily agreed.

I was given so many great opportunities to prepare myself and my Court Administrator to be a hands-on progressive Chief Executive Officer of the Arizona Supreme Court. I hope the Arizona Bar, as well as the public, feel that I was a positive influence in making our courts more understood and accessible, as well as more of a working partner in our state government.

10

CHIEF JUSTICE,
1987 - 1992

B The Chief Justice of the Supreme Court of Arizona is chosen by the members of that court, usually on the basis of seniority on the court. The job of Chief Justice of the Arizona Supreme Court is not only being the person in charge of seeing to the business of that court, the deciding of cases that come before it, moves smoothly, efficiently and as speedily as possible, but also being the Chief Executive Officer of all the courts of Arizona, including the Court of Appeals, Superior Courts, Justice of the Peace Courts, and City Magistrate Courts in Arizona. In addition, all probation officers in the Superior Court system are considered state officers, and thus under the administrative control of the Arizona Supreme Court. The Supreme Court also has the responsibility to regulate the admission of all new members of the State Bar of Arizona, and has the last word in disciplining them. Also, if judges misbehave or do not follow their Canons of Ethics, they are investigated by a special Commission on Judicial Conduct. After making a determination of improper judicial conduct, this commission can recommend sanctions against the judge, including reprimand, suspension or removal from office, which the Supreme Court could then impose.

As I have mentioned, one of my hopes and goals in being Chief Justice was to make the courts in Arizona better understood, more respected, and more accessible to the public, both physically and financially. Before I was elected Chief Judge, I developed a working agenda that pointed me in this direction, prepared by me and approved by my Court Administrator. When it was approved by my colleagues on the Court, I was off and running. But how was I to accomplish all of these things?

I knew of the availability of federal funds for improving the administration of justice, and I applied for and got some. My first project was to create the Commission on the Courts in Arizona. I appointed a 150-member commission to make an in depth study of the courts in Arizona. I knew that any suggested changes made by me or the court alone had little chance for approval if legislative approval was needed. I needed the well-researched recommendations of a broad-based public commission to convince the legislature and other judges that these changes needed to be made. The commission first was to compare Arizona's courts to those in other states and countries. In doing this, we had to find out what other states and countries did that was better than what we did, and to make recommendations on how to achieve the modernization of Arizona's courts to make them more accessible, understood and respected.

This Commission was made up of people from all areas of the state, from all occupations, all persuasions, balanced in political views and even with critics of the system partici-pating. We had lawyers, doctors, law professors, ministers, a lawyer-nun, police, business people, media representatives, legislators, mayors, city council members, members of county boards of supervisors, judges, law enforcement officers and every other job I can think of. The Commission was co-chaired by two very well-known and respected people, Eddie Basha, the grocery store magnate, and Jack Whiteman, of Empire Machinery, both from Phoenix. The Commission was divided into several areas of inquiry, each with a chairperson in charge. The Commission and its subcommittees were to do their research, hold hearings in order to obtain public input, and make recommendations for change within a certain period. Then the recommendations were to be printed, bound and submitted to the court for approval.

I chaired many sub-committee meetings as the project proceeded. The challenge to modernize the court system in Arizona was eagerly accepted and diligently pursued by all Commission members. They did their job well and promptly, and returned with 50 recommendations for change, of which the Arizona Supreme Court adopted all but three as I recall. I still have a copy of the Commission's Report and Recom-

mendations. Before I left the court, I was advised that 80%
percent of the recommendations had been accomplished,
either by court rule or legislative enactment. This was one
of my greatest accomplishments as Chief Justice, and one of
which I am quite proud. The public in general probably is
not aware of the changes made in the system as the result
of the Commission's work, but lawyers and judges knew. I
received many honors for this project, including ones from the
American Bar Association, the State Bar of Arizona, and the
Maricopa County Bar.

My colleagues on the Court: Vice-Chief Justice Stanley
Feldman, James Duke Cameron, Jack D. H. Hays, and William Holohan must have realized that my heart was more in
the field of court administration than the mundane task of
writing opinions for the court, as this new aggressive plan for
revision of the judicial system was taking a great deal of my
time. They therefore took on more than their shares of court
responsibilities in writing opinions so that I could pursue my
quest of improving the court system. They were great supporters, who although philosophically diverse, were a team
united to improve justice in Arizona.

Before taking that job, I explained to Joan that being Chief
Justice would add about 40% percent more work to my usual
duties, and that we probably would have little or no time to
ourselves during the next five years. She was gracious in ac-
cepting this. I promised at that time, however, when my five-
year term as Chief Justice was over, I would retire from the

300

court and we would spend more time together thereafter. I would be 63 years old then, and with my family's health history, I felt I might not be around too many years after that.

My prediction as to the demands on my time was nearly correct. I did a great deal of travelling around the state to different courts, and around the country on meetings of Conference of Chief Justices, or appellate judge seminars. Joan accompanied me on most trips. If we drove, she drove the car as I studied appellate briefs or prepared outlines of speeches I was going to make. I used her as a sounding board often to get her feelings as to whether certain changes in court rules would meet with favor. She was a good indicator of public reaction and a valued helper in my duties. Joan truly enabled my work on the Supreme Court. Without her patience, tolerance, encouragement, and sometimes consoling, I would never have been able to do the work or accomplish the things that I did.

One of the most interesting trips that Joan and I took soon after becoming Chief Justice was to attend my first Conference of Chief Justices, which that year was held in Rapid City, South Dakota. Joan and I decided to drive to that conference, as the trip would cover areas we hadn't seen. As an aside, I wanted to see the newly refurbished Navajo Supreme Court building in Window Rock, Arizona, which was on the way. I had heard that the courtroom of their Supreme Court had a marvelous series of paintings depicting their culture and system of justice. I wrote to Chief Justice Tom Tso of the Navajo Supreme Court, whom I did not know, and asked if

301

it would be possible for me to see "their courtroom" on our way to the Conference, and told him of the day of our arrival. The Arizona Supreme Court Administrator, Bill MacDonald was also going to the conference at Rapid City, so he accompanied us on our stop in Window Rock. What I did not know at the time was that no previous Chief Justice of the Arizona Supreme Court had ever come to the Navajo Supreme Court on any occasion, formal or informal.

Chief Justice Tso construed my letter of inquiry as one seeking a formal meeting with the members of his court. The Navajo Supreme Court was the highest judicial body of the Navajo Nation, but its powers were limited by the Navajo Tribal Council, which could overrule any decision made by the Court. Because of this, the Chief Justice had a special role: he spent a great deal of time developing and maintaining a working relationship with the Tribal Council, trying mightily to maintain friendly ties between the court and the Council. He rarely had time to write opinions for his court. He really did a great job in maintaining whatever separation of powers that existed between the legislative and judicial branches of government of the Navajo Nation. Tso was not a lawyer, as that is not a requirement to be on any level of court in Navajo Land.

One of his two associate justices was named Homer Bluehouse. Justice Bluehouse was a specialist in the common law developed historically in each and all of the Chapters of the Navajo Nation. A "Chapter" is the equivalent of a county in

Arizona. But each has the power to establish variations of the law of their Chapter consistent with the overall law developed by the Tribal Council and the Supreme Court. Whenever a case came to the Supreme Court involving a Chapter decision, Justice Bluehouse would normally be the author of the opinion of the court in that case.

The third justice of the Navajo Supreme Court was a Navajo who was a graduate lawyer, who had practiced in New Mexico for some years, and had served as a Judicial Clerk to the Chief Justice of the New Mexico Supreme Court. His name was Raymond Austin. Justice Austin, with his legal background, usually wrote the opinions of the Navajo Supreme Court which had to do with statutory construction of the laws passed by the Navajo Tribal Council.

Chief Justice Tso graciously invited us to visit, but we were not aware that he considered our visit to be one of State. We were dressed casually when we arrived, and unaware that Tso had gathered all his judges and representatives from the Tribal Council, and arranged a tour of their courts, with representative judges of trial courts, intermediate court of appeals and the Supreme Court. We were then treated to a luncheon at a restaurant with several media people in attendance. At lunch and after witnessing some traditional Indian dances, we were officially welcomed by the Chief Justice to the Navajo legal and judicial system. Joan was given a beautiful shadow box silver bracelet with turquoise, and I was given an inlaid bola tie. Judge Tso gave a warm speech pointing out the importance of our visit – the first meeting of two important courts and the building of a bridge of friendship that he hoped would lead to continued friendship and cooperation. I am sure he never imagined what his invitation later spawned.

In conversation after his speech, Judge Tso got around to asking me whether our court, the Arizona Supreme Court, took judicial knowledge of the decisions of his court. I mentioned that this would be difficult, because Arizona lawyers and judges would not know or be able to find what the law in Navajo Land would be, as their court's decisions were not regularly published and distributed in Arizona, and were not included in published periodicals such as West Publishing, or Lexis. He thought a minute and realized that was true. Even if the Arizona Supreme Court wanted to follow the latest decisions of the Navajo Supreme Court on any topic, such as grounds for divorce, division of marital property, child custody, or spousal or child support, we could not be sure we had the latest decision on any of those points. I decided we had to do something about that.

On my return to Phoenix, I spoke with Dean Paul Bender, then Dean of the Arizona State University School of Law, and he volunteered the cooperation of the Law School to become the official depository of the decisions of all of the highest courts of all Native American courts in Arizona. This was eagerly accepted by Chief Justice Tso, and many other Arizona tribal courts. As far as I know, Arizona was the first state to arrange such a mutual recognition of the decisions of the highest courts of Anglo and Indian courts. Judges and lawyers in Arizona now know how to find the law on topics, which might have to be applied in Arizona cases, or in Indian courts.

As Chief Justice, I allowed the Hopi policemen and judges to attend Arizona Judicial education programs at no charge. This was done at the request of Hopi trial Judge Delfred Leslie, whose family lived on the Second Mesa north of Flagstaff. Later, other tribes took advantage of the same educational possibilities.

As a kindness for inviting Hopi policemen and judges to meetings, Judge Leslie invited Joan and me to attend a spring-time traditional homecoming dance called the Bean Dance. Technically, the Indians allow Anglos to watch dances on the sidelines, but Anglos rarely do, as the time of the dances is not published and only the Indians know when they are going to take place. The name "Bean Dance" does not give a clue as to what this particular dance represents. At a certain age, I think at eight or nine years, Hopi boys are required to make some promises as to how they will live in the future – being good and faithful to their culture, and becoming warriors, etc. Then each year at the Bean Dance, the Ogre Kachina, a truly frightening tall Indian with a gruesome black and red headdress and a huge toothy mouth with fake blood around it, would visit the homes of each of those children to make sure the child had kept his promises for that year. The Ogre Kachina would come up the street on this high mesa dressed in gaudy colored paint, rattling her turtle shell gourds tied to her knees, wielding a huge machete, and chanting. The story is that if it is found that the boy has not kept his promises, Ogre Kachina will take the child away and eat him. Ogre Kachina is surrounded by Indians painted with black and white stripes. These are called "Koshares" and are clowns who dance along with Ogre Kachina and slap carpenters' metal saws on the sides of the mud buildings, making weird sounds and chanting.

The Hopi judge who invited us to this ceremony had his family provide us lunch in their home on the mesa. He had a six-year-old son, Juan, who had made his promise last year that he was ready to become a warrior. He had killed a sparrow with his BB gun and to prove it, he had his mother wrap it and keep it in their freezer for the occasion. He was the cutest thing you ever saw. He looked very much like children that DeGrazia painted. He had huge round, black eyes with hair that stuck straight up all over his head.

This annual ceremony was so important to the tribe that Hopi families from all over the world came back to re-live part of this validating occasion they had previously been involved in previously. The judge told us that there were only certain things he was allowed to tell us about this ceremony, as most of it was very secret. His father was the Chief of the Second Mesa, and was a highly honored person.

Sometime after introducing us to his family, the Hopi Judge left us, as did all the men from the homes. We assume they went into the underground kiva to be a part of the ceremony. This left only females in the homes with the children when Ogre Kachina came.

As we ate lunch, you could hear the Ogre Kachina coming up the street, visiting the homes of the other boys. Juan became nervous, knowing that he would have to face this very ominous creature at the front door, and if the Ogre Kachina did not believe his answers, he might get eaten. Juan decided to hide under the table, then in the closet, and then in other places. His mother told him that would do no good as the Ogre Kachina would find him. When Ogre Kachina arrived at our house, we were told we would be allowed to watch, but we had to go into the bedroom and watch through the door partially opened. When Ogre Kachina arrived, with saws slapping the walls and chants being sung just outside, Juan's mother answered the door and Juan reluctantly came forward. After some words we could not understand, Ogre Kachina grabbed the little boy and started to pull him out the door. His mother grabbed his legs and pulled back entreating the Ogre Kachina not to take him. The boy was terrified, crying, and shouting, "I'll be good! I'll be good! I promise to go to school and do my homework." Still Ogre Kachina kept pulling until Juan's grandmother brought out a case of soft drinks and gave it to the Kachina, who handed it back to the Koshares, who disappeared with it.

Then more conversation between Kachina, mother and boy, and with another shriek, the Kachina grabbed the child again and started out the door. Mother again grabbed the

307

child again and the tug of war resumed with much yelling and chanting. Grandmother again came out, this time with a slab of bacon, which caused the Kachina to put the child down and the Koshares were given this gift again. More discussion, more shrieking, more tugging and pulling, more things like loaves of bread and dozens of eggs all passed to Ogre Kachina until she appeared to be assuaged.

I am not sure whether the frozen sparrow had anything to do with it or not, but the stressful situation was over for Juan. While all this was going on, Joan and I noticed a 10 or 12-inch black and white TV in the bedroom that was showing the actual launch of the Challenger spacecraft, which exploded before our eyes, killing the astronauts inside. As Joan has said, we felt we had one foot in an ancient world and at the same time the other in the space age. Those were moments we shall never forget.

When we returned to Phoenix, I told Dean Bender about the ceremony, and because he and his wife were interested in Native American culture, he pleaded with me to get him and his wife, Margy, invited to the next ceremony that we might get an invitation to. Judge Leslie did invite us to a beautiful "Longhair" ceremony, again on the Second Mesa. Paul and Margy went with us and we introduced him to Judge Leslie. Bender was so enthralled with Judge Leslie and his court system that he saw to it that one of his second year law students spent an internship on the Hopi Reservation, helping Judge Leslie on cases and also making suggestions as to how to make the court system there more efficient and accessible.

The result of these serendipitous events was that Bender saw to it that Native American college students were encouraged to go to law school at ASU through a tutorial program and student loans. In addition, the law school at ASU began teaching subjects on Indian Law to Anglo, as well as Indian students. Also, Bender created a Native American Judicial Educational Program at ASU Law School. Judge Canby, a Ninth Circuit U.S. Court of Appeals Judge, formerly a law professor at ASU Law School, and I once taught a class at the law school for Native American appellate judges from all over Arizona. I had no idea these tribes had progressed so far in their judicial systems. And although few were lawyers, they were very skilled at their craft, and asked very intelligent questions, pointing out some of the good and the bad points of our Anglo system.

My experience with Native Tribes and their judicial systems and what happened after our trip to Window Rock for a "visit" to the Navajo Supreme Court made me feel very good about what good things can come about if you try.

During my terms as a Superior Court Judge, as well as my time on the State Supreme Court, it became very apparent to me that illiteracy was a big factor in recidivism. People would serve their time in prison or jail, and when they were released they went right back to their old criminal ways. We discovered that most prisoners could not read above a 3rd grade level, so when they were released from prison they could not read want ads for available jobs, nor could they read bus schedules to get to a job or interview.

Computers were a fairly recent innovation for learning to read, so at my instigation, Dave Byers (a court employee), researched the programs that were available and helped to start a learning-to-read program sponsored by the Supreme Court. It began first in Tucson, and then in other parts of the state. It was so successful that parents and siblings of the prisoners wanted to take the program as well. The program has since expanded statewide and continues to this day, with 34 learning labs, three of which bear my name.

The first George Bush was President of the United States at that time. His wife, Barbara, was very much interested in literacy. The President had a program called "Points of Light" where he honored different people at the White House for their contributions to society. I was among the fortunate few that he chose to honor. In 1993, our whole family – Joan, son Trey, his wife Ruth and their daughter Brandee, our daughter Candy, her husband Scott and their children Scotty and Elisha, were guests in the White House for drinks and refreshments and a wonderful ceremony where I was honored and given a medal and citation listing the literacy center accomplishments. What a night! The Marine Band played, and some members of the U.S. Supreme Court attended, including Sandra Day O'Connor. Many U.S. Senators and Representatives were there as well. It was truly a once-in-a-lifetime experience. Although I have received many awards, both state and national, this was a never-to-be forgotten highlight of my career.

Almost everyone has in his or her lifetime a "defining moment." I would have hoped that I would be most remembered as the leader of the Arizona Supreme Court in wide-ranging or important cases, such as those that decided the future use of Arizona's surface streams or underground water, or keeping the state from disposing of trust land to ineligible buyers, or that insurance companies had to pay more attention to the interests of people they insured, rather than their own. However, my "defining moment" came to me in the early part of 1988, when I heard that a house committee of the Arizona legislature was hearing evidence that might lead to a vote of a bill of impeachment by the House of Representatives against our then-Governor, Evan Mecham. Even though Governor Mecham had only been in office a few months after his election in November 1987, he had succeeded in his own inimical way in alienating all of his own party's support in both houses of the Arizona legislature and to such an extent that a large number of them were looking to find a way to rid themselves of the new Governor. The procedure they chose was to impeach him. The process to impeach an elective officer in Arizona is set forth in Arizona's Constitution, Article 8, Part 2, §§1 and 2, and Arizona Revised Statutes §38-311 and following.

Impeachment is an extreme and rarely used remedy. It is purely a political one, specifically reserved by the original drafters of Arizona's Constitution to the legislative branch of government in order to purge the state of an official found by the legislature to be guilty of high crimes or misdemeanors, or corruption in office. It is such a drastic remedy that Arizona's first try at being admitted as a state to the United States was rejected by then-President of the United States, Howard Taft, because in its first proposed constitution the Territorial Legislature included allowing impeachment of judges.

After rejection, the Territorial Legislature removed this provision and statehood was granted. The people of Arizona reinserted the impeachment clause by later constitutional amendment. Impeachment is available regardless of whether any other criminal or civil proceeding is available or being used. If the House of Representatives votes by a majority of its members a bill of impeachment against the Governor, the constitution requires a trial in the Senate, presided over by the Chief Justice of the Arizona Supreme Court. The Senate must convene for the trial and the Chief Justice must preside, whether he wants to or not. Neither they, nor he, have any say about it. If the Senate finds the official guilty of any of the charges in the bill of impeachment, that official is immediately removed from his or her office. It can also deprive him or her of the right to hold any public office in the future in the State forever.

As a member of the Arizona Supreme Court, I had participated in, or authored many decisions, affecting citizens and organizations in Arizona. Many of these were far more important to Arizona than whether this Governor should be removed from office. I would rate the impeachment trial of Evan Mecham as one of the least important proceedings I was involved in while on the Supreme Court. However, because of the political attention that resulted from the legislature's voting of a bill of impeachment against Mecham, I became better known for the Mecham trial than for any of my other accomplishments.

Mecham was truly a maverick. A successful Phoenix area car dealer with beginnings in Ajo, Arizona, and coming from a strong Mormon background, he and his family built a large car dealership in Glendale, Arizona, and was elected once before to the House of Representatives of Arizona, but served only one term.

Mecham lacked many qualities necessary for political leadership. He evidently did not feel he needed the Republican leadership in the House or Senate to further his agenda as he rarely confided in them before springing hare-brained schemes on them at the last minute. He frequently appointed political misfits to his cabinet or other public offices, and loyally supported them even after disclosures showed that they had flawed backgrounds or were corrupt. One was under present investigation for murder. Mecham hired an attorney, Jim Coulter, to advise him personally on his new duties and responsibilities. Coulter did not have the background, experience, knowledge or influence to keep Mecham out of the problems he brought

313

on himself.

Mecham displayed very little knowledge of politics in general and bitterly resented criticism by anyone for his missteps, especially by the media. The media, however, loved him, as he almost daily provided headlines for them by getting his foot caught in his mouth on some issue. He did not understand why people were shocked when he referred to black children as "pickaninnies." Once, when Pope John Paul II was to visit Phoenix, he was asked by a reporter whether he was going to meet the Pope at the airport and what he was going to say to him. He replied, "I don't even know if the Pope speaks English." Of course the Pope spoke English and six other languages fluently. Once if asked by a reporter whether his previous statement on an issue was true, he became so violently angry at the reporter that he shook his finger in the reporter's face and said, "Don't you ever ask me for a true statement again." For a while thereafter, that reporter was not allowed to attend press conferences.

Early on in his governance, Mecham became obsessed with the paranoid belief that Arizona's Attorney General, Bob Corbin, was spying on him through the windows of the Governor's office atop the Executive Tower, using some sort of radar beams aimed from his office a block away to the east. When Mecham met with anyone of importance, or when he interviewed people for appointment to office, he made them sit on the floor of his office so that Corbin could not overhear their conversation by way of radar through the windows above.

There existed in Arizona, by statute, a fund called the "protocol fund," which consisted of donations from private individuals and political supporters to be used by any Governor in office to put on a Governor's Ball soon after being sworn in, and for him to use to purchase gifts to be given to visiting dignitaries, or put on affairs of state for them. Mecham did give a Governor's Ball, but then decided to give the remainder of this fund to his car dealership, Mecham Pontiac. Typical of his arrogance, Mecham had not asked either the Attorney General of Arizona or his own private counsel whether this was an appropriate use of the money.

When the media found out about the use of this fund, Mecham's private lawyer recommended to him to return the money, or at least to treat the transfer of funds as a "loan" to Mecham Pontiac, sign a note with a return date together with interest. Mecham refused. It was then that the Attorney General's office was asked by a member of the legislature to give an opinion as to whether this use was considered a misuse of the protocol fund. The answer given was that it was, and could be considered a misappropriation of public funds. This fueled a search for other grounds to impeach Mecham. Later it was found that Mecham had not reported that he had received a large campaign contribution from a wealthy man named Barry Wolfson, which was a minor crime in Arizona. But the final charge added to the bill of impeachment was that Mecham had ordered the head of the Department of Public

Safety, Ralph Milstead, a Governor's appointee, not to co-operate with the Attorney General, Robert Corbin. Corbin's investigation concerned an alleged death threat made by one of Mecham's employees toward a female state employee who was being contacted to testify against Mecham. That, in the opinion of the legislature, was the crime of obstruction of justice.

All three of these allegations were characterized as willful and deliberate commission of high crimes and misdemeanors and malfeasance in office by the Governor, according the House of Representatives in its voted Bill of Impeachment filed in the Senate against him, which formed the basis of Mecham's trial in the Senate. The mere voting of the Bill of Impeachment had the effect of immediately removing Mecham from office as Governor of Arizona.

The Constitution of Arizona does not require that the Senate trial on impeachment take the full form of a court trial, with all its legal trappings. In fact, the format of the required trial is not set forth in the Constitution at all. Also, under the law the Senate did not need to have witnesses testify and be cross-examined, documentary evidence provided, or have lawyers represent the parties and argue before the Senate. The Senate could have, upon receiving the Bill of Impeachment, if it so desired, merely appoint a committee to investigate the truthfulness of the allegations in the Bill of Impeachment, and once its investigation was completed, whether using witnesses under oath or not, report to the Senate its findings.

The members of the Senate could then consider conflicting evidence and argument, debate the sufficiency of the findings in the report of the committee, and then vote, up or down, on whether the Governor had indeed committed any of those acts, and if so, whether this conduct constituted in its opinion "high crimes and misdemeanors" within the meaning of the law.

Mecham had quite a strong backing of hard-core conservative voters, mostly in rural areas of Arizona, who were convinced he was the ultimate common man, not a professional politician, one who was uniquely capable of protecting them from too much government and taxation. The leadership in both the House and the Senate were keenly aware that impeaching the Governor on the basis of the three grounds they were alleging, without going through the regular channels of having either the Attorney General or the Maricopa County Attorney file criminal charges against him, and proceed to conviction before removing him from office, would raise a tremendous hue and cry from Mecham's supporters. It would in effect nullify their votes in his election. The procedure would be legal, but not politically astute. It would not be wise to hold any closed door proceeding such as secret committee investigations, without letting the Governor have his full day in court with all the legal protections the public would expect in a trial. So, the Senate decided to have a full-scale public trial on all three counts of the Bill of Impeachment.

It was at this point that the Senate, for the first time, con-

317

tacted me to become involved in the preparations for the trial in the Senate Chambers. Many issues needed to be discussed and agreed upon: what would the Senate rules for the trial be? How would the Senate Chambers be converted into a working courtroom? What would my role be in the proceedings? Would cameras be allowed in the Senate Chambers during the trial? Would the usual court rules of evidence and procedure control the proceedings, and if so, to what extent would they do so? What type of record would be made of the proceedings? How would the identification and admission of documentary exhibits be handled? Would the senators be given an opportunity to ask questions of the witnesses after the attorneys for the parties were finished with their examinations? If so, what types of matters could be brought up? If new material, beyond the examination of the attorneys, was brought up by the senators' questions, would the attorneys be allowed to ask the witness on the stand further questions to clear up things? Did the senators all have to be present at all times during the proceedings? If they were absent for any period of time, would those absent be disqualified from voting on the guilt or innocence of the Governor at the end of the proceedings?

The Senate employs attorneys to assist them in procedure, and some of the issues above were brought out by these attorneys, who gave input to the senators in solving them. But quite a few of the issues had not been thought out completely and they needed my input.

The legislature in Arizona had only prosecuted one other

impeachment proceeding since statehood. This involved charges of impropriety against two members of the Corporation Commission a decade or more before. We were able to find some help in reviewing how those proceedings were handled. Ironically, William H. Rehnquist, who later became Chief Justice of the United States Supreme Court, had acted as the attorney prosecutor in that Senate trial. He later would be called upon to be the Presiding Officer in the United States Senate impeachment trial of President Bill Clinton.

Other than these prior proceedings, I was not able to obtain information about any other state's impeachment of its governor. Oklahoma was the only state we could find that had impeached their governor. In fact they impeached three governors, all involving quarrels over educational issues. But Oklahoma failed to provide information about procedure in those matters.

Before this, I had never known of the Constitutional provisions on impeachment, and knew nothing about how to proceed. My law clerks, Fred Petty and Danny Adelman, did extensive research and brought to my attention everything that had ever been published on the topic of impeachment, and we studied it together for several weeks before the trial. Their interest and enthusiasm was infectious, and we became a real team in preparing for the biggest political event in the history of Arizona. It became obvious to not only my law clerks and me, but to my colleagues on the court, that my time was going to be entirely devoted to preparation for the impeachment trial, the trial itself however long, and perhaps some time after. During this time I would not be able to carry my share of the load of the court's cases, and the other justices would be doing some of my work for me. Stanley Feldman, my Vice-Chief Justice, would effectively take my place on the court and arrange for other judges, whether on the Courts of Appeal or other Superior Court judges, to sit in my place to hear and decide cases that normally came before the court during my absence. Little did I know that my absence from the court would be almost three months long.

I also predicted that there were bound to be objections to procedures in the Senate impeachment trial raised by the Governor's lawyers, which would be brought to the Arizona Supreme Court in the form of Special Actions, for judicial answers. Of course, being the Presiding Officer in the Senate trial, I could not participate in those matters with the Supreme Court in answering these questions.

The two weeks before the Senate trial were particularly interesting to me. The Senate had me come to discuss the issues and make recommendations. The Senate acted in separate caucuses in different rooms to discuss proposed rules of procedure for the trial and either agree or disagree with recommendations made by me or the other caucus. Each caucus invited one of my law clerks to be present in their discussions on rules so that they could bring to me the thoughts of the caucus on each issue and get my recommendations. The senators became so impressed with my clerks and their knowledge of the procedures in impeachment, that they became quite attached to them. In fact the senators started asking my clerks questions that should have been answered by their own employed counsel. I had to warn the clerks about being too available to the senators in that respect, and to suggest to them that their own counsel should be giving them help on those matters.

One of the easiest issues to resolve was that of whether media cameras should be allowed to film the proceedings, and if so, under what conditions. It was apparent to the senators that the media had to be able to report the proceedings live, as the public was so interested that the senators would be voted out of office if it were known that they were the ones that precluded full coverage. After all, the spectators' section of the Senate chamber only seated about 100 persons. How would the rest of Arizona know what was going on? Actually, those 100 seats were in great demand, and were filled with dignitaries and members of the media from all over the world every day. It was with difficulty that I was able to get Joan and a few friends tickets to be able to attend only one of the sessions.

Fortunately, the Arizona Supreme Court had recently adopted its rules for cameras in courtrooms in Arizona, and with some minor adjustments the rules were just what the Senate needed. Channel 8 of Arizona State University was chosen to film the proceedings. They were to use four silent cameras which could function without adding additional lighting to the Senate chambers. Two cameras would be stationed in the front corners of the chambers, facing toward the witness chair, and counsel for the parties, presiding officer's chair, and the clerks of the Senate. The other two cameras would be in the rear of the chambers, in the spectators' portion of the room. All print, audio and television media would feed off the footage taken by Channel 8, which made an archival copy of the entire proceeding for historical use.

Next was the hairiest of all the issues. What role would the Arizona Supreme Court's rules of evidence and procedure play in these proceedings? Very few members of the legislature were lawyers, and I am not sure any of the senators were at that time. One member, Peter Kay, had obtained a law degree from a night school somewhere, had not passed the bar exam and had never practiced law. Other than Kay, whatever knowledge of courtroom procedure the senators had must have been obtained through watching television programs, such as Perry Mason, or Judge Judy. So, most of the members of the Senate were unfamiliar with, and opposed to, the rules of evidence of the Supreme Court controlling the proceedings. They considered the rules of evidence as getting in the way of bringing out the truth. In their opinion no evidence of any type should be kept out of the proceedings.

This caused me some concern, as the senators were proposing a trial format with sworn witnesses testifying and being cross-examined. Keeping the questions of the lawyers and also the senators within bounds of relevant testimony would be impossible without the help of the rules of evidence. These ancient and time-honored rules keep out evidence that is not material to the issues, or which would not be relevant to the inquiry, or which would be unnecessarily repetitive or overly prejudicial. After a lot of urging on my part, the caucuses agreed that I could use the rules of evidence in the conduct of the trial in my rulings on evidence, but that the Senate had the right to overrule any ruling I made by a majority vote. That was all right by me, as this was their call on what rules of procedure would govern the trial, not mine. But it would lead to some confusion later on in the trial.

In civil, as well as criminal trial court proceedings in the Superior Court, a rule requires lawyers prior to trial to exchange information about their cases to each other, and to divulge the names, addresses and the substance of testimony of witnesses to be called at trial. This disclosure is to keep the proceedings from being a trial by surprise or ambush. I obtained special authorization from the Senate by rule to hold a pretrial conference in the impeachment proceedings, with counsel from both sides. I felt that, as in court trials, all parties should know in advance how many and which witnesses would be called, generally what they would testify to, and what documentary evidence would be offered. That gives the presiding officer a great insight as to the length of the trial and the major issues that will crop up in the course of the proceeding. Also, opposing counsel will be aware of what evidence they will have to counter. It was a very useful proceeding, which I used to much advantage.

I had the lawyers meet at our home at 321 East Marlette several days before the trial. We met in the cool of the afternoon next to my swimming pool, under our ramada. It was a fruitful exercise, much to the advantage of all concerned, and which saved a great deal of trial time in the process. I would venture a bet that no other impeachment trial in history utilized this helpful procedure.

The lawyers representing the House of Representatives who handled the presentation of evidence to prosecute Governor Mecham in the trial, were Paul Eckstein, of the Brown and Bain Phoenix law firm, and Bill French, a former Superior Court judge in Maricopa County. Both are and were excellent attorneys who had done their homework in researching the law for the House of Representatives proceedings and were entirely prepared for the Senate trial. Governor Mecham originally hired Murray Miller, a local lawyer experienced in criminal trials. For some reason, Mecham changed lawyers, and had Jerris Leonard and Fred Craft represent him in the trial itself. Leonard had been a state legislator in Wisconsin, and thus had some political experience. He handled most of the witnesses. The Governor's attorneys were no match for the cool, logical, well prepared and unemotional presentation of witnesses by Eckstein and French. The Governor's attorneys rambled on cross-examination, brought in unimportant matters and matters that provoked justified objections by Eckstein and French.

One law enforcement officer who testified was cross-examined about his treatment at a mental health institution for a mental breakdown 10 or 15 years prior, which had been a temporary matter and had nothing to do with his present competency as a witness. That was objected to as irrelevant and immaterial, and I sustained the objection, meaning that this line of questioning was improper. At this point the senators asked for a vote as to whether to overrule my decision. The vote was to allow the questioning that I had said was improper, and when the lawyers pursued the line further, it became apparent that my ruling was correct and that the witness had fully recovered from a temporary breakdown. The senators pursued the inquiry so far that it embarrassed them, as it brought out a totally unnecessary and previously unknown medical episode in the witness's life. At the next recess during the trial, one of the Republican senators came into my chambers and said this had shown them that the rules of evidence were and should be important and he felt that I would not be overruled again in ruling on evidence. I was not overruled from that time forward.

The senators were not used to being told when to be present and under what conditions. They were pretty independent, setting their own timelines and agendas. I sensed they did not really want me to be there, telling them what to do. They had their own President of the Senate, whose chair I took, and who they were used to. They became accustomed to me gradually, and most even became quite friendly.

I did not know any of the senators on a first-name basis, and had to become accustomed to their rules of procedure, which were quite different from courtroom procedures. I discovered that seniority of membership is extremely important. The ones who were members of the Senate longest were entitled to deference. That was difficult for me as I have a problem even remembering names in the first place. My law clerks made a paper cover for my desk, which had pictures of all the senators in the seats they normally occupied, with their names and dates of taking office under each.

Senators seeking recognition from the chair were required by the rules to stand and hold his or her microphone up to be recognized. This rule was only partially obeyed, as they did not stand. They would just raise their microphone above their heads and then lay it down. I had to rely on my clerks to alert me when some senator was signaling for recognition, as I was busy watching a witness testify, or a lawyer asking questions of a witness or taking notes. When my clerk would point out who had raised their microphone, I would recognize him or her. If two or more raised their microphones at the same time, it was my obligation to recognize the senator most senior first. This was awkward and sometimes I made a mistake and had to apologize for not acknowledging the correct one first.

I also had problems getting used to the senate's special rules of order, which were different from Roberts' Rules of Order, the meeting rules I was used to. I made sev-

326

eral mistakes in how to handle votes on motions in which amendments had been requested to be made, and other unusual requests. After I apologized for my awkwardness a couple of times, I asked Senator Peter Kay to be my "parliamentarian" to whom I could refer to for answers to my questions. Senator Kay agreed, and humbling me in this way seemed to gain me some respect and compassion from most of the senators. It also seemed to make the senators friendlier toward me.

I was pretty tense during the first few days of the trial. In such unfamiliar territory, I needed advice even beyond that which my clerks could provide. The Senate President's bench, which I occupied, had in it two very comfortable swivel chairs. I used one. I don't know what the other one was used for. Sometimes when I was most troubled, I had the eerie feeling that my father was sitting in the empty chair, holding his cigar, smiling, with his head cocked to one side as he used to do in pensive moments, as though he approved of the way I was handling the matters. This gave me comfort.

I was disappointed with the conduct of some of the senators in the trial. After the lawyers asked questions regarding the matters in the bill of impeachment, some of the senators insisted on asking inane questions that had nothing to do with the issues being discussed. Some of these were obvious attempts to get before a television camera and make a speech that might aggrandize them and to try to make them look good to their local constituents. You could tell that someone else had crafted some of the questions.

During the first few days of the trial, a few of the senators arrived late. When I started on time, their empty seats with their names on them were obvious to the folks back home watching on TV. I understand that many phone calls from constituents were made after that day's trial.

The senators had to give up their usual practices of reading newspapers at their desks during the proceedings and taking stretches at the back of the room. These brought phone calls, too.

Having the benefit of a pretrial conference, I knew what witnesses would be called on which days, and generally what they would testify to. When we closed for the day, I would discuss with my clerks what the next day might bring up. I would then tell them to give me a memo on any possible objection that might be made to evidence, or document offered. Sometimes they worked late at night anticipating and giving me citations of authority on what my ruling should be on each point. Then at eight the next morning, I would find and read the various memos they had written the night before. They were so good at their predictions that they never missed a single objection. They even briefed objections that were not made and should have been. Danny and Fred were great. Sometimes we made bets of a quarter on what issues would be raised and which ones would not. We kept the winnings in a jar and spent them on margaritas after the trial.

In hindsight, all three charges in the articles of impeachment were frail reeds with which to support an impeachment proceeding. The evidence on the obstruction of justice charge turned out to be weak and hearsay. The failure to report a campaign contribution had never been raised by the legislature against anyone else before. The improper use of the protocol fund would probably not have been considered if the Governor would have admitted a mistake in interpretation of an unclear law and offered to refund the money.

All in all, when added together after all the evidence was in, there was barely enough evidence to support the Bill of Impeachment. In fact, criminal charges brought against Mecham after the trial based on the exact same charges resulted in a jury finding in Maricopa County Superior Court that Mecham was not guilty on all three charges. The impeachment proceedings showed a weak evidentiary support for the use of such a draconian procedure to rid the state of a governor who undoubtedly was guilty only of being minimally qualified to hold the office. Were it not for the fact that Carolyn Warner was defeated by a candidate running against her in the Democratic primary, and later ran against her as an Independent in the general election thus splitting the votes against Mecham, he would not have obtained the majority of the votes and would not have become governor in the first place. Most lawyers believe that the reason Mecham's criminal charges resulted in not guilty verdicts was probably the result of juror sympathy for Mecham having already suffered enough by being removed from office so abruptly and awkwardly by the use of impeachment.

During the proceedings, my secretary received dozens of telephone calls about how I was conducting myself as Presiding Officer. Some were complimentary. Some were derogatory, and even threatening. I received one letter with a live round of ammunition in it. As a result, I was assigned a DPS officer to be my bodyguard. His name was Van Jackson. He would be with Joan and me whenever we were in public, and would be with me when I was away from home. He drove me to work and brought me home, and even jogged with me in the mornings. He was a nice young man in his late twenties, about 6' 4" and handsome. He was a little out of shape, however, and was embarrassed when the old guy he was guarding was able to outdo him at jogging for the first couple of weeks of the trial. After that, he got back in shape and had no trouble keeping up with me for several miles each day.

I had to walk from the Supreme Court's second floor office in the Executive Tower to the Senate building each day, and back again in the afternoon. A group of some of Mecham's supporters one time mistook me for Bill French who was one of the lead prosecuting attorneys, and made disparaging remarks about how I was treating Governor Mecham. I had to tell them I was not Mr. French. Some folks thought we looked a lot alike, although I didn't agree.

One of the Clerks of the Senate was Shirley Wheaton, a lovely lady. She frequently handed me pieces of candy during the trial. Once, during a very long and boring cross-examination of a lawyer, Robert L'Ecuyer, one of Mecham's witnesses, she handed me a fairly large piece of hard candy which I had just put into my mouth when one of the cross-examining lawyers objected to L'Ecuyer's refusal to answer a question that had been repeatedly asked of him. I had been ready to say something to the witness for some time, as he had been evading the question, but the State's lawyers were, in my opinion, making a tactical decision to let him do this in order to hurt his own testimony. But unexpectedly one of the lawyers objected. I had to say or do something right away. There I was with a rather large piece of candy stuck in my left cheek, and I said as I picked up my gavel, "Mr. L'Ecuyer, see this gavel? I have been a judge for about 27 years. In all that time I have never had to use it to hold a lawyer in contempt of court. Now you are tempting me!" The TV cameras had focused on me, and pictures of me with a swollen cheek and my to-become-famous words were front page news in the papers the next morning.

Another witness who would not answer a question posed by a prosecuting attorney created a problem for me — Governor Mecham. He had taken the stand in his own defense and was being cross-examined about the financial condition of his car dealership to prove the need for using the protocol fund. He avoided answering specific questions, and even when I had told him he had to answer the questions, he ignored my warning. At that point the prosecuting attorney asked me to hold Governor Mecham in contempt of the court for not answering.

This caught me by surprise. I didn't know for sure whether I, as the Presiding Officer of the Senate trial, as opposed to a judge in a regular court trial, had the authority to do that. It was after four o'clock in the afternoon that day, so I called the trial at recess to the next morning to do some research. As I was walking to my car in the basement of the Executive Office Building, I saw the Chief of Police of the Capitol Police. He was a very cordial man, directly appointed to his job by the Governor. I didn't think about that at the time. I asked him whether the Capitol Police had a place where they confined people accused of some crime on Capitol grounds before turning them over to the City of Phoenix Police. He said he did. It was a storage room in the corner of the garage, where trespassers or other minor criminals would be held for a few hours before the police came for them. The storeroom had no bathroom facilities. I said to him, "No, I mean do you have a room suitable for you to take custody of Governor Mecham and detain him for an indefinite time if I hold him in contempt of court until he decides to answer some questions?" He looked shaken. He said he would look into the matter.

The next day I resumed the case, armed with research that indeed I had the power to hold the Governor in contempt. I really did not want to do it, because that alone would become a side issue in the trial that would cause a lot of political turmoil. That morning, for some reason, when I asked Mecham if he had reconsidered his refusal to answer the question, he said he had, and answered the question fully.

The reason could have been that the Chief of Police probably went to Mecham and told him about our conversation. Or maybe he and his counsel made that decision on their own. I will never know.

The impeachment trial took over six weeks, five days a week, from 9:30 a.m. until about 4:30 p.m. each day. It was the most important thing on local news, and achieved quite a bit of national and international attention. Most citizens were glued to their television sets throughout the whole trial. Some people stood in the streets, watching television being shown in store windows. It was a live civics lesson for all Arizonans, where all three branches of government, legislative, executive and judicial, participated in the same courtroom. My grand-daughter, Elisha Lander, was pre-school age at the time, and usually watched Sesame Street on television in the morning. Sesame Street had been blacked out during the trial to show the live impeachment proceedings. When Elisha first noticed it, she called to her mother, Candy, "Look, Mommy, Grandpa is on TV." After a few minutes, she would much rather have watched Sesame Street. I am sure many others would have as well.

One day before the trial started, I found out that Mrs. Al Leader, who, with her husband, was friends with my parents, and who had acted as a babysitter for me when I was an infant, was celebrating her 100th birthday in a Kingman rest home. She evidently was an avid watcher of the impeachment trial. At the beginning of that day's session, as Presiding Officer I asked for a "Point of Personal Privilege" to wish Mrs. Leader a happy 100th birthday and to thank her for being a part of my life. Mrs. Leader died a week or so after her birthday.

Over the period of the trial, the senators came to accept me as their leader for the trial, and most became very cordial to me, even strong Mecham supporters. At some point in the trial, a few senators made some very critical remarks about lawyers and their actions representing clients. I heard enough of them until I could not be silent any longer. I took an opportunity to tell them that I was a lawyer, and was proud of it. I told them that this country would not have become independent from Great Britain had not the majority of the signers of the Declaration of Independence and the Constitution of the United States not been lawyers, and that I was proud of the legal profession in protecting the rights of minorities and the poor. My statements were published in the press and I received awards from several lawyer organizations as a result. My comments put a stop to derogatory lawyer remarks thereafter in the proceedings.

After all the witnesses had testified, both for the legislature and the Governor, the attorneys argued the case to the senators, who were in essence acting as jurors in the case. The senators were instructed by me on the law. One of the instructions was that the Board of Examiners (the team of representatives and their attorneys) had the burden of proving that the Governor had in fact committed one or more of the three charged offenses in the Bill of Impeachment, and if they found that particular offense constituted a high crime or misdemeanor amounting to malfeasance in office, the burden of proof had to be carried by "clear and convincing evidence." This burden was greater or more onerous than "a preponderance of the evidence," which is the standard in civil cases, and less than "beyond a reasonable doubt," which is the standard in criminal cases. Those standards were properly defined to the senators, although I doubt that many of them understood the true distinctions between them.

After hearing counsel's arguments, the senators returned a verdict of guilty against Mecham on Counts One and Three (misappropriation of public funds and obstruction of justice). They found Mecham not guilty on the count concerning non-reporting of the loan by Wolfson. Having been found guilty on those counts, Mecham was automatically removed from his office as Governor, and there was no appeal from them to any other court or legislative body. By law, 2/3rds of the Senate was needed to return a vote of guilty on any count. On the counts they found Mecham guilty, there were only six or seven senators that voted not guilty.

When the verdicts of the senators were announced in open court, each senator was allowed an opportunity to explain his vote. Those voting guilty usually made short statements of their reasons, but those voting not guilty were much longer. The announcement of their reasons for their votes was a very difficult point in the trial, as Mecham's supporters had threatened to vote out any senators who voted in favor of a guilty finding at the next election. In fact, several of those suffered that fate.

At the end, even before recessing for the day, the senators were obviously relieved that the trial was over. A formal motion for a resolution was made by one senator expressing the Senate's appreciation of my handling of the trial. The motion was passed and later I was given a copy signed unanimously by all members of the senate.

Sometime thereafter, I was invited to sit in on the regular senate agenda as an honorary "Senator for the Day." This was a great honor, never before bestowed on anyone, much less a sitting justice on the Arizona Supreme Court. The day I sat in on senate proceedings was very interesting. It happened that this particular day was the one that had secret proceedings as to whether the State of Arizona should be authorized to buy the land on which the Kartchner Caverns are located, and which was purchased and made into a wonderful Arizona state park. The secret had been kept for over 14 years since the caverns' discovery by spelunkers, and until the Kartchner family decided that it would be better for the state to make a park out of them, rather than to allow them to be commercially developed. It was a wonderful decision, one that will undoubtedly make it possible for the caverns to be far better protected for posterity. What a thrill when some 16 years later Joan and I were able to visit the caverns for the first time in 2004.

The friendship that I engendered with the House of Representatives and the Senate paid off handsomely for the court system. Chief Justice Duke Cameron for many years had entreated the legislature to grant us funds to build a new courts building for the Supreme Court and the Court of Appeals just east of the Capitol complex. Each time our project came to the top of the waiting list, it was bumped to the bottom for some reason. After the impeachment trial, the court's and Chief Justice Cameron's plans were put at the top of the list and the building now housing those courts and the Court Administrator's offices were built and dedicated in January, 1992, just before I resigned from the Court. It is a marvelous building, built with only one condition imposed by the legislature – that no judge's office (including his law clerks and secretary's space) be larger than each senator's office.

After the trial of Mecham, I was a very popular official in Arizona. I was besieged by many friends, some from both parties, to consider running for Governor of Arizona at the next election. I was very flattered, as was Joan. I gave the matter some thought, and even did a little investigating as to what a run for Governor would entail. I consulted with quite a few politically connected people and decided against running. The reasons were many. One was that I was told that in order to make a good run against Fife Symington, who was at that time the most likely Republican candidate, I would need at least $1 million dollars in the bank before I made a formal announcement. How to raise that huge amount of money was the first problem. The small amounts that individuals could make to a campaign by law would require months of contacting people, making requests of individuals I did not even know, and some of which I would not want my picture taken with. The time element would mean I would be required to resign from the Supreme Court, which I hated to do. I still had a lot of things that the Commission on the Courts had recommended to bring to fruition.

But the biggest reason I decided not to run for Governor was that in my almost 30 years of service as a judge, I had never had to make any promises to people that I knew I could not keep. I just had to promise that I would work hard and decide cases fairly and impartially. Also I was never in a situation where I was called upon to violate my code of ethics or compromise my judgment because of a constituent's demand.

Joan was unhappy with my decision, and still is. She jokingly blames me for everything that she believes has gone wrong in Arizona since then, believing that I could have handled whatever problem came my way better than whoever else was Governor at the time. I know that is not true. I have not regretted my choice, as I truly did not have the needed "fire in the belly" to run in a heavily contested race. Also, I believe the pressures of the Governor's office would have been bad for my health.

In February of 1992, after the completion and dedication of the new courts building, I resigned from the Arizona Supreme Court.

11

LIFE AFTER THE SUPREME COURT

After retirement from the Arizona Supreme Court, I acted on my promise to Joan that we would spend more time together, travel and have fun. We started out to do that, but I realized that our meager savings and my pension might not be enough to do everything we wanted to. I found that because of our judicial retirement pension to which I had contributed over the years, I would have only a small amount of Social Security pension benefits when I became 65. What I needed was a part-time job in which I would pay into self-employment taxes for about 12 quarters to bring my monthly Social Security checks up to maximum. After some hints dropped, some friends in law firms invited me for interviews for post-judicial work. This sounded good to them at first, but when I told them what type of things I wanted to do, most were not interested. Actually, I didn't want to become a full-time trial lawyer — litigation specialist. I knew that would be too stressful at that stage in my life, and would interfere with trips that Joan and I would want to take.

What I envisioned was that some firm would want me to be highlighted on their roster as "of counsel" and pay me for about three years to do pro bono work to help develop charitable organizations such as, the United Methodist Outreach Ministries in developing a greater ministry to homeless families; the Maricopa County Volunteer Lawyers Program in obtaining funds and lawyers to furnish free legal services to the poor; and to further promote literacy for those who were functionally illiterate. These are not money-making pursuits for a law firm, but with my name recognition and public exposure in helping these programs, I believed that I would bring in business for the firm.

Only one law firm, Roush, McCracken & Guerrero in Phoenix, believed that what I had in mind would be a worthwhile asset to their firm. They hired me effective February 1992, and kept me on their payroll for the next three years. After that, and to the present, they have kept my name on their firm as "of counsel" and allowed me to use their offices when I needed them, and to call upon their secretaries and paralegals when I needed their assistance in doing arbitrations and mediations, which became and were my sources of supplemental income.

The RM&G firm was and is a highly respected and successful personal injury plaintiff's law firm. The firm has been very generous to me, and allowed me to contribute to the community in ways to help the poor and unfortunate. Besides, the lawyers and their staff are wonderful people, and have included Joan and me in firm outings and trips, even one to Ireland, at their expense.

Right off the bat after leaving the Arizona Supreme Court, Joan and I went on a trip with Ernie and Shirley Scott, and Shirley's brother, George, to New Zealand and Australia. Shirley researched and arranged the whole trip and made it one of the most memorable that we have taken. We spent 10 days on a bus tour of New Zealand, which was fabulous. New Zealand is a British colony with strict immigration laws, keeping out undesirables who they believe might become a burden on their society. Whether intended or not, this keeps out most non-white people, the poor and those with criminal backgrounds.

The country is gorgeous, with rolling hills of grass where sheep graze everywhere, and where high mountains with glaciers overlook lakes and streams. Beautiful, clean cities. We bungee jumped there on the north island near Queenstown at a jumping station (the Wairau Bridge) which was touted as being the original home of commercial bungee jumping. The bridge you jumped from was 163 feet over the Shotover River. There was at that time only one higher bungee jump in the world, in North Australia – 200 some feet. The jump was Joan's idea, as she figured it was time: I was retired, the kids were grown and married, our dog had died, and we had no real responsibilities to keep us from doing wild and crazy

Horseback riding with Roush, McCracken & Guerrero in southeastern Arizona

things. This, coming from a lady who hadn't dived off anything higher than the edge of a swimming pool! I realized I
could never live it down if she jumped and I didn't, so I agreed
to jump also. Joan did the most beautiful swan dive I have ever
seen. She said she really didn't try to dive; she was so scared
she was actually trying to fly. We both survived and have a
video to prove it. The jump was free if you were 65 of age or
more or would jump naked. Joan decided to lie about her age
to avoid the latter.

After New Zealand, we visited cities in Australia from
Sydney in the south, then along the east coast all the way to
Darwin on the northwest corner of the continent. On the way
we visited scenic attractions, like bird sanctuaries, koala bear
compounds, and indigenous people's villages. We also had a
five or six day cruise on a ship that visited several islands on
the Great Barrier Reef, where we snorkeled and saw coral reefs
and fish in abundance. On the northeast part of the country,
we stayed in the Kakadu National Park, which the government
of Australia created for the benefit of the indigenous people,
the Aborigines, who had lived for centuries there surviving by
hunting and fishing. Their ancestors left fascinating x-ray type
petroglyphs on rocks and in caves. The locals call these people
"Abo's."

We stayed in a three-story hotel made in the exact shape of
a huge crocodile, with rooms down the sides of the crocodile
and down its tail. You registered by driving your vehicle into
the mouth of the croc, and walking into its throat to the front

desk. The legs were stairways. The whole animal was covered with a roofing material that made it look like crocodile skin. If you were in an airplane looking down on the hotel, you would see an opening on the crocodile's back or roof, through which you would see a stream with pools and rocks winding down its body, depicting the alimentary canal (gut) of the animal, with pools where there would have been a heart, lungs, stomach, etc. It was definitely a most unusual piece of architecture. There were signs warning you not to walk about outside at night because you might meet a live copy of the hotel wandering around, looking for his dinner.

On this trip, we were amazed by the friendliness of the Australian people. They appreciate the fact that it was the Americans in World War II who stepped in to protect their country when Great Britain gave it up as not being defensible against the Japanese. They like American tourists and are helpful and cheerful people.

Our next fun trip was in 1993, when we bought our new Holiday Rambler 27-foot travel trailer to go with the Scotts, Hoovers, Freidays and Wrights on a six-week trailer pull all around the Baja Peninsula in Mexico. That was wonderful also, as we went from one beautiful campsite to another on sides of the Sea of Cortez and the Pacific, fishing, relaxing and enjoying the people.

After these two trips I felt that I needed to go to work and make some money. I found that I had some skills as a professional neutral to work through the American Arbitration Association to act as an arbitrator or mediator in civil disputes. I had considerable success in that field, and enjoyed the work. My training as a trial and appellate judge comes in handy, and makes me in demand for complex civil cases. To date, I have been selected to handle those types of matters in Arizona, Nevada, Louisiana, Connecticut, Texas and Colorado. It is fascinating work; I was able to keep up my legal and judicial skills, get paid handsomely for it, get to pick and choose what cases I wanted, and to arrange most of the time for the hearings to be held when they wouldn't interfere with our trips or summers in the mountains.

I have been given two singular honors and experiences that have given me lasting memories. The first occurred, I believe, in 1994, when Russia, or the Union of Soviet Socialist Republics, dissolved. (The second was a trip to China, which is described later on.) When that happened, all the states within the Soviet Union suddenly became independent nations, needing to set up their own separate forms of government. Many nations, including the United States, wanted to influence these states to adopt forms of government like their own. I was asked by the U. S. State Department to be part of a team of two judges, two constitutional law professors and two lawyers to visit the country of Belarus, to meet with a committee of their Parliament, to evaluate their constitution and to make suggestions that might change their country from a totalitarian socialist state to one of a democracy.

I think my being invited was due to the suggestion of Sandra Day O'Connor. The team members I can recall were a U. S. Federal District Court Judge from the State of Washington, Judge Cohenour; and a nationally known constitutional law professor then from U.C.L.A., now of Duke University, Erwin Chimerinsky. The others I cannot remember. We met each other at a briefing session in Hamburg, Germany, and went from there by air to Minsk, Belarus, where we lived in a government compound outside of Minsk for nine days, meeting with 11 members of the Minsk Parliament each day to learn from each other. It was a fascinating experience.

My job was to convince the Belarusian committee to accept suggested constitutional amendments that would create an independent judiciary similar to that in the United States. Our team met with lawyers' groups and judges. We were allowed to witness a criminal trial that was shocking to us. The two defendants charged with stealing some tires from a government plant were guarded in the courtroom by two uniformed soldiers with automatic rifles pointed at them. The prosecutors were located in the courtroom facing the defendants and were asking them incriminating questions without their attorneys objecting. (In the U. S., defendants cannot be required by the state to take the stand to testify.) The defendants' lawyers were way in the back of the room, talking among themselves, apparently not taking part in the proceedings, or even paying any attention that we could observe.

Judges in Belarus are appointed by the government and can be removed by the government at any time if they do not decide cases the way the government wants them to. A telephone call from the State Attorney General before the trial might advise the judge outright what his or her decision in a pending case should be. If he did not obey, he would probably find himself back on the line in his old job in a tractor factory. Judges there had little or no legal or judicial training and were paid poorly.

Lawyers were at that time minimally trained in law schools which had only small, basic libraries. Because the government owned all the land, buildings, factories, apartments, etc., concepts of mortgages, leases, title conveyances, bankruptcies, operating agreements or any other business agreements, were unheard of. If Belarus were going to attract private foreign investments for new businesses, these legal concepts and a host of others were going to have to be incorporated into law, and the owners or operators of these businesses must be able to rely on the fact that their agreements will be enforced in courts of law where judges are trained and ethical, and whose judgment will be fair, impartial and without political interference. That would require earth-shaking changes to be made in their existing system. Our task was a difficult one; changing into a free society seemed dangerous to everyone we spoke to.

We were in Minsk quite close in time after the nuclear disaster in Chernobyl, which was very close to Minsk. We saw people fishing in a river that probably contained radioactive fish. We were told not to drink the local water, or even brush our teeth in it. Bottled water was supplied.

Judge Cohenour and I were joggers at the time, and were allowed only to jog around inside the government compound. We were not allowed outside the wire fence. We were guarded the entire time, and had interpreters with us when we met with other government officials. We discovered that one of them was a former KGB officer, who was leaking all our discussions to the government, which wanted very much not to change from the Soviet system of government.

Five other governments had sent teams to Belarus to meet with the parliamentary committee before we got there. The ones I remember were Italy, Germany and France. Those countries have parliamentary forms of government quite similar to the one that existed under Russian rule.

After meeting several days with the committee of Parliament, our team was to report our suggestions of change to the legal and judicial departments of their government. I was to give my presentation to a panel of judges of several levels, including their high Constitutional Court. We met in a beautiful huge courtroom decorated entirely in the color of Russia, red: the carpet, the drapes, the chair upholstery, everything red. I was seated at one end of a huge conference table in the center of the courtroom. The table was so long that it must have been able to seat 40 or more judges. Other judicial officers sat in spectators' seats. At the other end of the table was the

Chief Justice of the Constitutional Court, which is the highest court in Belarus. He was a tall, thin, handsome man with a Mongolian V-shaped face. After my comments on how judges should be impervious to threats by other government officials, be trained for their work, abide by strict codes of ethics and behavior, and other things that filled about 15 minutes of my time, the Chief Justice said, through the interpreter, "Your Honor, with great respect, I must tell you that I could not require these things of my judges until they are paid more than taxi drivers."

In our day, it is difficult to imagine the differences between our two systems, and the chasm that would have to be bridged in order to change them.

At the end of our stay, our team borrowed a typewriter from the American Embassy in Belarus, and typed up a list of the changes we felt would need to be made in their laws and constitution in order to guarantee the rights of the rule of law to their citizens and businesses. We soon found that none of our recommendations were accepted, and that the new form of government in Belarus was fashioned to clone the old Russian system. The State Department of the U.S. was, however, able to establish an office in Minsk to assist lawyers and law schools in adopting some teaching methods and rules that have hopefully had an effect on the future practice of law in Belarus. Programs of the Central and East European Law Initiative and Institute (CEELI) in other countries of the Soviet Union were more successful than we were. Some were able to convince their parliaments to make considerable change. I am kept aware of the progress in those countries.

Although apparently unsuccessful in major ways, it is possible that our team planted some seeds of change that may sprout at later times in Belarus, after that country sees the changes that are occurring in other, more progressive Soviet states.

Joan and I have been able to enjoy several trips to other countries outside the Americas. We cruised the Greek Isles and parts of Turkey, including Ephesus, where the apostle Paul spoke to a crowd of thousands in an old Roman amphitheater entreating them to abandon their Roman gods and idols and was nearly arrested. The marble seats in the theater were so carefully arranged in tiers that at a certain point on the ground, a speaker could be heard clearly by all without amplification, regardless of where he or she sat, even if the speaker spoke only in a whisper. On a cruise and bus tour trip in Italy, we visited Corinth, where Paul started home-type Christian churches. Besides seeing Rome, and historical parts of Italy, it was fascinating to actually be in parts of Europe where the apostles risked and lost their lives in the name of Christ.

We also took a bus trip in northern France, where the beaches of Normandy bring silence to anyone visiting them who have heard of the American and British invasion of France on D-Day in WWII, at a loss of thousands of lives. Paris and other quaint villages were also pleasing. Joan says she isn't through with Paris yet.

We toured Spain for a month with the Tathams who had purchased a used Bentley in England and drove it to Madrid, where we met them for our trip all around Spain. Using that car, we had lots of interesting experiences. It was a right-hand drive automobile in a left-hand drive country. Chuck would drive and I would usually sit in the front passenger seat on the left. In order to pass any vehicle, I had to peek around it and signal to Chuck when to pass. Sometimes Joan, with a yell, would disagree with my signal and Chuck would duck back in position. Joan would sometimes blame me for the driving because I was in the seat where she was used to seeing the driver. We saw Toledo, Barcelona, Seville, Madrid and others. Great fun. We ended our tour in Valencia, where a former law clerk of mine, Pamela Franks and her husband Bram, attending Spanish instruction there, took charge of the Bentley and had it shipped back to the U.S. where Chuck and Joyce drove it for some time before selling it at a profit, according to Chuck.

On our Baja trip, we bought a two-week time share in a hotel in Cabo San Lucas with the Scotts. We were only able to exchange it twice outside the U.S. — once in Portugal, on the ocean, where both Ernie and Shirley got food poisoning and Shirley was in the hospital most of the time. The other was in Recife, Brazil. The Portugal trip was a disaster. The Brazil trip had some interest – we were able to experience

352

a practice parade for their annual celebration, Mardi Gras. The parade consisted of dozens of huge 18-wheeler trucks converted to hold a samba band and dancers on top of the trailer, with huge (eight-foot) sound speakers all around their sides, blaring music so loud that you could feel the bass concussion on your body while standing on the sidewalk. Those sidewalks were so packed with people that you were crammed against each other like fish in a can. I don't think you could fall if you tried to. What a great opportunity for pick pockets. Ernie felt his wallet being removed and grabbed at the guy who attempted the take, but he pulled away and was lost in the crowd.

Most of the rest of our trips were to the various islands of Hawaii, which Joan enjoys. She says she can be ready for a Hawaiian trip on five minutes' notice, and thinks that in a former life she was a Hawaiian.

When we were not traveling, Joan and I enjoyed our summer cabin in Munds Park, Arizona, about 17 miles south of Flagstaff. In 1989, we purchased an old frame two-story home there at 540 Sundance, but could only enjoy it on weekends until about 2002 or so, when we started spending more time there and less in Phoenix, sweltering in the 110 degree plus weather. There, I could still do arbitrations and mediations – some in Phoenix and some even in Flagstaff, where Phoenix lawyers were not averse to presenting their cases where it was cool. In Munds Park, we made a lot of friends who play golf or bridge and also live in Phoenix in the winter.

We play a lot of golf and enjoy the cool pines and our new friendships.

The one other business type trip that I would like to mention is the one Joan and I took to China in October, 2006. The Fellows of the American Bar Association is a branch of the American Bar Association, dealing with research and education. The program, People to People Ambassadors of the American Bar Association, was founded by former President Dwight D. Eisenhower. A large team of lawyers and judges from all over the U.S., plus one from England and one from Poland were selected to spend two weeks in China, in three different cities – Beijing (the capital city), Shanghai (the industrial and business center of China) and Guilin, a beautiful farming and rural city decades behind the other cities in business or industrial development. Our team met with lawyers, judges, members of chambers of commerce and embassy officials in these cities and discussed the "rule of law" in China, as it was before and is now, and the progress being made. The information I obtained on this trip was valuable to me in my handling of future mediations in business disputes.

China, like old Russia, owns all the land, buildings, apartments and even the homes people build. Businesses and even families must lease the property from the socialist government. During the Cultural Revolution, about 40 years ago, all professional people, doctors, lawyers, teachers, ministers, and accountants were either imprisoned, killed, or run out of the country. Everyone was supposed to be on an equal status, no one above the other. All were employed by the government, and all they produced belonged to the government. In order to reduce the population explosion that was occurring, married couples are allowed to have only one child. The government provides schools, hospitals, medical and other needs the people have, and this control is supposed to reduce the cost.

People who lived in the country were supposed to raise the food for the people in the city. People in the city were employed in factories and got to live better. They were paid more money, had free housing, education, and medical services. No one born in the rural areas were allowed to move to the city. As could be expected, the country people were unhappy about the inequality of their situation, so they did not work hard at growing their crops or animals.

Only within the last decade, the government gave the country people a little incentive to work harder. The government put a quota system in place for farmers which established a level of production for each farmer. If the farmers grew crops or animals in excess of that quota, they could sell the excess and keep the money for themselves. Almost instantly, the farmers greatly increased their production, and with the money they earned they could now buy farm equipment, automobiles, more food and better clothes. With this, production increased even more. What a radical change this made for the farmers. And for the government, additional money was available from new taxes. Capitalism had been created in China.

By this change in policy, a surprising increase occurred in the gross national product of China. The Chinese government then allowed even small businesses to keep their profits, after paying taxes. The government, however, maintained owner-ship of transportation, mining operations, and large busi-nesses, like manufacturing of trucks, tractors and other farm equipment, automobiles, as well as electronics.

Today, Communism still is strong in China, controlling all businesses, both local and foreign. But with capitalism, the need for education grew and flourished. There are now 130,000 lawyers in China, when during the Cultural Revo-lution there were none. There are 170,000 judges in China, whereas in the Cultural Revolution there were hardly any. The government is allowing foreign industry and business to come to China, under very strict conditions. The U.S. desires to build industrial plants there, where Chinese labor is still very inexpensive.

The conditions put upon foreign businesses doing business in China are very strict and difficult to comply with. The most successful method of getting permission for a U.S. firm to set up a business is to agree to make the Chinese government a business partner, sharing in the profits of the enterprise. Then things go along rather rapidly and smoothly, and with government protection of intellectual property rights.

What we saw in China in Beijing and Shanghai was an exploding economy, with handsome, well-dressed city people looking every bit like westerners, talking on cell phones and driving vehicles on roads so congested that it takes hours to go a few miles. The air is so polluted in Beijing that you cannot see a half of a mile. Pollution is so great because 85 percent of China's electrical energy comes from coal-fired generators. Because Beijing would host the 2008 Olympics, we were told that all plants or industries would be shut down two weeks before the games so the air would clear temporarily.

Several of the members of our team, including me, spoke to a class of judges in training at a judicial school. Judges in China are functionaries, as they were in Russia. They are appointed by the government and hold office at the pleasure of the government. Decisions made by judges against the interests of the government may cost the judge making them his job.

At our gathering of almost 300 judges to be, we were told that the students were interested in how judges were trained, selected and disciplined in the United States. Our presentations were converted into Chinese by our interpreters. After we gave our speeches, the students were allowed to ask questions, which had to be interpreted also. We were impressed that the questions were soft ones, which were not very deep or interesting. We found out why. A Communist Party official was present, who required each questioner to state his name and sign a book before asking his question. When our team left, we had to walk about two blocks to our bus. On this walk, we found ourselves surrounded by small groups of the students, who spoke very good English, and asked more penetrating questions that were not being reported. I sensed a new breed of judges that were seeking more information about justice as it is administered in other countries.

Joan got to spend more time in seeing interesting sights and events in China than I did. We finished our trip to the east with a two-day stay in Hong Kong, which 10 years before was ceded by England to China on the condition that for a period of 50 years, the existing form of government could remain as it was before. A beautiful city, blending the new with the old. It will be interesting to see what will happen to Hong Kong when the 50-year period has passed.

In Hong Kong Harbor we had lunch on a three-story floating restaurant with very beautiful Chinese decor that could serve 2,500 people at once. We were taken to the restaurant on a sampan, which is a small covered wooden boat with a motor. Ours was driven by an ageless Chinese woman who showed us the hundreds of old houseboats on which some people live. She was driving with one hand on the tiller of the boat, a foot on the accelerator pedal and a cell phone held to her ear by her other hand, shouting orders to someone like a boss to her workers. What a contrast.

We had wonderful seafood at an island where we were taken one evening for a cruise. The food we were given on our trip was great. Mostly traditional Chinese, beautifully presented. I understand it is very reasonable in price. I am not sure what we ate, and pretty sure I don't want to know. One thing unusual was deep-fried large scorpions, which tasted like potato chips. Very good Chinese beer is served at lunch and dinner in quart bottles. Chinese really like beer. Bottled water was always served also.

Our hotel accommodations were better than any I can recall in any other country. Usually television in English is available on BBC, but the content is highly censored. You can be watching the news and when something is shown about a happening in China the screen goes blank, returning when the subject is changed. Nothing derogatory about China is allowed to be aired, even natural disasters. Everything in the media is pre-screened. The party employs thousands of censors to ensure that nothing critical about the country or its politicians will be publicly aired.

My impression of the youth of China is that city people are far better educated than our children are, especially in science and math. It is obvious that they are driven by their culture to get as much education as possible. The children and their parents appreciate teachers and respect them. Most all of them want to get as much education as they can and to excel in their courses.

We learned in China that American lawyers are not permitted to practice law on their own or have their own law firms in China. They can, however, work in a Chinese law firm helping mainly with matters concerning American industry coming to China. At meetings held with the Bar Association of Shanghai, we found that most of the successful Chinese lawyers were trained in the best law schools in the United States, and charged as much as successful lawyers in their fields in our country.

I feel it will not take long for China to pass the United States as the wealthiest country in the world. She already owns over 60 percent of the debt of the United States.

12

THE PURPOSE OF THIS MONOGRAPH

I have felt cheated that I never met either of my grandfathers or my paternal grandmother. I know very little about them. I only met my mother's mother once when I was nine years old in Chicago. Mother and I visited her and quite a few of my Polish uncles, aunts, and cousins for about a week in the summer. I saw my maternal grandmother once more at her funeral. I never got to know why and how my grandparents immigrated to the United States, where they first lived in the U.S., very little about how they made their living, what was important in their lives, and other things I have told you about myself.

Over the years, I feel I have not been able to spend enough time with my children while they were young and I was building my practice. I let Joan do most, if not all, the child-rearing then. Before I knew it, Trey was grown and on his own, Scotty had died, and Candy was ready to marry.

It was much like the Jewish song, "Sunrise, Sunset." Where have the years flown?

We moved to Phoenix after both Trey and Candy were married and had their own lives. Brandee was in her mother's arms then. Over 180 miles separated us from our grandchildren Brandee, Scotty and Elisha, who we saw only on visits to Kingman a few times a year. Now they are all grown and married, having their own lives, with only little input from the Gordon grandparents.

The next generations have come along with three grandchildren and 12 great-grandchildren. Again we are far apart and missing important changes in their lives.

I started this monograph years ago, thinking I would give Trey and Candy the benefit of the things I hadn't told them during the time they were growing up. I did not find the time to write this tome, and now Trey and Candy have either heard or experienced many of the things mentioned here. Time has flown and now two new generations are appearing, and I won't be around much longer. I won't be able to tell my great-grandchildren the things they ought to know about the lives of their great-grandfather and grandmother on the Gordon side. We may not even meet some of them.

I take this opportunity to give all of you, from children to great-grandchildren, the picture of our lives that either I didn't have time to tell you because of our busy lives, or because I am not around or able to tell you now. Some of this material may be too deep or uninteresting for the youngest of our brood, but they may find it interesting later.

I have had a wonderful, remarkable and rewarding life. I wouldn't change any part of it, with the exception of losing Scotty. I didn't start out this project for the purpose of tooting my own horn. I have had the greatest gifts that God could have given me – good health, wonderful parents, the unconditional love of a wife whose beauty and intellect I have seen no equal in this world, children who have grown into adults who have solid marriages and who are respected in the community in which they live, grandchildren who have given me great pleasure and will in the future. What more can a man ask for?

I do this monograph only to fill in the gaps, which I may have left in your knowledge of my life, so you don't feel cheated as I do about the lack of knowledge of the details of my grandparents' lives. If you have already heard many of these things in my telling you before, forgive the repetition. This is really for those to come who have not heard them.

In conclusion, I would like to list some of the things I have learned that I feel are important rules to live by:

1. Remember that there are always two sides to a coin. In my years as a judge I have found that you should never accept one person's version of a dispute without hearing from the other side. There always is something you need to know about the other side of the controversy before you make up your mind.

2. Be humble, honest, truthful, loving, caring of others, and willing to be helpful in your community. These go a long way in establishing your reputation. It takes a long time to develop your reputation – it does not come about quickly. It is, however, perhaps the most important asset you own. Once lost, it is very difficult to restore. Small mistakes in judgment can be very harmful to it. Be very cautious in all you do and say.

3. An act of kindness to someone in need is a very powerful force, bringing good will to both the giver and receiver. We ought to make this a priority in our daily living. Joan and I see this trait already developing in our family, and we are very proud. It may be the "pearl of great price" that will live as our legacy.

4. Don't be afraid to start at the bottom of the ladder in a job, doing the dirty work no one else seems to want to do. Those above you in that work will be watching as you stand out among those who feel it beneath them to do those things, and they will reward you with rapid advancement.

5. Some people are by nature very negative. They look at everything and enjoy finding fault. These people have very little to add to a conversation other than critical or caustic comments. They are also very depressing. Don't waste your time with them. Find people to associate with that are positive

and with a bright outlook, who can find good in any situation or person, and forgive their faults. These people leave you with good thoughts and not bad ones. You feel better after being with them.

My first year in law school I became acquainted with Burr Udall, a classmate, and now an extremely successful lawyer in Tucson. Competition in law school tends to make people critical of others. I remember how frequently our coffee discussions brought up someone most of us disapproved of for some reason or another. That seemed to make us feel justified that we were not that kind of person. However, no matter how hard we tried, you could not make Burr say a bad word about anyone. He would just smile, and instead find something, no matter how small it seemed to me, to be good about the person we were discussing and then change the subject. When he did this, almost always we felt bad about what we had just said. I think that was one of the most important things I learned that year, and I try to follow Burr's example. I still admire Burr for that gift, and am thankful for it.

6. Don't harbor grudges. The longer you hold onto a disagreement with someone the harder it is to get rid of it. One of our ministers equated grudges to rocks in a bag around your neck. The more you put in there the heavier the bag gets, until your back becomes bowed with them. If you can't pick one out and talk about it with the person you are having that disagreement with, toss it away and forget about it. Get on

with more important things in life without this bag of rocks around your neck.

Joan and I tried early in our marriage to get rid of our disagreements before we went to bed each night. The longer you carry the grudge, the heavier it gets and the harder it is to get it out of your subconscious.

Many times when I performed a marriage ceremony for friends or children of friends, when they offered me money for the ceremony, I would refuse, asking them to take the money and put it in a jar up in a closet, not to be opened until they had such a problem in their marriage that they thought they would seek a divorce. Then I said if on serious thought they really, really thought divorce was the answer, take the jar down and use the money to go out for a nice dinner together, on me, before signing papers for divorce. On several occasions I was told by couples that they thought they had reached that point, but before they reached for the jar, thought it over again and changed their minds. That always pleased me.

7. On occasion, Joan and I would arrange to go to the lake for a day by ourselves. This provided us time to spend together and refresh ourselves. As married couples, especially with the time children take in your lives, schedule some time, even a little bit, for yourselves for renewal. Do it often and on a regular basis, as part of a bargain with your children. You need time for renewal of yourselves apart from

the demands of the kids.

These are my words of wisdom to my family. I hope you will find them helpful and encouraging. I hope your lives will be as fulfilling as ours have been.

Joan and me, Sonoita, AZ

StoryTerrace®

Made in the USA
San Bernardino, CA
14 January 2020

63177067R00227